Kirsti

TRAVELS IN THE SCOTTISH ISLANDS

THE HEBRIDES

MacD
Books

Come in the evening,
or come in the morning.
Come when you're called for,
or come without warning.

Old Celtic invitation

Kirsti MacDonald Jareg (1966) is a Norwegian-Scottish author with a background in psychology and social anthropology. She grew up in Norway, Sweden, Botswana and Scotland. From her childhood onwards in the 1970s she made frequent visits to the Hebrides, and later Shetland and Orkney.

Travels in the Scottish Islands. The Hebrides is the first part of a book that was published in Norwegian by Cappelen Damm (2011, 2014). The second part, *Travels in the Scottish Islands. Orkney and Shetland,* is due in English in 2017.

This book was first published in Norway thanks to Norwegian editor Sverre Aurstad at Cappelen Damm Publishing House Oslo. My Scottish mother Elizabeth then took on the huge task of translating into English the sections on the Inner and Outer Hebrides, while my father Pål retrieved and checked all the references. Annabel Drew did a wonderful job in editing and proofreading. A warm thank you to my Scottish/English part of the family, especially Pearl and Mary, for always welcoming us to the isle of Tiree. As a member of Mezcla 06, my writing group, I am grateful for your encouragement and help. Last but not least, a sincere and grateful thank you to all those I met in the Hebrides, who over countless cups of tea generously shared their time and rich heritage, and allowed me to glimpse their personal stories. A true treasure awaits those who brave the winds and visit these emerald isles in the Atlantic Ocean.

Copyright © 2016 MacD Books
Copyright © 2016 Kirsti MacDonald Jareg
www.macdbooks.com

First published in Norway by Cappelen Damm (2011, 2014)
Original title: Øyene i vest. Hebridene, Orknøyene og Shetland
This edition published by MacD Books 2016

The author has received writing grants from
The Norwegian Non-fiction Literature Fund and Fritt Ord Foundation.

ISBN 978-82-690404-0-1
First edition 2016

Author photo: Sverre Aurstad. All other photos: Kirsti MacDonald Jareg
Map: Cappelen (1935)
Typograghy and design: Walter Grønli
Proofreader: Annabel Drew
Translation: Elizabeth M. Jareg, except for the following chapters translated by Guy Puzey:
Kintyre – a peninsula, Scotch, Burnt Eigg Rolls, A German artist by the name of Maruma, Massacre Cave,
Creditors, The Eigg Heritage Trust can't believe its ears, makes a bid and receives a gift from Talisker, Ex-
odus from Rum, John Bullough and George Bullough, The Boer War, Sir George Bullough, The Luddites,
Kinloch Castle, The factor, Lady Bullough: Divorce, rumours and scandals, A morning at Kinloch Castle,
Deer and alligators, Dinner at Kinloch Castle, A ball at Kinloch Castle, The circle is closed, From Mallaig
to Skye, Loch Coruisk, 'Cuillin for sale', MacLeod's Tables, Sleat, Trumpan Church – 'Remember the cave
on Eigg', The Fairy Flag – or the Land-waster, The decisive meaning of censorship, A 'rude speech', The
Highland Clearances, An encounter with a weaver, From famine to the catwalk, A peculiar odour

CONTENTS

9 Preface
The Hebrides

Inner Hebrides

13 Kintyre – a peninsula
15 Scotch
16 Port Charlotte
18 Uisge-beatha
19 The battle of Duich Moss
20 Geese
The Kildalton Cross
22 Home brewed
23 Malting
24 Smoke and Peat
26 The grain is milled and fermented
Distillation
27 The truth or a damned lie?
28 Kilchoman farm distillery
Oak casks
30 The Lord of the Isles
31 Finlaggan
33 Paps of Jura
34 On unmarked paths
35 George Orwell
36 Corryvreckan
37 1947
38 Home again
Oban
40 Duart Castle and Scottish Nationalism
42 The Lady on the Rock
43 Tobermory

45 James Boswell and Dr Samuel Johnson
and their journey to the Hebrides in
1773
47 Tour of Mull
49 'We came too late to see what we were
expecting'
51 Bonnie Prince Charlie and the battle of
Culloden
53 Revenge
54 'No Jews, negroes, gipsies, foreigners,
or persons born in England'
55 The rural watchdog
57 From Tobermory to Ulva
The Clan Chief MacQuarrie
58 'Uncover red panel'
59 David Livingstone
60 The kelp industry, the Napoleonic wars
and forced evacuation
62 Inch Kenneth
63 The Mitford family
65 Modern pilgrims
66 St. Columba
69 Queen Victoria's tour to the Hebrides
70 Large demand, little on offer
71 St.Columba hotel
72 Healing hands
74 Pilgrimage
78 On route to Staffa
79 Erraid
80 The Northern Lighthouse Board
81 Dubh Artach
83 Kidnapped

84 The Ross of Mull and pink granite
86 Hebridean Princess
   Basalt columns on Staffa
88 Fingal's Cave
89 The plague of the seas
91 Children of the Romantic Age
92 Tiree – the land beneath the waves
94 The arrival of the potato
95 The struggle against emigration
96 *A'bhliadhna a dh'fhalbh am buntàta*: The
   year the potato went away
98 Slum or Patagonia
99 Foster children
101 Skerryvore
104 Eigg – the island that bought itself
105 'We don't have rules like that here.'
106 'The case of Eigg'
107 Singing Sands and a meeting with a
   descendant
108 A round dance of buying and selling
109 Schellenberg buys Eigg
111 Eigg for sale – again
112 'Burnt Eigg Rolls'
113 A German artist by the name of Maruma
   Massacre Cave
117 Creditors
118 The Eigg Heritage Trust can't believe
   its ears, makes a bid and receives a gift
   from Talisker
119 Exodus from Rum
120 John Bullough and George Bullough
121 The Boer War
122 Sir George Bullough

123 The Luddites
124 Kinloch Castle
125 The factor
126 Lady Bullough: Divorce, rumours and
   scandals
127 A morning at Kinloch Castle
128 Deer and alligators
   Dinner at Kinloch Castle
130 A ball at Kinloch Castle
   The circle is closed
131 From Mallaig to Skye
133 Loch Coruisk
134 'Cuillin for sale'
135 MacLeod's Tables
136 Sleat
137 Trumpan Church – 'Remember the
   cave on Eigg'
138 The Fairy Flag – or the Land-waster
139 The decisive meaning of censorship
141 A 'rude speech'
142 The Highland Clearances
143 Courage, myths and shame
144 The Napier Commission and the
   Crofter Act
146 Seannachaidh George MacPherson
148 Telephone catalogues from Jamaica
150 The Lord Lyon
151 Professional ethics
152 The original kilt – the fillimore

Outer Hebrides

156 Kisimul and Foster Children
157 Mussels from the Traigh Mhòr Airport
160 Castlebay Bar
161 Ceilidhs
162 Anonymous Alcoholics
163 An Honest Incomer from Glasgow
164 Vatersay and the brig, Annie Jane
165 Eriskay
166 SS Politician
167 Hold #5
168 The Rescue Operation
170 Whisky Galore
171 CalMac from Oban to South Uist
173 A865
175 Troublesome Conservation
176 Ferries on a Sunday
177 Sunlight and Quicksand
178 Luskentyre
179 An Encounter with a Weaver
181 From Famine to Catwalk
183 A Peculiar Odour
184 The Orb
186 Emigration
188 Tarbert
    A Bug on Stornoway Airport
190 Cairns
    Problematic Farmed Salmon
192 Scenic Cruises
193 The Hurricane in 2005
194 White Slaves
195 The Boat Builder John MacAuley
196 St Clement's Church

197 Ljodhus
198 Chessmen
199 The Stone Circle of Calanais
201 The Free Church
203 Gaelic Gospel
205 Arnol Blackhouse
208 The Year the Tweed Disappeared
211 Sheepdogs and Uncooperative
    Sheep
214 St Kilda—the Myth at the End of the
    World
216 Noa Words
217 Hirta
218 Houses
219 The Evacuation
220 Soay Sheep
222 Feathers and Oil
223 Grief
224 Sickness of the Eighth Day
225 Priscilla
226 The Myth of St Kilda
227 The Myth that Took UNESCO
    The Parliament
228 Boreray
230 Heavy Metals
    Supper

232 Works Cited

Preface

Can islands be an obsession? Of course they can. And there is even a term for this affliction: *islomania*. The mania expresses itself as an irresistible urge to continually explore islands and even to write about them. It's difficult to pinpoint exactly when I was bitten by this bug. Probably it started around the time I was shedding my first milk teeth. My earliest childhood memories from the Hebrides revolve around the eternal search for what my Scottish relatives aptly named 'a sheltered spot.' After long saunters on blinding white sands lapped by turquoise seas, we kids running with our kites, or bent over searching intently for coloured shells, it was at last time for a picnic sheltered from the ever-prevailing winds. Lunch huddled behind old, dry stone dykes. Sometimes we set up our tent after a chat with the landowner. Perhaps we would get a welcome gift, a pail of milk fresh from the cow, or maybe we'd agree on a deal to borrow a boat and fish for mackerel.

At other times we stayed in cosy comfort with our relatives in Tiree, surrounded by whitewashed, thatched Hebridean cottages. Sky melted with sea, and the sun shone over the green *machair* turf, alive with daisies and clover, merging with sand dunes from which generations of children before us had jumped, howling with joy, down to the beach.

We ran into the sea for a quick, chilly, but utterly refreshing dip. Afterwards we lay with the sun warming our backs, dusted with salt crystals, tracing letters with our fingers in the sand.

When I became old enough to travel in the Scottish islands by myself, off I went with boyfriends (one at a time), friends, and eventually my own family. I stayed the night in old Ardvasar Hotel on the Isle of Skye, which my grandparents, Jeana and William (Bill) MacDonald, ran just after the war. I visited the birthplace of my great grandmother Margaret MacLeod on the isle of Lewis, and was shown around by the present gamekeeper the old house where she was born and brought up. It was here in the grounds of the hunting and fishing paradise Morsgail Lodge, where her father, my great-great-grandfather Angus, was himself a gamekeeper. Before leaving Morsgail, my children swam in the loch a stone's throw from the house. For a second, I had an image of my great-grandmother wading, perhaps swimming, in the clear waters of this peaceful loch.

This book is about the Scottish islands. It is neither a guide nor history book. Instead I invite the reader to accompany me on a journey of discovery: of stories, hovering between myth and reality, which expose and explore the whole range of human emotions; the need to belong, and the deep sorrow of leaving behind; epics of love and hate; the pride of the clans and their fall from grace; the aching backs of a people toiling to survive under lean circumstances; the terrible fatigue of starvation. The joy and exaltation bestowed by the beauty of the Hebrides.

I have not gone 'island hopping,' as if I were playing hopscotch. On the contrary, the stories are gleaned from excursions made over the years. Some islands I have visited many times, others only once. I have not covered the entire archipelago, which runs into hundreds of islands, but I have been to most of those with ferry connections. My starting point is the Inner Hebrides, sailing westwards to the Outer Hebrides.

One of the fascinating things about islands is that just like us they have unique characteristics, a blend of subtle as well as precisely-defined features which make up their personality or soul. As with people, some immediately arouse my sympathy and affection, even enthusiasm. I want to know them better. On a few occasions they trigger feelings of irritation and dislike. Hang on, some may object, aren't your impressions of an island and its people always coloured by your own personal lens? Every traveller carries baggage undetected by X-ray security checks: positive expectations, prejudice, scepticism, a yearning to learn, a belief in one's fellow men, or a patronising approach. Some travellers meet new places with a trusting, open mind; others with their arms crossed guardedly. An island can be experienced and described in totally different terms by visitors, or even by the same visitor at various times in life. In this vibrant space between the traveller, the islands, and their people, memories are made.

THE HEBRIDES

When Dr Johnson, author of *A Dictionary of the English Language*, decided to leave behind his comfortable existence in London and travel to the Hebrides with his Scottish friend James Boswell, Boswell's wife objected. What business could they have on these islands west of the Scottish mainland? She received the following answer: 'Madam, we do not go there as to a paradise. We go to see something different from what we are accustomed to see.' Much has changed since Dr Johnson's expedition in 1773, but many people still travel to the Hebrides for the same reason: to experience something *different*. Priceless qualities. People with time to chat and to say hello. Unlocked doors, bicycles and cars. Clean air and the heavens full of seabirds, purple heathered moorlands with wandering herds of deer, and a golden eagle gliding on the updrafts. Beaches with clear turquoise water that even the Thai tourist board has used in its brochures. An embarrassing advertising blunder by Thai authorities, of course, but what else could it be, asks VisitScotland, but a 'compliment in disguise?'

The Inner Hebrides lie along Scotland's west coast and stretch from fertile, whisky-marinated Islay in the south, to mountainous Skye in the north. To the west of Skye lie the Outer Hebrides across a stretch of open sea: the Little Minch. This is where blue men from the Gaelic underworld drown adventurous seamen voyaging to the outer isles, or *Innse Gall*, 'the isles of the foreigners,' after the Norsemen who colonised the Hebrides. The Outer Hebrides extend in a long arc out towards the open Atlantic. The next stop beyond their unbroken white beaches is America.

Dougie MacTaggert digging peat for Laphroaig distillery

Kintyre, a peninsula – almost an island

The Kennacraig ferry landing on the Kintyre Peninsula is little more than that. A ferry landing. Places like this are without lives of their own. They are parasitic. They come to life when ferries dock, and for an allotted length of time they feed off the greasy exhaust of diesel engines, the bleating sheep staring out from behind the bars on the back of pick-ups, wet cyclists shivering, babies crying impatiently, and tourists drumming on their steering wheels, feeling as though they've been waiting an eternity.

'The ferry to Islay was due to leave at 5.30 p.m., but it's been delayed,' says the lady behind the desk at Kennacraig. It's Easter. I'm in the low building that houses a waiting room and the ticket office. The windows are steamed up with the respiration of wet, waiting passengers. On the wall behind the desk someone has hung up small trophies - banknotes from Sweden, the United States and Italy.

Outside, the cars stand queued up in parallel lines. It's raining and it's getting dark. Far out in the Sound of Islay, I can vaguely make out a vessel. A car ferry belonging to Caledonian MacBrayne, or CalMac, to its friends. The state-subsidised berated and praised CalMac, linking together the Hebrides. Black and white ferries frequenting over twenty ports. For many people, this day marks Jesus' last supper with his disciples, but for CalMac this is just the last day of the winter season.

The ferry's belly opens and out roll its contents: cars with kayaks on the roof, others with bikes tied behind, the gangway clanging as the cars drive ashore. Men in yellow high-visibility vests and red helmets wave the waiting cars on board. There's space for them all, the patient and the impatient. The drivers put on the handbrake and get out of their cars. A lone car alarm soon starts to wail – somebody locked his car in a moment of distraction – and other alarms soon join in, like a pack of wolves. A final farewell as the ferry slips away from the pier. Left behind, the ferry landing makes no fuss. It takes strength to be the one always left behind.

Once upon a time, Norway was about to annex the entire Kintyre Peninsula from Scotland. The whole thing was down to a blunder by Edgar, King of the Scots. In 1098, he and King Magnus Barefoot of Norway signed a peace treaty. 'You shall have the Hebrides, or what you call the Sudreys,' said the Scottish king. The Norwegians had already controlled the islands for a long time, so it seemed appropriate to formalise a contract for these Norwegian territories. 'But,' added

Edgar, thinking he was being crafty, 'you shall only have the islands that you can sail round with the rudder shipped.' By messing with the definition of what makes an island, the Scots lost Kintyre, or Saltire as the peninsula was then known to the Norse. Because who could have imagined that King Magnus would be equally cunning, that he would sit at the tiller while his boat was dragged across the narrow isthmus joining Kintyre to the rest of the mainland? The ancient Icelandic poet and historian Snorri Sturlason describes the incident in the *Magnus Barefoot saga*:

> [...] when King Magnus came north to Cantire [Kintyre], he had a skiff drawn over the strand at Cantire, and shipped the rudder of it. The king himself sat in the stern-sheets, and held the tiller; and thus he appropriated to himself the land that lay on the farboard side. Cantire is a great district, better than the best of the southern isles of the Hebudes [Hebrides], excepting Man; and there is a small neck of land between it and the mainland of Scotland, over which longships are often drawn.

Snorri and the *Orkneyinga saga* both maintain that King Magnus actually conquered Kintyre. Modern historians claim that this creative attempt at conquest was not entirely successful. Oh well. Even if King Magnus tried to remove Kintyre from the map of Scotland, nobody has done more to put Kintyre back *on* the map than Paul McCartney. If I had driven beyond the Kennacraig ferry landing to the end of the road, I would have ended up in the small town of Campbeltown, near Sir Paul McCartney's former holiday home, High Park Farm. Paul and his family travelled here after the Beatles broke up in 1970. It was here he licked his wounds and recovered. When, a few years later, Wings released the song 'Mull of Kintyre,' the effect was overwhelming. It sold more in the UK than any previous single. The music video for 'Mull of Kintyre' shows Linda, Paul, and Wings' guitarist Denny Laine singing as they stroll down to the shore. In the distance, bagpipers can be made out. The local pipe band, the Campbeltown Pipers, swirl up the sand as they march straight towards the three band members. Song, guitar, and rubber wellies meet drums, pipes, and kilts: 'My desire is always to be here, oh Mull of Kintyre.'

Soon, children, old women in headscarves and well-built farmers join the little band. As it turns dark, they all stand gathered around a large bonfire singing their tribute to Kintyre, a secluded and uncontrived place where the McCartney family was allowed to stay more or less in peace. The Mull of Kintyre lies right at the end of the Kintyre Peninsula, off the beaten track. An old lighthouse flashes warnings in the night. Northern Ireland can be glimpsed on the other side of the narrow strip of ocean separating the two islands.

Scotch

But I'm not off to Campbeltown or to the Mull of Kintyre. I'm heading for the whisky island of Islay.

The crossing from Kennacraig on the MV Hebridean Isles takes around two and a half hours. This Easter evening, a bitter Atlantic wind is blowing. The voyage isn't for those without their sea legs, but as always some people take a nap, even on short distances like this. Passengers lie sprawled out on sofas and benches. Why are they so tired? Are they bored? Have they been working shifts? Or have they travelled far? It's only the locals who sleep. They're easy to spot, already wearing summer shoes in March, all golden sandals and bare, pale calves. The tourists, on the other hand, look like they're going on a long Arctic expedition. Windproof, waterproof, warm clothes. Many with cameras and binoculars. If the weather's nice enough they stand on deck, their binoculars searching for killer whales and dolphins.

There's also a bar on board. I order a whisky from Islay, a Lagavulin. A young passenger in the bar drinks an Irn-Bru, Scotland's other national drink. This orange fizzy beverage looks poisonous, tastes artificial, and has been produced since 1901. It's well-loved in Scotland but is poorly suited to the export market. Unlike whisky.

But what *is* whisky, Scotland's foremost national drink? Put simply, whisky is distilled beer, without hops. Scotch whisky must be made in Scotland and matured for at least three years in oak barrels. Its alcoholic strength must be at least 40% volume at bottling. How many whisky regions there are in Scotland depends upon whom you ask, but one of the traditional classifications distinguishes among whiskies from the Highlands, Lowlands, Islay, Speyside, and Campbeltown in Kintyre. There are two main types of whisky: grain whisky made from various types of grains, and malt whisky from malted barley.

So far so good, but hold on tight, as it's about to get a bit more complicated. If you're holding a bottle where it says 'malt whisky' on the label, then it's made from malted barley. If all the whisky comes from one distillery, then you've got hold of a single malt. And if the whisky also comes from the very same barrel, you're holding a bottle of single cask. If, on the other hand, you pour yourself a glass of blended malt, then you're drinking a mixture of malt whiskies from different distilleries.

Why all this hair splitting, you ask? For one simple reason: if you're going to get something out of a tour of Islay's whisky distilleries, you have to have done your homework first. All right, so if you've poured yourself a blended Scotch, then you're drinking a mixture of grain whisky and malt whisky, and it's highly likely that the malt whisky in this blend comes from Islay. At one time, most of the whiskies from the island went into blends, to big names like Johnny Walker, Chivas Regal, Bells, White Horse or Famous Grouse. Then something dramatic happened. Pure malt whiskies became sought-after items. The market can't get enough. Whisky pilgrims flood to Islay like never before.

Port Charlotte

Islay. The ferry glides in to Port Ellen, the gentle swell reflecting moonbeams. Once on land I follow the signs out of the little harbour town, heading north. Mile after mile of totally deserted 'peat bogs,' as they're called here. The road is uneven, the tarmac almost floating on heaving turf. If a heavy lorry thunders past while you're walking along the road, you can feel the surface undulating underfoot.

The weather changes rapidly from a clear moonlit sky, to what can only be described as a monsoon rain, except of course, there is no monsoon season here. The expression 'raining buckets' suddenly makes sense. It's exactly as if someone is throwing buckets of water at the windscreen, threatening to smash the struggling wiper blades. The windy gusts hurl water in haphazard sploshes, the rain falling in

Port Charlotte, Islay

horizontal sheets. Compliments of the Atlantic. I drive cautiously. Partly because I can barely see anything, and there are also sheep on the road. It's as if those animals are attracted by car lights, exhaust and tarmac, totally ignorant of any danger. A few minutes later the madness is over. The wind has not died down, but the rain clouds have decided to work their way eastwards, maybe to the Sound of Islay, where they may shower the cupola of the old lighthouse on the Mull of Kintyre.

Islay is a big island. It takes three-quarters of an hour to reach Port Charlotte where I am staying for the night. White painted houses huddle together. The town is named after Charlotte Campbell, the mother of Walter Frederick Campbell, who owned Islay in the 1800s. She was said to be beautiful. And so is Port Charlotte.

Uisge-beatha

Whisky arrived in Islay from Ireland around the 1300s, probably brought by monks who used the drink medicinally. It was unlikely that it could be used for anything else since it took time before it was understood that whisky matures in casks. The Gaelic name, *uisge-beatha*, or *uisgebaugh*, pronounced uske-va, gradually became shortened to whisky. It means 'water of life.'

Southwest of the ferry township of Port Ellen lies the Oa. A deserted wilderness of tall steep cliffs and white beaches, where illegal distilleries thrived, far removed from the excise man's notice. A concerned minister from Islay, Archibald Robertson, wrote towards the end of the 1700s:

> We have not an excise officer in the whole island. The quantity therefore of whisky made here is very great; and the evil, that follows drinking to excess of this liquor, is very visible in this island. This is one chief cause of our poverty; for the barley, that should support the family of the poor tenant is sold to a brewer for 17 s.

A downward spiral which led large sections of the population to succumb to starvation and disease. And alcoholism. When the potato blight from Ireland also hit the crops on the Scottish islands in the 1840s, many packed up the little they owned. The prospects of a better life led many smallholders to accept free tickets from private landlords; tickets for passages on overfilled boats to Australia, New Zealand, the USA and Canada. Landowners on the majority of the Hebridean islands, including Islay, collaborated in the mass departure of thousands of people. Poor farmers, unable to pay the rent, or whose holdings were not profitable, were simply thrown out of their homes by force. The period is known as 'the Clearances.' Large areas were cleared of 'unprofitable' people, and were replaced by imported, very profitable breeds of sheep, producing much more wool than the skinny, hardy, black Hebridean breed.

People do not emigrate, neither then nor now, if they don't expect a better future. But often the reality did not live up to the expectations. Canadian winters and the never-ending toil of clearing the forests were probably worse than the conditions the Scottish crofters had left behind. However, some did make a better life, and encouraged their countrymen to follow on. New York State, at that time a British colony, presented itself as attractive, and advertised for 'good Protestants.' It enticed folks willing to risk death from epidemics or shipwreck with the promise of good farm land.

In the 1830s, about 15,000 people lived on Islay. Today the island has a population of around 3,500. Islay is no exception. This drastic reduction in population happened in virtually all the Hebridean islands. The only differences were that emigration could be more or less voluntary, or more or less violent.

The battle of Duich Moss

Today large tracts of Islay are still in the hands of a few private landowners, as are many of the Hebridean islands. Even though the inhabitants hold completely different rights than former times, many still feel at the mercy of the landowners' lack of respect for and knowledge of local conditions. On Islay, the biggest conflict, however, has been between conservation organisations and the local population.

A case from the 1980s started when the distilleries were trying to find new areas from which they could cut peat. The peat is burnt to dry the barley grain, and also impart that smoky taste which characterises several Islay whiskies. Well and good. The distilleries were given the all-clear to dig for peat in Duich Moss, a marsh near the airport, according to the whisky writer Andrew Jefford. The national nature conservation organisation, Nature Conservancy Council (NCC), protested against the plans. They insisted it was an important feeding ground for a threatened species of bird, the barnacle goose. The whole situation reached a climax when environmental activists from Friends of the Earth came over to Islay and demonstrated against the peat extraction. It must have been a spectacular culture clash. Down-to-earth islanders against idealistic townsfolk. It ended in a big community meeting in 1985 in Bowmore community hall, arranged by Friends of the Earth. Six hundred and fifty people attended. When the leader of the activists, David Bellamy, remarked that it was the birdwatchers who kept the ferries running, he was met by laughter. But it was when he described the environmentalists as 'brave people,' and the people from Islay as 'an angry horde,' that things clicked for the usually stolid islanders. When Bellamy returned to his hotel that evening, his luggage stood outside Machrie Hotel. A plea for police protection did not arouse any sympathy: 'You make your own way, mate.'

The islanders lost the Battle of Duich Moss, in spite of their conviction that the combination of peat cutting and birds was unproblematic. Their logic, naturally, was as follows: Since we have so many protected species that want to spend the winter here, this must mean that we are living in harmony with nature, in contrast to the places where the nature conservationists live. There are hardly any animals left there. So they should clear up their own backyard and leave us in peace!

But the issue migrated abroad. The bird protectors sent a complaint to the EU Commission in Brussels, which stated that Great Britain was not upholding its obligations towards threatened species. The pressure on the Islay distillery from British authorities increased when the press leaked that the representative from Brussels would present the case to the EU court. The distillery then found other places to dig for peat. But this did not end the battle with the bird lovers.

Geese

Many on Islay still have mixed feelings about environmental protection, due to the powerful, well-endowed private organisation, the Royal Society for the Protection of Birds, RSPB. This organisation has become an influential landowner in the Scottish islands in its own right, Islay included. A positive product of its never-ending fight to protect the geese is the RSPB bird reserve in the north of the island which attracts tourists. Naturally, this is a good thing. The tourists spend money in the summer which allows empty bed and breakfasts to survive the winter. The problem is that the birds are so numerous they overgraze their surroundings.

One evening I took a walk with Mark Piper who owns and administrates the deer forest, Gearach Forest. We were searching for deer in the twilight. I asked him what he thought of the whole geese affair, and he sighed resignedly. 'They're smart. The geese add two and two and figure out that where there are scarecrows, the best grazing is to be found.' On the other hand, geese are often more profitable than sheep because of the compensation paid to owners for their overgrazing. But compensation leads to more than money; it can also lead to conflict. According to Piper, compensation is dependent on the geese actually being present when the RSPB arrives to confirm where they are grazing. He has not always been so lucky himself. When the RSPB comes to count the geese, the birds have often already flown.

Compensation or not, the number of visitors to the bird reserve at Loch Gruinart, northwest Islay, competes with many of the distilleries. And even people like Ian Mitchell, the author who lived many years on Islay and who is a strong critic of RSPB, admits that the organisation has improved its attitudes towards the local population. It no longer instructs local farmers on how they should cultivate their land. And it contributes to the smooth running of island society's cogwheels, albeit with some irritating sand left in the machinery.

The Kildalton Cross

Long ago, after the last ice age but before peat carpeted the islands and the geese were threatened with extinction, the Hebrides were covered by deciduous forest. There are still pockets of this ancient forest to be found on some islands, for example in the area around Kildalton, southwest Islay. The road there passes three whitewashed distilleries lying along the shoreline, where the high tide laps at old pier constructions: Laphroaig, Lagavulin and Ardbeg. The mountains shelter this part of the island from the Atlantic Ocean. Trees dare to grow here. Ash, willow, rowan and hazel. The gnarled trunks and new green shoots on the trees protect the wild primroses, and Scottish bluebells cover the forest floor in an intense carpet of blue. The familiar scent of wild garlic wafts through the car window.

Loch Indaal, Islay

The road ends at the medieval church of Kildalton. The walls are covered with patches of grey and yellow lichen. The roof has crumbled, but walls with round-headed windows still stand to protect the graves of the forgotten. Some of the oblong gravestones lie in the grassy enclosure, others are cemented into the walls. One of the reliefs shows a man in armour, eyes closed, his sword held against the length of his abdomen.

Kildalton church dates to around 1200, but the gravestones are much older. The churchyard is home to the Kildalton Cross, Islay's best-known attraction besides the distilleries. It stands more or less where it was erected in the 700s and is the only intact Celtic cross in Scotland. Far taller than a grown man, it is carved out of a single piece of stone. For a thousand years it held a macabre secret, at least if we are to believe Sir Arthur Mitchell who restored it in 1882 and found the remains of a woman and a man beneath it. According to Mitchell, the man had suffered a brutal, unnatural death. It is possible that he had been the victim of blood-eagle, a method of execution used by the Vikings when they plundered and colonised the Isle of Man, the Hebrides, Orkney islands and Shetland, starting at the end of the 700s. The saga from the Orkney islands, *Orkneyinga Saga*, tells us how the son of the Norwegian king Harald Fairhair was killed by his opponent the earl Einar: '[...] they found Halfdan Long-Leg. Einar had his ribs cut from the spine with a sword and the lungs pulled out through the slits in his back. He dedicated the victim to Odin as a victory offering.' In other words, the victim lay on his stomach and the lungs were torn out and spread on his back like bloody eagle wings. Not everyone had the honour of being killed in this way. The victims were of high rank, as was Harald Fairhair's son. And the fellow under Kildalton Cross? Was he a priest on the island, gruesomely killed by the Vikings who plundered Islay in the 800s? Or did he meet his end another way?

Some historians doubt that blood-eagling really occurred. They maintain that horror stories such as this fit in only too well with the church's attempts to demonise the heathens. Others think there has been a basic misunderstanding of saga texts. Roberta Frank, for example, asserts that even during saga times, the poetry of the Nordic bards was misunderstood. Metaphors were often interpreted literally. What these early poets *really* meant was that victims had their backs torn up by eagles as they were left for carrion on the battlefield. So is Frank right? Did the Christian monks simply get carried away? Was it just too tempting to paint so lurid a picture of the bloodthirsty Vikings?

Home brewed

A cold wind grabs hold of me, even in this sheltered part of the island. I'm off to visit the first of the three distilleries along the road: Ardbeg.

In the 1880s the writer Alfred Barnard visited all the whisky distilleries in Britain. This resulted in a richly-illustrated book, *The Whisky Distilleries of the United Kingdom*. Naturally Barnard also went to Islay and visited seven distilleries which are still going strong. Some of them had already existed for a hundred years, such as Bowmore, from 1779. Others were new and modern, like Bruichladdich or Bunnahabhain from 1881. When Barnard visited 'the isolated' distillery of Ardbeg, the place had officially existed since 1815. Officially? Like many other distilleries, Ardbeg whisky was at one time identical with the home-brewed variety. Many small farms on Islay and elsewhere in Scotland brewed whisky as a cottage industry, an additional source of income which was very welcome in the cold months when there was otherwise not much else going on.

As late as the 1700s, whisky was the prerogative of country folk, far from the national drink it has become today. Townspeople, on the other hand, enjoyed beer and wine. Cities grew as industrialisation spread, and with increased economic growth new habits developed. A demand for malt whisky ensued. The authorities seized their chance for new sources of income; they introduced taxes on malted barley, a grain also used to brew beer. This action proved an exceedingly unpopular one. There were riots in Glasgow, soldiers were deployed against the demonstrators, and blood flowed in the streets. On Islay and many other places, whisky production went underground. Or more accurately, into caves and isolated shacks. Those who produced legally and openly went broke.

Islay probably had more unlawful distilleries and extensive smuggling than any other place in Scotland. It was not until around 1800 that an excise man plucked up the courage to go to the island and investigate the situation. The catch was formidable. Two hundred thirty-three persons were convicted of illegally distilling alcohol; some were family members of the founders of today's distilleries and forebears of present-day managing directors.

However, fines and the confiscation of moonshine equipment were not effective. The thirst proved too great, and smuggling far too profitable. Two changes in the law were necessary to whitewash the whole enterprise of whisky making. In 1823 it became affordable to buy a license, and the taxes were halved. So what happened when the producers were enticed out of their caves and shacks? To start with, the quality of the whisky produced in the professional distilleries improved immensely. It was high time. An early traveller to the Hebrides, Martin Martin, described the drink in his journal from 1695: '[…] which at first taste affects all the members of the body: two spoonfuls of this last liquor is a sufficient dose; and if any man exceeds this, it would presently stop his breath, and endanger his life.'

Another consequence of legalisation was that the distilleries then employed a large segment of the population. Not only that, but small villages with schools, churches, and workers' houses established themselves around the big distilleries. And apparently, paradoxically, alcohol abuse declined, in spite of workers' rights to three to four glasses a day. This custom lasted so long that even today's distillery, workers remember those lively times with a smile and a sigh.

Malting

Malt whisky is made of barley, yeast, and water. But yeast can't work miracles with barley straight from the field. Grain is mainly composed of starch, but yeast needs sugar to be able to do its stuff. So how to conjure starch into sugar? By malting the barley. By cheating nature, leading the golden grains astray. To start the germination process the grain is put into water. For two days it lies there soaking, while the water is continually and conscientiously changed. And as the grains bathe, they start to germinate. The starch slowly breaks down to sugar. After a couple of days the water is finally drained from the soaking wet barley.

The wet grain is spread out over the malting floors. 'Spring!' the hopeful seeds think, and start to germinate under a sun that isn't there. And as they lie there, trustingly sending out tiny shoots and roots, the starch continues to turn into sugar. Sugar which will nourish the plant as it grows. Or so the barley thinks. But alas, it will never be a slender stalk bending in the summer breeze.

So what next? Lynda Grey is a guide at Bowmore, Islay's oldest distillery, which looks out over the sea loch, Loch Indaal. I park the car and get out reluctantly into a shower of hail, my cheeks stinging. Lynda awaits, lightly clad, outside the Bowmore's door, until all those who have booked the tour have assembled. She asks us to turn off our mobiles and camera blitzes due to the fire hazard they represent. Hanging on the white wall of the distillery, a black and yellow plaque underlines Lynda Grey's request: 'Highly inflammable liquid.'

Bowmore has three malting floors. Birds flap under the roof as we enter into the half-dark area of one of the floors. The barley spreads like a golden carpet, germinating willingly. The smell awakens a childhood memory: a hand reaching out into the grain field, closing around damp stalks, stripping off the hard seed heads and holding them up to the nose.

The grains of barley lie in peace for twenty-four hours before they get the full treatment. The germinating barley is raked night and day, every four hours. This prevents the damp grain from going mouldy, and the tiny roots from becoming entangled in each other. It also maintains the correct temperature in the thick, living blanket.

Smoke and Peat

Just as the barley is lying there germinating and looking forward to a mild spring, it becomes intolerably hot. Some spoilsports have laid the grain out to dry on huge racks in the heat of Bowmore's peat ovens. Lynda Grey opens the oven door; glowing lumps of peat burn quietly. Not like common firewood, sparking and crackling, but gently and with dignity. The grain is dried twice: first with peat smoke at a low temperature to give the malt a smoky taste, then with hot air without smoke to complete the drying process. The amount of smoke needed and the time the smoking process lasts depends on which brand of whisky the malted barley is to become.

Ardbeg whisky destillery, Islay

The classic peaty whiskies from Islay would not taste the same without this magic fuel, although surely the world would have continued on its way without 'peated' whiskies. However, the situation for those living on the Scottish islands would have been much worse had they been without peat to keep them warm through the wet autumn storms and howling hurricanes of winter. For several thousand years, the well-known smell of peat has filled earthen huts, traditional 'blackhouses,' newer 'white houses,' and modern homes. Wood was generally not available, except driftwood washed ashore from shipwrecks or far-off continents. Coal first arrived with the ferry traffic in the middle of the 1800s. That is, if there *was* a ferry. For many, buying coal was in any case not an option; it was just too expensive.

So what is peat? If you see a greenish-brown boggy landscape on the Scottish isles, there's a high probability you're looking at a thick blanket of peat. Slowly, patiently, layer upon layer over ancient rock it has accumulated, for many thousands of years. So what happened? Climate change. As the grip of the ice age slackened, the climate in the islands gradually became milder, allowing trees to take root and form deciduous forests as far west as the Outer Hebrides. But in the millennia before our era it became wetter and colder. The wind increased in strength. *Sphagnum capillifolium*, a sphagnum moss which thrived in these conditions, has an insatiable appetite for water, a greedy little sponge, always craving more moisture. It can suck up water corresponding to eight times its own weight.

Peat is formed when the moss grows faster than it decays. But if the moss makes a serious attempt to rot, it has to give up. It will suffocate under its own weight. The decaying plant material becomes an oxygen-deprived acidic sludge, instead of composting decently and becoming proper earth. On Islay the peat is up to ten metres deep. The more the peat has been processed, the heavier and more compact it becomes, and the more heat it produces when burnt. Peat is therefore usually cut out a couple of metres below the surface in big bricks, then expertly stacked in large piles to dry.

So what's the connection between these black, wet, organic remains, and whisky? Every visitor to a whisky distillery will hear about the unit of measure 'parts per million,' in short, ppm. This indicates the level of phenols in the different whiskies. So what do phenols do? The chemical compound imparts the smoky, peaty taste. Ardbeg held the record for the world's smokiest whisky, right until the Bruichladdich distillery decided it would make 'The World's Peatiest Whisky:' Octomore. A bottled smoke bomb.

The smoke from the peat ovens swirls up the pagoda-formed chimney. The flat roof on the top captures the invaluable peat smoke on its way out, and persuades it to filter back to flavour the malt just a wee bit more. Most distilleries on Islay have this distinctive-shaped chimney, reminiscent of Nepal and Buddha. White-painted, maritime temples.

The grain is milled and fermented

When the malted barley has dried, it is sent through a mill. The rough meal, which tastes smoky and sweet, is then poured into a large mashing tank of steel, filled with warm water. This vessel has one purpose only: to extract as much sugar as possible from the coarsely-ground flour.

This sweet water, or 'wort,' is collected in a tank, leaving behind the remains of the grain robbed of all its sugar. The sugarless residue is now ready for a new, worthy task: to be pressed into pellets to feed Islay's cattle (and geese, who have also developed a taste for the leftovers from the distilleries).

The smoke-imbued wort travels in pipes to large containers for fermentation. Depending on the distillery, such receptacles, 'vats,' are either made of pine or rust-proof steel, and can measure up to six dizzying metres deep. In Ardbeg, the vats are lined up against a huge hall with large windows looking out to sea.

'We use wooden vats,' says Lindsay MacArthur at Ardbeg distillery. 'We think this is best. But it means we have to keep production going 365 days a year. If the containers dry out, they crack.' On this point the whisky producers differ. Some believe that rust-proof steel is just as good as wood, and besides, steel is easier to keep clean. Steel doesn't dry and develop cracks. So does it make any real difference whether the wort is fermented in steel or wood? Better leave it to the experts.

Steel or wood apart, fresh yeast is added to the sweet liquid and the yeast eagerly absorbs the sugar. The result is alcohol and carbon dioxide. Bubbling gasses cause the beery brew to foam under the lid of the wooden vats. Rotating arms keep the brown, foamy froth under control, while the beer works itself up to an alcohol percentage between five and seven. Fairly strong beer, in other words. MacArthur opens a little hatch on one of the vats and submerges a steel bottle dangling on a string. The bottle fills with a thin, yellow soup and is sent round the group of onlookers. Warm beer without hops. A bland, sickly taste. Lindsay invites me to pop my head into the opening of the vat. My nostrils sting, my head jerks backwards. Carbon dioxide in concentrated form literally takes my breath away. 'If you fall into the vat, you're finished,' she says. She's right. Whisky production can be dangerous. There have been several distillery accidents on Islay. In 1847, Donald Johnston, the founder of Laphroaig, fell into one of his own distillation apparatuses and died of burn wounds. A similar accident befell a tax collector the following year in a Port Ellen distillery which is now no more. He died after falling into a vat filled with boiling, yeasty wort.

Distillation

It's time to distil the flat beer. Twice. First in a wash still and then in a spirit still. Both distillation tanks are made of pear-shaped, shining, polished copper. The condensers too, where the distilled steam will be cooled down to be transformed again into liquid, are made of copper. The reddish-brown metal gives off a warm glow in the distillery room. As we shed our wet rain clothes, the warmth from the huge, rounded containers seeps into our pores.

Malt whisky is always distilled in an apparatus made of copper. Snobbery? Not a bit. The metal reacts easily with other substances. When the evaporated alcohol passes through copper, the metal halts the steam to take what is known in the distillery world as a 'chat.' The longer the chat lasts, the more the copper binds the impurities, and the lighter the whisky becomes. And the contrary holds true as well—a short chat gives a robust whisky.

But not all impurities bind to copper. If so, one would end up with pure alcohol, not whisky. Brewing balances the art of keeping the good impurities in and eliminating the bad, giving malt whisky its iconic taste.

The truth or a damned lie?

Still the mystery remains. What makes the malt whiskies from Islay so special? Water runs smoothly in a white-painted canal along the entrance to the distinguished Lagavulin distillery. It flows from the hills, from the peat-coloured Sholum Lochan, and runs through bogs and heather on its way to the sea. Just before the brownish water unites with the clear salt water, it is siphoned off into the distillery canal to be used for whisky-making. Several whisky producers try to kill a persistent myth about whisky: that the peaty taste of the water contributes to the distinctive taste of malt whiskies. 'Myth and myth,' says Andrew Jefford, who has compared water from bogs against clear spring water. The water from the bogs has a distinctive, organic and grotty taste. So why should it be surprising that the water adds to the flavour?

Some Islay whiskies also have an unmistakeable maritime taste and smell: of sea, iodine and seaweed. Where does it come from? Surely not from the bogs? All the distilleries on Islay, apart from the newcomer Kilchoman, lie by the sea. Or like Laphroaig, almost *in* the sea, with seaweed clambering up along the walls of the storage building. They lie by the shore for one completely logical reason: right up until the 1960s the barrels of whisky were sent by sea to Glasgow. Small, flat-bottomed steamboats sailed close to land and moored at the piers belonging to the distilleries.

The steamboats have gone, and today the whisky is transported in trailers on the ferries, but one thing remains the same: the sea air. The smell of seaweed and salt. Which some say forces its way into the seaside cellars and creeps into the oak casks. The explanation is apparently obvious: every year 2% of the whisky evaporates from the casks. It's said to be the angels who benefit from this disappearing act. At least 'the angel's share' is the term used for the evaporation. The more the angels help themselves to the whisky, the more room for air in the casks. Damp, salty, sea air. There's just one detail which seems to contradict this theory that the flavour of the sea in Islay whisky is imparted through the air. Lagavulin stores much of its whisky on the mainland, far from salt water. And Diageo, who owns Lagavulin, insists that it cannot tell the difference between whisky stored on Islay and that which is stored on the mainland. Those storing whisky only on Islay naturally disagree. How is it possible for whisky *not* to absorb the taste of salt spray carried by the wind?

Kilchoman farm distillery

Visitors to Islay can be misled to believe that whisky distilleries traditionally lie by the sea, as is the case today. But as mentioned before, whisky used to be made in sheds near the smallholders' homes. Or in caves or hideaways in the wilderness if distilling was illegal. It was only when the distilleries began to produce large quantities legally that export and access to the sea became important. Thus Kilchoman distillery, west on Islay, is proud to be able to call itself Islay's only traditional *farm* distillery. A distillery which does almost everything itself: grow the barley and tend to the malting, store the casks on Islay, and bottle the whisky. The first single malt on Islay from Kilchoman went on the market in 2009.

The manager of Kilchoman shows me around. The distillery is small and has three employees. 'But we don't produce for just anyone,' the director assures me. 'We aim for the whisky enthusiasts,' he says. 'Not those who only drink whisky once a year at Christmas.' I feel somewhat uncomfortable. Does the director find me sufficiently 'enthusiastic'?

Kilchoman sells only single malt. When I visited the distillery, the first whisky was still maturing in its casks. Therefore, there was no tasting at the end of the tour, as is the custom in the other distilleries. Since whisky needs to be stored for at least three years, it takes time before investments pay off. The only thing Kilchoman had sold to obtain capital were 250 unfinished casks of whisky to private buyers. As a business, whisky is risky. You need optimism, knowledge and money to go ahead. As a rule only big companies have enough capital to run distilleries.

After the visit to the dark storage room where the casks were stacked on top of each other, the director continues, 'We are concentrating on limited edition and are only interested in mature markets, customers who are used to whisky. This is not a whisky for the hoi polloi.' I took the hint and left.

Oak casks

Kilchoman experiences the same challenges as all start-up whisky distilleries; they know what they have, but not what they get. Whisky does not mature in bottles. It

Kilchoman whisky destillery, Islay

does so only in casks, which flavour the whisky as it ages. The production of malt whisky can well be compared to having children. It takes just six days to make the liquor, but you are not done looking after it until it has spent ten, fifteen or twenty years maturing in its cask. Sometimes it lives at home until it is thirty or more.

It's the casks which give colour to the whisky, because new whisky is colourless. Previously the most common and approved practice was to use old sherry casks. Today, most use former American bourbon casks made of oak. Some distilleries give their whisky a so-called 'finish,' or double-maturing, some months before it's bottled. An intense experience for the whisky, which perhaps has been lying peacefully for up to ten to fifteen years, and it soon finds itself in comfortable surroundings. It is tapped from ordinary bourbon casks over to ones steeped in aromas, in casks which in their earlier life have lovingly held sweet port wine or sherry. Or wine from Sauternes, such as a sweet Château d'Yquem. The sweetness mingles with a spicy, somewhat fiery and smoky Lagavulin Distillers Edition, or a faintly peaty Bruichladdich, but the result is the same. The whisky becomes smooth and full-bodied, absorbing mellowness from casks from southern lands.

The Lord of the Isles

One of Ardbeg's whiskies is sold out. 'The Lord of the Isles' is now a collector's item. Nose: nuts, sea air, calfskin, smoke, marmalade. The name on the label has a very special connection to Islay and the MacDonald clan.

In my childhood home, an old stitchwork piece framed in glass hung on the wall, the motto of the MacDonald clan, delicately embroidered by my great grandmother: *Per mare per terras; by sea and by land.* The biggest and most powerful clan in Scottish history.

The founder of the MacDonald clan was a Hebridean chieftain who ruled in the 1200s, Domhnall mac Raghnaill, or, if you will, Donald, child of Reginald, or Ranald. He had inherited his power mainly thanks to his grandfather, the Norse-Gaelic hero Somerled, who in a gigantic sea battle outside Islay in 1156 won the Hebrides and the west coast from a petty Norwegian king. Somerled now called himself Ri Innse-gall, the 'King of the islands which are ruled by the foreigners;' Norwegians, in other words.

When Somerled died in 1164, his three surviving sons divided the islands, formally under the Norwegian kingdom, and the west coast, under the Scottish king. The sons became the founding fathers of several of today's clans. Ranald took over Islay and Kintyre, and it was his son Donald who became the founder of the MacDonald clans.

The islanders perhaps had misgivings about Norwegian state ownership of the islands, but were even more concerned about the thought of living under the Scottish feudal system. Thus it was perhaps not so strange that the son of Donald, Angus Mor MacDonald, supported King Haakon Haakonsson when his fleet met the Scottish soldiers at the Battle of Largs in 1263. Angus Mor fought loyally together with the Norwegian king, who on his side recognised Angus as the first Lord of Islay. The Battle of Largs did not end as King Haakon had hoped. His fleet was scattered by bad weather and the king and his men sought refuge in the Orkney Islands, where he fell sick and died in Kirkwall. In a peace agreement three years later, the Norwegians had to relinquish the Hebrides to the Scottish throne.

The same throne, however, could not stop chiefs of the MacDonald clan from becoming autonomous petty kings, ruling over the Hebrides and large parts of the west of Scotland. In fact, it was more difficult for the Scottish than the Norwegian king to control this self-declared kingdom. There were no roads. The mountains in northwestern Scotland, the Highlands, divided the towns in the Lowlands from the islands. Deep sea lochs made the western seaboard formidable. Many of the islands lacked suitable anchorage, and the heavy Scottish warships were difficult to manoeuvre and navigate in the dangerous waters, strewn as they were with rocks and islets. On the other hand, the clan chiefs sailed about elegantly in their *birlinns*, improved Scottish copies of Viking boats, where a side rudder was substituted by a stern rudder. Thus from the 1300s, the power over the Hebrides was in reality shared between the Scottish king and the kingdom of the Lords of the Isles, a state within a state, managed from Islay. For the majority of the Scottish population, the island and western coast was a *terra incognita*. Primitive and dangerous.

Finlaggan

Usually the castles of the Scottish clans were by the sea, typically on some crumbling clifftop with a good view to all sides. Thus the Macdonald clan made an original decision when they established their seat of power at Finlaggan, a loch northeast on Islay. Today there is very little to show that it was here that the Lords of the Isles held court, applying in all probability their own system of justice according to Celtic law.

There are two small islands lying east in the loch, close by land, which were previously connected by narrow stone causeways barely above the surface. Now a bridge leads over reeds and muddy water to the first island. By the ruined chapel, I try to capture from the low stone walls memories they have been storing for 500 years. Neighing horses, fumes from red deer grilling on the spit, boisterous men with wine glasses raised. *Slainte bha!* To your good health! But all I hear is the endless wind.

The chapel roof is of course long gone. Gravestones rest on what was once a floor, which over the years has become a carpet of grass. Here, the wives and children of the Lords of the Isles were put to rest. The Lords, however, were carried by boat to the Holy Island of Iona and buried there. Not far from the chapel was the hall where the lord entertained his guests. The chiefs of the different branches of the MacDonald clan took their places at the lord's table in Finlaggan. The hall had a large hearth, the smell of burning peat filled the room. Gaelic bards entertained the guests in the soft light of oil lamps, the musicians playing on Jews' harps, bagpipes, and drums.

The MacDonald clan also had a combined castle and stronghold by the sea. The remains lie on a cliff overlooking the approach to Lagavulin distillery. So why do the court at Finlaggan and the castle at Dunyvaig lie in ruins? Opinion is divided on this particular issue. The story of the demise of the clan depends on who writes it.

One version holds that the MacDonalds squandered their properties. They went to bed with the enemy. The fourth and last Lord of the Isles, John II, made a secret pact with the English king Edward IV in 1462, a revealing contract which laid down how they would share Scotland between themselves if the English managed to evict the Scottish king. Some years later, the deal was exposed. In 1475, John II was condemned for treachery and some of his property was forfeited to the crown. Strangely enough he was allowed to keep the islands and his life, in return for promising loyalty to the Scottish king. This could all have ended peacefully

Mr. L. Powell and his peat stack, Islay

and agreeably. But John's relatives were enraged that they had lost land. They had not pledged any form of loyalty, and rebelled.

Finally, in 1493, King James IV, fed up with the quarrelsome clan, confiscated the MacDonalds' land, influence, power, and title. Once more John II escaped with his life, as long as he promised never to return to the islands. He lost the title of 'Ri Innse Gall,' and died a king without a kingdom.

In hindsight, the period under the MacDonalds is seen as a relatively peaceful one in the Hebrides. The power struggles between the earlier rival groups from Ireland, Norway, Scotland and England had died away after the Lords of the Isles became rulers of the Hebrides in the 1300s. Thus the king of Scotland acquired new problems when he destroyed the lordship of John II. One important fact remained unchanged: it was no easier for the central powers to exercise control over the islands and Highlands in the 1500s than the 1200s. The power vacuum which arose following the clan-based kingdom on Islay would lead to a violent chapter in the history of the Hebrides, a period that was to last about 250 years. Clan battles. Bloody massacres. Assassinations. Intrigue and betrayal.

Titles seldom disappear. They wander on throughout history. So what happened to the title 'The Lord of the Isles?' It was confiscated by the Scottish crown when the MacDonalds lost power in 1493. So in 1603, the English and Scottish thrones shared the same monarch, King James VI of Scotland, who was also James I of England. Now, 500 years after the Scottish chiefs lost their title, the Laphroaig-loving Prince Charles is the present 'Lord of the Isles.'

Paps of Jura

'This isle is perhaps the wholesomest plot of ground either in the isles or continent of Scotland, as appears by the long life of the natives and their state of health,' writes Martin Martin in his travel journal from the Hebrides in 1695. The mountain air on Jura is given the credit for the longevity of its people, and indeed, a fellow by the name of Mac Crain is said to have celebrated no less than 180 Christmas Eves in his own house. It's not only that we live long, the people tell Martin; not a single woman has died in childbirth in the last thirty-four years! No cases of madness have been registered, and, the islanders add not without pride, the neighbouring islands of Islay and Gigha have many diseases we don't even know about.

A steep bend leads to the deserted ferry terminal of Port Askaig on Islay. There is a cycle path for the last 200 metres, probably the only one on Islay, or in the Hebrides for that matter. A hotel with mossy windowsills and walls waits for customers. Merry flags fly perpendicularly from lines straining to hold them down. The owners appear to have abandoned trying to freshen up the faded notice boards, which inform one that the hotel also has a bar. Nevertheless, the view is impressive. Across the Sound of Islay, the three Paps of Jura tower—breast-shaped, pale, quartz mountains. Those very mountains which, according to Martin Martin, were the source of that wonderfully healthy breeze. When I last saw them, the north wind had borne snow and left its cold burden on the Paps.

Eilean Dhiura, the small open ferry which struggles through the strong current in the sound between Islay and Jura, chugs confidently towards Port Askaig, berthing alongside the pier as it has done countless times before. The crossing takes only five minutes.

On unmarked paths

It has not been easy to prepare for this visit to the Paps of Jura. A green brochure, 'Jura—a guide for walkers,' simply states: 'There are no clear or obvious routes. Different walkers—whether residents or visitors—have their own preferred route.'

Let me confess right away: I underestimated how steep the mountains were. Their rounded breast-like forms are deceptive. An hour's walk from the road through boggy holes and heather lies a small loch: Loch an t'Siob. By the foot of Beinn Shiantaidh, the holy mountain, huge stepping stones lie in a row across the river, which meanders from the loch through peat bogs and quartz on its journey to the sea, lying leaden far below. Crossing the river, the next thing is to find 'the preferred path.' 'Take care not to get too high up the slope of Beinn Shiantaidh,' warns the green guide, leaving me wondering about the fate of those who ignore this advice. And how high is 'too high'?

The paths are muddy and downtrodden. Yesterday the Isle of Jura Fell Race took place here. During my considerably less ambitious expedition, I meet a straggler from yesterday's event. An Englishman in shorts and joggers is bouncing in my direction. Fifty metres away he plunges into the mud, struggles up, and undeterred, hastens on like a hare hound which has got the wind. 'I was in the race yesterday,' he pants in civilised English, 'but I got lost in the mist. So I only managed to climb two of the three Paps.' Naturally, he was disqualified. Today, he ran up to the last top. A matter of pride? Or practice for next year's run?

Respect for these determined people rises as fast as my pulse as I start to climb Beinn Shiantaidh. The terrain gives nothing away freely. The spongy surface sucks and grips my boots, and barely lets go before it greedily swallows them again. There are deer tracks in the mud, hoof prints from one of the 5,000 of its kind wandering freely around Jura. A golden eagle sails in the currents above me. Seven pairs nest in the mountains.

I am on my way up to the pass between Beinn Shiantaidh and Beinn an Oir, the Golden Mountain. This, according to the 'wee green,' is route number 2. 'Once you reach the saddle you can decide which one to climb. Sometimes the one will be in cloud but not the other.' Right enough! The top of Beinn Shiantaidh is hidden in mist.

The surface of the path has become hard quartz and is taking me along a small, dried out streambed. Or is it a path? Soon I find myself clambering with hands and feet. The wind has picked up and tugs at my rucksack. My grip becomes unsteady. The rest of Jura and the neighbouring Hebridean islands slowly come in to view. A traveller by the name of Walker relates enthusiastically that through the haze he could see the Isle of Man in the south, and the Isle of Skye in the north. He even caught site of the northern part of Ireland towards the west, and mainland Scotland to the east. Arriving on the final plateau, just below the cairn on the summit, a gust of wind blows me off my feet.

Martin Martin attributed the islanders' good health to the height of the hills and the fresh breezes that come off them. Perhaps it was the rumour of health-bringing breezes which 250 years later tempted a dying writer to settle on Jura.

George Orwell

When George Orwell landed on Jura in the spring of 1946, he was a sad, worried, and sick man. Sad because he had become a widower; worried because he now had the sole care of his two-year-old adopted son Richard; and both ill and worried because his lungs were affected by a serious disease.

The original plan had been to visit the island with his wife Eileen in 1945. They intended to locate and visit a farm, Barnhill, to decide whether they should move to Jura. They planned to stay on the island for ten days, he wrote to Mrs. Nelson, who owned Barnhill. Eileen just needed time to recover after a forthcoming operation, Orwell explained. Soon Mrs. Nelson received a new letter. Eileen was only thirty-nine years old when she died following a routine operative procedure in the spring of 1945. Their baby Richard was not yet one year old and the publication of *Animal Farm* only months away. Eileen never made it to Jura and Barnhill.

Orwell's main reason for going to Jura was that he needed a place where he could work in peace. He had a book in mind. The idea had been there for some time, it wasn't new. 'I first thought of it in 1943,' he wrote in a letter from Jura. At home in London, however, he was weighed down by journalistic work for the newspaper *The Observer*, leaving him no time left to write a novel. He also lacked the same energy as before. His illness was stealing away his strength. This was, however, nothing new. In 1938 he was already coughing up blood; writing the book was now becoming a matter of urgency. He had cheated death once before, when a sniper bullet from Franco's army struck him millimetres away from the carotid artery in his neck. When he moved to Jura in 1946, Orwell must have realised, in a pessimistic moment, that death would soon cheat him out of a long life. He could not get to Barnhill fast enough.

The farm lies on the north of the island. To get there you drive on the only road there is, as far as it goes. Then you have to walk six kilometres, unless you have a four-wheel drive. Barnhill provided Orwell with the isolation he craved. It was almost forty kilometres from the island's only shop, doctor, post office and telephone. His nearest neighbours, Mrs. Nelson and her family, were ten kilometres away.

Mrs. Nelson's memories from the time are recorded in a thin yellow pamphlet: *Jura and George Orwell*. Barnhill had been deserted during the war and was rather run down. For several days before the author arrived on the island, Mrs. Nelson made sure the place was put in order as far as possible. The furniture was sparse; in fact, the whole place was very basic. A camp bed, a table, one chair, and some pots and pans. 'He said he would be all right,' she says in the yellow pamphlet, 'and preferred to manage on his own. I had the impression that he was content as long as he had a roof over his head and a loaf of bread to eat.' However, she was worried. How would this tall, gaunt and sad-looking man manage on his own?

Orwell's life as a hermit did not last long. Soon he was joined by his son Richard and sister Avril. According to Mrs. Nelson's memoir, the little family received many visitors during that first summer. Friends often turned up without notice, since they, and the letters they had sent to announce their arrival, often arrived simultaneously. 'Therefore, if you proposed coming on, say, June 15th,' wrote Orwell to a friend, 'it wld [would] be as well to write abt [about] June 5th because, according to the day of the week, it may be 4 or 5 days before your letter reaches me, & another 3 or 4 days before I can send a message. It's no use wiring because the telegrams come by the postman.'

Corryvreckan

One August day in 1947, Orwell and a couple of guests made an excursion. On board the small boat was also Richard, then three years old. It could be that the little group of four had been visiting one of the author's favourite places. In a letter he described the deserted bays and 'the beautiful white sandy beaches.' On the return journey he failed to take account of Corryvreckan, the world's third largest whirlpool, on the north end of Jura. It can behave quietly and calmly, but when tides and wind combine their strengths, the currants in the sound become roaring, whirling masses of water, which can be heard at a distance of six kilometres.

Orwell's row boat had an outboard engine, but that was quickly torn away by the strong current. It must have been a terrifying experience. Orwell wrote in a letter: 'Recently four of us including Richard were all but drowned in the famous whirlpool of Corrievrechan [...]' The small crew managed to row the boat to a deserted little island 'where we might have been stranded for a day or two, but very luckily some lobster fishermen saw the fire we lit for a signal and got us off.'

The young Norwegian prince Breackan, after whom the whirlpool is named, had a much worse fate. As with all legends, this one also has many variations. Prince Breackan was in love with a local princess, but to gain her hand in marriage was no easy matter. The father of the chosen lady challenged the suitor: He could have his daughter's hand if he managed to set anchor in the whirlpool over three days and three nights.

Breackan returned to Norway and had three ropes made: one of hemp, one of wool, and the third pleated from the hair of virgins. Such a rope would withstand anything, and the virgins willingly gave up their long plaits. Back in Jura, Breackan anchored up in the whirlpool and secured the boat with the various ropes. On the first day, the hemp rope snapped; the second day, the wool rope gave way. All went well on the third day, the rope of pleated virgins' hair still held, thanks to the magical powers associated with the donors' purity ... right until a strong wind managed to destroy even this last rope. The boat and Breackan were quickly sucked into the whirling masses of water. When his body floated ashore, the crew carried the drowned prince to a cave, and laid him to rest in what to this day is known as Breackan's Cave. When news of the prince's death reached Norway, one of the virgins was overcome with guilt. She was perhaps not quite as virginal as she had claimed, after all. It might be her hair, she had to admit, that had caused the rope to finally give way.

1947

George Orwell, or 'Eric Blair,' his real name and as he was known on Jura, survived the Corryvreckan. But the accident, exposure to cold, and soaking wet clothes made him sicker. During the autumn of 1947 he often lay in bed banging away on his typewriter in the upper storey of the isolated, spartan house. In December 1947, a specialist came all the way from Glasgow to examine him. For the first time he was diagnosed with tuberculosis. In a letter the same month he wrote: 'I was conscious early this year of being seriously ill & thought I'd probably got T.B. but like a fool I decided not to go to a doctor, as I knew I'd be stuck in bed & I wanted to get on with the book I was writing.' A couple of months later he adds in a letter from the hospital: 'This disease isn't dangerous at my age [...]'

In October 1948, Orwell wrote in a letter, now from Jura: 'I am not pleased with the book but I am not absolutely dissatisfied [...] I think it is a good idea but the execution would have been better if I had not written it under the influence of T.B. I haven't definitely fixed on the title, but I am hesitating between "Nineteen Eighty-Four" and "The Last Man in Europe".'

The popular explanation is that the title *1984* is simply a reversal of the year the book was completed. According to the journalist Robert McCrum in the newspaper *The Observer,* this myth started with a statement from the American publisher of the book, and not from Orwell himself. McCrum points out that there could have been several sources of inspiration for the title. One theory is that the figure represents the 100-year anniversary of the establishment of the British socialist

Fabian society in 1884, of which Orwell was extremely critical, and to some degree is the model for the society described in *1984*. Others point out that the year figures in writings by authors such as Jack London, where a political movement comes to power in 1984. Or perhaps Orwell could have been inspired by another story of the future, *The Napoleon of Notting Hill*, which also takes place in 1984.

In 1949, Orwell had to give up Barnhill and Jura and was admitted to a tuberculosis sanatorium in England. He died on the 21st of January 1950. Inscribed on an unpretentious, grey gravestone in Oxfordshire are the simple words:

Here lies
Eric Arthur Blair
Born June 25th 1903
Died January 21st 1950

Home again

Climbing up Beinn Shiantaidh, I did not look back to memorise the path. When descending, I followed what *looked* like a path, but which ended in a steep overhang, forcing me to turn back. Finally I slithered down a gulley in the mountain, slipping on quartz pebbles; it might have been either the bed of a stream or a rough path. The unrelenting mist from Beinn Oir soon embraced the Holy Mountain, enveloped the cairn, and mingled with the stormy gusts.

On my way back to the ferry I drove through the little village of Craighouse, which, at a stretch, could be considered the capital of the island. Jura whisky distillery was closed for the day. Mountain tents flapped in an improvised campsite, looking miserable in the rain. The tents were struggling to keep upright, tugging impatiently at the guy ropes. The participants in yesterday's race were preparing to go home. They packed primus stoves and pots and pans, stuffed muddy clothing and boots into plastic bags, all the while thanking each other for yet another great race on this remote island, promising to return next year. The sprightliest were biking to the ferry and further up the shortest cycle path in the world on arrival at the ferry terminal on Islay. Peace settled once more on Jura's 220 inhabitants.

Oban

North of Kintyre on the west coast of Scotland lies the harbour town of Oban—the point of departure for most of the ferries to the isles. With the establishment of the Oban whisky distillery the town grew rapidly, and during the 1800s it became a busy port. The ferry company MacBrayne opened up the isolated islands to the wider world, and the steamships became loaded with post and tourists. Today the CalMac ferries glide smoothly back and forth between destinations in the Inner

Hebrides: Lismore, Mull, Coll, Tiree, Colonsay; as well as to Uist, Barra, Harris, and Lewis in the Outer Hebrides.

Finding a parking place here in the summer is a nightmare. On this, the *Rough Guide* and I totally agree. However, the author of the same appears to find no reason to stay a night in Oban. On the contrary. There is every reason to spend a night here. The town is perfect for wandering aimlessly about. The promenade along the waterfront takes you past bobbing fishing boats and stalls selling fresh seafood. Victorian sandstone houses rise in terraces up the hillside. From the promenade, across the street you will see McTavish's Kitchen, an establishment with a high tartan factor, bagpipes, drums and sing-a-longs.

The eye is drawn to a building perched high up on the hillside. McCaig's Folly. It is totally out of place on the Scottish west coast, but rich men throughout the ages in these parts have been inclined to leave behind grandiose monuments in their name. Castles and mausoleums, and now here, a mini-Colosseum. It was erected by the businessman McCaig around 1900. His grand plan was to erect statues of the family in each of the rounded windows of the Roman-inspired monument. The Folly was also a humanitarian project with three objectives: to ensure McCaig's everlasting memory, that jobless stonemasons had an income, and that Oban got a museum and art gallery. However, McCaig died before the monument was finished, and his relatives saw no reason to complete it.

The hotels in Oban are remnants of another age. The rather shabby but dignified Caledonian Hotel from the 1800s could deservedly be included in the Norwegian author Kjartan Fløgstad's *Hotel Tropical,* where hotels from colonial times, often Victorian in style, appear in all their former beauty. However, the Caledonian is obviously not in the tropics: quite the reverse. Neither is the hotel in Oban representative of an archaeological and cultural meeting between colonisers and the colonised, as Fløgstad puts it. Or perhaps there *are* some parallels here? Could it be going too far to compare the power elite of England and the Lowlands of Scotland with colonial oppressors? Undoubtedly, abuse of power against the Gaelic population was present in the 1800s. And could there not also be a slight racist angle? A perception that the 'Gaelic race' was less developed and needed to be civilised? The hotel in Oban is certainly not a product of Gaelic architecture. It's a symbol of a time when lowland Scotland and England were fascinated by the wild and primitive Celts, simultaneously aspiring to both tame and civilise them.

Caledonian Hotel was built when the railway reached Oban from Glasgow in 1880. It was then known as The Station Hotel. The railway brought tourists, giving a new lease of life to the ferry traffic to the islands. Mirrored in the eyes of the tourists, many of the islanders glimpsed a distorted image of themselves. A romantic vision, or a people to be wary of, subjects of either contempt or pity.

Old, grey, Caledonian Hotel has seen ladies of the Victorian age strolling along the promenade under flimsy parasols, arm-in-arm with gentlemen in top hats. Perhaps some had spent the night in one of the airy rooms overlooking the promenade and harbour. Maybe one of these ladies had followed the advice given to women of those times: 'to lie back and think of England.' The following morning, she and her husband would take the steamship to the islands, far from civilisation, to explore sublime, intimidating, and overwhelming nature.

The ferry, Isle of Mull, which plies between Oban and the island of Mull, takes forty minutes. Placards encouraging passengers to follow the 'diet circle' are posted in the cafeteria, which reeks of fried food. Fishermen in long yellow rubber boots are guzzling fatty doughnuts and black tea. The cafe offers the usual CalMac breakfast: eggs, bacon, fried tomatoes, sausages, baked beans, and for the brave, black pudding. I long to get away from the smell of stale cooking oil, which saturates the air and clings to my pores, hair and clothes. A government report from 1999, *Towards a healthier Scotland,* concludes that the traditional diet is dangerous. In short, it has far too much fat, salt and sugar. In addition, continue the health authorities, the Scots eat too few fruits and vegetables. State-subsidised CalMac tries to keep up with the times and sells salads, but the breakfasts and dinners continue their deep-fried tradition, ignoring government recommendations.

On deck, the air is much fresher. On the starboard side the ferry glides towards a lighthouse built by one of the engineers from the Stevenson dynasty. Through 250 years and four generations, this family illuminated the Scottish coastline, saving thousands of lives from underwater rocks and wreck robbers. A BBC series, *Seven Wonders of the Industrial World,* presents the seven greatest achievements in the field of engineering. The Bell Rock Lighthouse on the east coast is one of them. It is the oldest existing offshore lighthouse in the world, built by Robert Stevenson, the founder of the dynasty. The lighthouse we are now passing on the ferry, built in Lismore in 1833, is also one of Robert's.

There was a black sheep in the family of engineers: the grandchild of Robert Stevenson, the author, Robert Louis Stevenson, 'R.L.S.' to his friends. After his father pressed him to study law and engineering, which he was not at all interested in, Robert Louis rebelled, not very successfully, against the familial expectations. But R.L.S. had made up his mind; he wanted to write. In retrospect it is he who emerges as famous in the Stevenson family. The eight engineers who built ninety-seven manned lighthouses are forgotten by most. On the other hand, *Treasure Island,* *Kidnapped* and *Dr Jekyll and Mr. Hyde* remain as classics in the world of literature.

Duart Castle and Scottish nationalism

There on the port side lies the Isle of Mull, dressed in brown, lifeless colours. It's Easter and the hills are barren. The snow has just melted. Duart Castle dominates a promontory overlooking the Sound of Mull. Through my view-finder I see a beautiful, stereotypical postcard from Scotland, a cliché with roots in reality.

Duart castle, Mull

The unassailable stone castle stands on the edge of a cliff, with the high, deserted mountains of Mull as a backdrop. This is the clan seat of the Macleans, and was the location for the film *Entrapment*, with the Scottish actor Sean Connery in the leading role. The daily reality is less dramatic. The present chief, Sir Lachlan Maclean, is number twenty-eight in the line. The saying 'My home is my castle' is appropriate in his case. This is Sir Lachlan's home, but the castle is open for paying visitors. It costs a lot to maintain a castle.

Sean Connery, whose mother was also a Maclean, is a fervent nationalist, and gives economic support to the Scottish National Party, SNP. Some would have it that there are none more nationalistic than Scots who live abroad, like Sean Connery. SNP characterises itself as a centre/left party whose main goal is Scottish independence. Scotland established its own parliament in Edinburgh by popular vote in 1997. However, the Scottish parliament has only a limited law-making mandate. In reality it is the British parliament in Westminster that decides which sectors the Scots can regulate. Perhaps it was no coincidence, then, that the National Party did well in the 2007 landslide election. It coincided with the 300-year jubilee of the union between the Scottish and English parliaments. Prior to this, Scotland had been an independent nation. There are clearly many who would like to return to this proud past. [Since the first publication of this book, in Norwegian, a referendum in 2014 on the issue of independence for Scotland has opted by a narrow margin to stay on as part of the UK.]

What would independence mean in practice? The newspaper *The Independent* discusses some scenarios. All Britons would choose which nation they belonged to, and everybody would have to have a new passport. Scotland might adopt the Euro as currency, while England would continue with pound sterling. There could be border controls. The present unhindered flow across the border would never be the same again.

Many *English* voters would like to see Scotland become independent too. Anti-Scottish sentiment has increased following the establishment of the Scottish parliament and the growth of the SNP. 'Parasites!' declare a few Englishmen contemptuously, and point out that more pounds are spent on Scottish heads than English. Don't the Scots have a welfare system on par with the Scandinavians based on tax returns at an American level? So let them have their independence! Then we will not have to subsidize them and all their deserted windy islands and districts! Like the Hebrides, which would not have been viable without considerable economic transfers.

The SNP retaliates: Independence will mean that Scotland can better steer its own economy. We will also receive EU support and expand our contacts with our neighbours, the Nordic countries, Norway, Iceland and Denmark. And anyway, we have all the income from our oil industry! As if England would let go of its share of the oil income, just like that, *The Independent* comments dryly.

On deck I can now discern the details of Duart Castle. The stone walls, the cannons, the chimneys from innumerable fireplaces. The castle was restored in 1911 when the then Chief of the Maclean clan bought it, after it had been out of family ownership for over 200 years. The centuries without the protective oversight of Clan Maclean had taken their toll of the stronghold. It lay in ruins. Today it includes a museum which tells the history of the clan.

The Lady on the Rock

Like all other Scottish clans, the Macleans also had their share of more or less eccentric or gruesome chiefs. The small, salt-coated windows set in the thick walls of the castle provide a good view of the sound separating Mull from the mainland. From there one can glimpse a black, wet rock. The Lady's Rock.

In the 1500s the eleventh Chief of the Maclean Clan, Lachlan Cattanach, married Catherine Campbell. A Campbell! The enemy clan! She was also the sister of the third Earl of Argyll, Colin Campbell. The Campbells had taken over most of the lands of the once-powerful MacDonald clan. Through cunning, strategic alliances and brutal force, they had acquired properties from other clans as well.

The marriage between Catherine and Lachlan was a failure, as is often the case when husband and wife are forced together for the sake of political alliances. Theories about what went wrong abound. Some say that the relationship soured when she did not bear him a son. Yet others claim she tried to poison her husband. The end of the story was that Lachlan plotted to quit himself of his wife once and for all, by drowning her. He would have her placed on a rock which disappeared under the waves at high tide. Soon Lady Catherine found herself standing, abandoned and helpless, on a black slippery rock within sight of Duart Castle.

The tide rises quickly in these parts. The difference between high and low tide is about four metres. A fishing boat appeared, and Catherine was unsure whether this was a good or a bad sign. The Earl of Argyll and the Clan Campbell were not popular in this area. However, the fisherman took pity on the doomed woman and she found her way home to her brother's castle in Inveraray. The Earl in all probability could hardly have controlled his anger when his sister told him about her abominable treatment. However, he played innocent when he received condolences from his brother-in-law, who visited him, bringing the tragic news: 'My dear wife, your sister, has tragically been drowned at sea.'

Dinner was served and Lachlan Maclean was about to sit down at the table when he suddenly saw Lady Catherine. A ghost? She was safely seated beside her brother. The dinner proceeded with apparent calm. Lachlan probably thought this was his last supper. The Earl, on the other hand, thought perhaps the shock of seeing his supposedly drowned wife alive was punishment enough. Or perhaps it was simply not worth starting a feud with the Macleans. Lachlan went free, for a while. One evening in 1523, in Edinburgh, another of Catherine's brothers spied the ageing Lachlan as he was on his way home to bed. The brother followed him. He had certainly not forgotten how the Maclean chief had mistreated his sister. Lachlan ended his life between bloody sheets, stabbed to death by Lady Catherine's avenger.

Tobermory

The ferry Isle of Mull docks at the pier at Craignure on Mull, a village divided by the main road, boasting some houses, a pub, the tourist office, a small SPAR shop and a petrol station. The road heading west passes through a dark pine forest plantation and finally ends in the main town of Mull, Tobermory. Much remains unchanged in this charming little place, but I do notice one change. Poles and other Eastern Europeans work behind the bar and in the kitchens of the restaurants.

In 1787 Tobermory was chosen to be the hub of the fishing industry. One of the many organisations involved in information, improvements, or advocacy in the Hebrides was *The British Society for Extending and Improving the Sea Coast of the Kingdom*. Wisely, the organisation changed its name to The British Fisheries Society. The Society envisaged the village of Tobermory becoming a base for commercial fishing, if only it had a decent harbour. Herring abounded around the Scottish islands and soon the little harbour grew into a small town. Tobermory

Tobermory, Mull. Detail from Tobermory (bottom)

began to take the form it has today. A kind of maritime amphitheatre. The old houses, which today are painted in bright blue, pink, yellow, red and black, lie in a half-circle around the bay, standing shoulder to shoulder along the promenade. Behind this row of houses the terrain rises sharply, and the next generation of dwellings creeps ever higher up the hillside among wild ivy and holly. Of the 3,000 or so inhabitants of Mull and the small neighbouring islands of Iona and Ulva, about 700 live in Tobermory.

James Boswell and Dr Samuel Johnson and their journey to the Hebrides in 1773

Readers of books about the Hebrides will sooner or later come across two gentlemen by the names of Samuel Johnson and James Boswell. When this unlikely pair travelled around the islands in the autumn of 1773, the development of Tobermory had not yet begun. It was the Scottish, travel-happy lawyer Boswell who took the initiative. But he did not want to travel to the islands in the west without the company of Dr Johnson, his old friend and mentor, and double his age. Many years passed between when they first began to fantasise about the journey until the plan was realised. Later, they would both publish journals from the experience.

Dr Johnson was very home-bound; it was difficult to lure him away from London: '[…] when a man is tired of London, he is tired of life, for there is in London all life can afford.' Thus he was sixty-three years of age before he finally accepted Boswell's invitation, and travelled by horse-drawn carriage to Edinburgh to meet his younger friend.

Samuel Johnson was a highly-respected and very well-known man in his day; essayist, poet, editor, and literary critic. After he died in 1784, no less than seven biographies about him were published in England. Today, Johnson is mostly known for his work *The English Dictionary,* found in all respectable homes along with the Bible.

I have read somewhere that Dr Johnson is the most quoted person in the English language, after Shakespeare, of course. True or not I do not know, but I do recognise some of his sayings: for instance, 'The road to hell is paved with good intentions.' If one is to believe another Johnson adage, '[…] the conversation of the old and young ends generally with contempt or pity on either side,' then the friendship between young Boswell and the elderly Johnson could have come to a bad end. During an arduous journey, as we all know, relationships can become strained. But the journey to the Hebrides strengthened the twosome's friendship. True enough, Boswell was a great admirer of his older mentor, a helpful attitude in a friendship spanning a generation. But his admiration was not uncritical, and here and there in his work, *The Journal of a Tour to the Hebrides*, he exposes Johnson's weaknesses, moodiness, and prejudices about the Scots.

Boswell admits that now and then he had to challenge the Englishman and those who shared his opinions, when he felt contempt for the Scots had gone *too* far. Johnson's low opinion of his northern neighbours was evident in his dictionary when it came to defining the word *oats*: 'Oats: A grain, which in England is generally given to horses, but in Scotland supports the people.' Johnson does admit, however, that 'much may be made of a Scotsman if he is caught young.'

On the other hand, Boswell agrees that Scotland lags behind England in certain areas. His good friend Dr Johnson is right about that! Take, for example, the evening the two friends meet in Edinburgh before their day of departure and walk home together in the evening. True enough, there were then laws which forbade inhabitants in the old town, where the narrow stone houses towered upwards many stories, from throwing dirty water and emptying chamber pots out of windows onto the heads of those below. But there were still open sewerage gutters, and Dr Johnson murmurs into Boswell's ear, 'I smell you in the dark!' Now this could sound like a comment on Boswell's personal hygiene, which it was not. It was meant instead as a criticism of Scotland's capital city.

On the 13th of October, Dr Johnson and Boswell sail into Tobermory on Mull and have a meal at the inn, one of the few buildings existing at that time. In 1773 Tobermory was a well-known harbour, deep and sheltered. 'An excellent harbour,' Boswell wrote. They are not alone; many sailing vessels lie at anchor. Boswell immediately feels happier. After some days on the remote island of Coll, they have now landed in the middle of international marine traffic. Languages from many countries fill the air and they soak in fresh news from the world's capitals. All this is exalting for young Boswell.

Dr Johnson, on the other hand, is starting to miss the mainland. He feels no joy in seeing the busy harbour. In his chapter from Mull, he writes: 'All travel has its advantages. If the passenger visits better countries, he may learn to improve his own, and if fortune carries him to worse, he may learn to enjoy it.'

What exactly does Dr Johnson have in mind when writing this? Perhaps he is comparing his London life to what he observes on Mull, and feeling deep gratitude for what awaits him at home. The contrast between the wild, barren and impoverished Mull, and Johnson's comfortable life in the English capital, is formidable. In his journal he reflects on what it is like to exist, or barely survive, on the absolute minimum. Life in the Highlands and islands of Scotland was, in many respects, at the mercy of the whims of nature. There were no safety nets against poor harvests, no compensation for the loss of roofs or boats in a gale, no insurance against livestock perishing of hunger or disease. Even in the most productive years, the climate meant that there was just enough food to survive at subsistence level. Two years ago, writes Dr Johnson, both Mull and Skye, the islands with the highest mountains, experienced an extremely hard winter. The ground was snow-covered over a period of eight weeks. The cattle, which were the most important source of income, perished, since snow covered the meagre winter fodder. The poor animals were also tapped alive for blood when people had no food in the early spring. The blood was mixed with oatmeal, so the islanders could make the typical food of the poor, blood pudding. Dr Johnson writes: 'The consequence of a bad season is here not scarcity, but emptiness.' He continues: 'If to the daily burden of distress any additional weight be added, nothing remains but to despair and die.'

Boswell becomes anxious that perhaps the gloomy Dr Johnson will pull out of the planned journey to the Holy Island of Iona on the southwest coast of Mull. How can he cheer him up? A cup of tea, served with fresh bread and butter, helps to lift the spirits. Boswell teases his elderly companion. He thinks it's amusing to recall how everybody has described Dr Johnson: 'A good man! He is happy with everything! He is always satisfied!' 'Little do they know,' says Boswell to Johnson, who responds laughingly, 'You rogue!'

The inn where they stayed is still to be found behind the co-op shop. A local historian, Jean Whittaker, who works at Tobermory's small museum, showed me the passageway where the insignificant, anonymous old house lies. Nothing indicates that this was one of the township's first buildings, let alone an inn, or that Dr Johnson and Boswell stayed the night here. 'And,' says Whittaker, pointing to the neighbouring house, 'that's where the composer Felix Mendelssohn spent the night when he visited Mull.' But that occasion occurred long afterwards.

Tour of Mull

'We travelled diligently enough, but found the country, for road there was none, very difficult to pass,' wrote Dr Johnson. He would probably have nodded his approval of the road network on Mull today, all 500 kilometres of them. The roads, most narrow single-track, twist and turn following the coastline, generally without any form of safety barrier.

One October day I took the ferry to Mull to experience an annual event. Tour of Mull car rally is organised by an enthusiastic English rally club sponsored by the biscuit maker giant, Tunnock's. The event is nevertheless completely dependent on local volunteers, and turns the island upside down. I order a taxi, but it never arrives. The driver is in the rally. I go to the pub. The owner is not behind the counter as usual - he's now a rally driver.

The ferries to Mull are fully booked long before October approaches. In Tobermory there are No Vacancy notices in the windows of all the hotels and B&Bs. I phone the place I'm booked to stay the night. A pause on the telephone, then the voice, panic-stricken, of my hostess. She has cancelled my booking. 'I am awfully sorry,' she says. 'So am I,' I answer, perplexed. I have visions of spending the night

Getting ready for the Tour of Mull

in the pub on a flowery wall-to-wall carpet stinking of beer. But the landlady knows other landladies, and the problem is solved.

The rally begins the same evening and lasts for three days. Every day and night the participants drive different routes and the respective roads are closed. The rally starts off in Tobermory, then passes through Calgary, which lends its name to the city in Canada. The route continues from the white, sandy beach in Calgary, along the cliffs of Gribun, and west on Mull.

I spend the day exploring parts of the rally route before the roads close. MacKay's Garage, from which I hire my car, warns me. Loads of others will be on these roads today, practising for the evening's race. Luckily, the mechanics at MacKay's are wrong. I meet only a few rally drivers but the roads are challenging: sheer drops down to the sea on one side, mountain walls on the other. The road has barely room for one car, and the verges are not trustworthy. My respect for the rally drivers increases as I drive. I am struggling in daylight; they will be driving in darkness.

I think back to a conversation I overheard on the bus to Tobermory. A participant from last year's rally told her fellow passenger that she was unaware that the twisting single roads were closed to other traffic during the race. She thought she risked meeting cars coming towards her at any time: mile after mile, hairpin bend after hairpin bend, along sheer cliffs with no room for swerving, in pitch darkness, all in a kind of Celtic roulette.

Night falls. The roads are closed. Down at Mull's only whisky distillery, Tobermory distillery, the cars are lined up in a queue in front of a ramp. One hundred and sixty rally cars are waiting for their thirty seconds in the limelight before start time. They drive up the ramp one by one. 'She looks like a flying machine!' the Master of Ceremonies tells every third driver. It's not easy to come up with unique encouragement for 160 drivers.

The performance is over. Old Mr. Tunnock, of Tunnock's biscuit factory, gives the all-clear signal with the red and yellow flag, and the cars spin away to await their turn in the queue at the starting line outside Tobermory. There are headlamps and high-visibility vests everywhere. Revving up, lights inside the cars illuminate the map reader's place. The adrenaline levels are soaring. Out in the darkness nobody knows what lies in store for him or her.

In the pub I ask about the rules of rally racing. What happens, for example, if someone right behind blinds you with his headlights in the rear-view mirror and wants to pass? An eighty-two-year-old ex-rally driver, and his son of around sixty, treat me to a beer and offer me a short introduction.

'The unwritten rule is that you let the car behind pass. If you don't go with this, that car can shove you off the road.'

'Jesus. Are there many accidents?'

'Some.'

'Fatal?'

'Sometimes.'

'We came too late to see what we were expecting.'

So what was the corpulent Dr Johnson doing on these inhospitable yet hospitable islands, with bad knees, on horseback, on foot, or in open row boats? He writes that he had wanted to do this for so long he can no longer remember where the idea came from. Boswell, however, since he had noted Dr Johnson's words over so many years, writes that Dr Johnson was given Martin Martin's travel diary by his father when he was a child. Martin came from the island of Skye in the Hebrides. He was well educated and spoke both English and Gaelic. His journey to the Hebrides at the end of the 1600s described people and animals, nature and culture. Perhaps Johnson had also been inspired by some of Martin's statements, which appear to be just as valid today as they were three hundred years ago:

> It is a piece of weakness and folly merely to value things because of their distance from the place where we are born; thus men have travelled far enough in the search of foreign plants and animals, and yet continue strangers to those produced in their own natural climate.

Dr Johnson wanted to explore his immediate surroundings, in other words, the Hebrides. However, even though the islands are in geographic proximity to the rest of Great Britain, they appeared somewhat daunting and foreign to Dr Johnson. When he and Boswell were about to start their journey, it was found that he had equipped himself with a pair of pistols, bullets and gunpowder. Boswell reassured him. There was nothing to be afraid of! The pistols were left behind in Edinburgh.

Boswell, on the other hand, presents himself as well travelled and more open to other people and ways of life, in contrast to the English and anxious Dr Johnson. Boswell describes himself as a citizen of the world, and 'sincerely loves all clans, languages, peoples and nations.' In the years preceding the tour to the Hebrides, he travelled around Europe. In France he became acquainted with the philosophers Rousseau and Voltaire. In 1764, nine years before the journey to the Hebrides, he confided his travel plans to Voltaire. Boswell writes: 'He looked at me, as if I had talked of going to the North Pole, and said, 'You do not insist on my accompanying you?' 'No, sir.' 'Then I am very willing you should go.'

To do Voltaire and Dr Johnson justice, their view of the Hebrides did not diverge from the views prevailing at that time. Martin Martin wrote at the end of the 1600s that the lowland Scots viewed the Highlanders as barbaric, and that those who lived in southern Scotland knew as little about the peoples of the Hebrides as the inhabitants of Italy.

So, did they find what they were looking for? Dr Johnson writes:

> We came thither too late to see what we expected, a people of peculiar appearance, and a system of antiquated life. The clans retain little now of their original character, their ferocity of temper is softened, their military ardour is extinguished, their dignity of independence is depressed, their contempt of government subdued, and their reverence for their chiefs abated. Of what they had before the late conquest of their country, there remain only their language and their poverty.
> Their language is attacked on every side. Schools are erected, in which English only is taught ...

Johnson the tourist is in fact disappointed that the primitive but heroic way of life was disappearing. Gone is the power of the clan chiefs, the clash of sword meeting sword, the skirl of the bagpipes urging on to battle, the shrill war cries as the men storm down from purple, heather-clad hillsides. The clan chiefs and their heirs are now educated at Eton and other English establishments, and have flats in Edinburgh and London. Meanwhile, their subjects have begun to emigrate to America. They no longer feel the ancient, blind loyalty to the chief. The bonds of the clans have become brittle and broken, the leaders and their people have grown apart. Money, which not so long ago was an unknown currency, has come between them. The land, cultivated or not, until recently held in common by the clans, had now become the personal property of the chiefs and traded with the highest bidders.

The ancient Highland culture was disintegrating right in front of their eyes. The most immediate cause of this fragmentation was that many clan chiefs in the Hebrides, including the Maclean clan on Mull, had supported the wrong man in the fight for the British throne. They fought for the exiled Catholic Prince Charles Edward Stuart, who tried to win the royal house back for the Stuart family. This decision would cost the chiefs and their subjects dearly.

Bonnie Prince Charlie and the battle of Culloden

To fully comprehend the ground-breaking changes which took place in Gaelic society in the Highlands and in the Hebrides, one needs to understand the rebellion which began in 1745 and ended with the Battle of Culloden in 1746. This is such an important and well-known milestone in Scottish history that the period is referred to as 'before or after Culloden,' and the rebellion itself is known as 'the '45 rebellion,' or simply 'the '45.' This last battle on British soil took place twenty-seven years before Dr Johnson and Boswell visited the Hebrides. The defeat was still an open wound for many of the people the pair met, and even today Culloden is a symbol of humiliation and suppression of Scottish-Gaelic culture.

To find the precedents of Culloden, one must go way back to the winter of 1688, when the Catholic king, as both James VII of Scotland and James II of England, was forced into exile in Italy by the Protestant William III of Orange. But the exiled King James, from the Scottish royal line of Stuarts, still had loyal supporters, termed the Jacobites after the Latin version of the king's English name. In the ten years following King James's flight there were several Jacobite rebellions, but none which regained the throne.

When the relationship between Great Britain and France became very strained in the 1740s and the two states went to war, the grandchild of the exiled king, twenty-three-year-old Prince Edward Stuart, hoped that King Louis XV of France would invade his enemy on the other side of the Channel. With the help of the Catholic French he hoped to win back the English throne for the Catholic Stuarts. However, times had changed. Now it was King George II who sat on the British throne. He professed to the Protestant Presbyterian Church. A 'foreigner,' folk said, wrinkling their noses; the family was from the Continent. The British Royal house now hailed from a small German state: Hanover!

The French, however, were reluctant to invade their neighbour on the other side of the Channel, according to the historian James Hunter. They wanted support from a Jacobite rebellion in Britain if they were to consider invading. The Jacobites on their side hesitated to start a new rebellion without support from French troops. So both sides waited for the other to make up their mind. The young heir to the throne, Prince Charles, became impatient. He took a risky chance. With only seven followers his boat scraped onto the white sands of the island of Eriskay in the Outer Hebrides. For the first time in his life, the prince who grew up in Italy set foot on Scottish soil. The date was the 23rd of July 1745.

In the Hebrides he was in Jacobite country and he immediately began to rally supporters among the clan chiefs and their subjects on his way to the Scottish mainland. Forgotten was the Jacobites' condition of having the French army to back them up.

Prince Charles, or 'Bonnie Prince Charlie' as he became known in Scots-Gaelic history, managed by means of his convincing and enthusiastic personality to recruit a clan-based army. The soldiers marched in and took Edinburgh on the 17th of September 1745. However, Charles Stuart wanted more, and the army marched on over the border to England. They advanced without serious resistance, but the prince's advisors began to get cold feet. The plan to take London was too ambitious, they said, and advised him to turn back to Scotland. The Londoners breathed a sigh of relief, as did King George II. However, he finally proceeded to mobilise his own war machine, appointing his son the Duke of Cumberland, to lead his army.

The two armies met on a cold day in April 1746, on Culloden Moor, a flat, windy field outside Inverness in eastern Scotland. Prince Charles's army was crushed. The Battle of Culloden was nothing short of collective Gaelic suicide. Prince Charles fled from the battlefield and was soon once more in the Hebrides. Soldiers and warships searched the islands hunting for the fleeing prince, and a large reward was promised for his deliverance to the government. However, those who knew his hiding places did not allow themselves to be tempted by blood money. They remained loyal to the prince as he sailed from isle to isle, sheltering in barns and caves. He was on the run for five months until a French ship picked him up and brought him safely over the Channel. By October 1746 the prince was back on the Continent. He never again set foot in Scotland.

Many historians are baffled about the popularity of Bonnie Prince Charlie, as he was later dubbed. Was he really that 'bonnie' and brave? Was he not in truth an egotistic, spoilt swaggerer from Italy, with no knowledge of the people he was aspiring to rule over? How noble were his intentions? Did he want power no matter how many lost their lives in the process? These sceptical and probably partly justified questions never really became rooted in the national consciousness. Even his flight from the battlefield and the abandonment of his own soldiers were presented in a romantic light. Forgotten were the errors of judgement, his arrogance, and his cowardice at the critical moment. A Scots folksong is said to express a hope that Bonnie Prince Charlie and the Scottish Stuart dynasty will once more return to conquer the throne:

My Bonnie lies over the Ocean,
My Bonnie lies over the Sea,
My Bonnie lies over the Ocean,
Oh, bring back my Bonnie to me!

For many years after Culloden, the Jacobites gathered in caves and houses where they felt safe from prying eyes. They drank to the exiled prince. Even though there was a death penalty for doing so, they raised their glasses in protest and hope: 'To the Bonnie Prince!'

Revenge

The '45 rebellion had consequences which continue to affect the Hebrides to this day. The revenge enacted by King George II, the Duke of Cumberland, and the Scottish-English London-based parliament, was brutal. The historian James Hunter talks about a collective, undifferentiated punishment. The clan-based society had to be destroyed forever. Dissolved. Murdered. Raped. Burnt. The terms used during retaliatory action are those used today to justify what we now know as ethnic cleansing. The Gaelic-speaking inhabitants of the Highlands and islands were 'animals,' 'wolves,' 'monsters' and 'vermin.' There were even those demanding that the whole Gaelic nation be starved to death, whether or not they had supported Prince Charles. That would be the final solution to the problem. Alternatively, 'flames and swords' would do.

The final death blow to the culture came in the form of laws passed by the British parliament at that time. Dr Johnson and Boswell encountered the consequences of these new laws when they arrived in the Hebrides twenty-seven years after the Battle of Culloden. The parliament and king together aimed to destroy the social structure of the Gaelic peoples. The disloyal clans should never again be allowed to threaten the seat of power. Enough was enough! We are, after all, a nation state. Catholicism and the Gaelic language became synonymous with traitorship. Children were punished for speaking Gaelic in school; Catholic priests were persecuted.

The lands of the clans which had supported the rebellion were confiscated by the British state. Thus the majority of the clan chiefs in the Highlands and Hebrides lost extensive territory. However, it was not the land in itself which was the main issue. After all, there were limits to what profits could be eked out of mountains and barren valleys. The true power of the clan chiefs lay in how many fighting men they could mobilise. Thus all chiefs lost their right to keep their own army. Everything connected to soldiering was outlawed: weapons, of course, but bagpipes as well, the instrument which gave courage in battle while drowning out screams and the clash of swords. Even wearing of the kilt was forbidden. It was high time the barbarians learnt to dress like proper people. No matter whether the kilt was the only clothing they possessed.

'No Jews, negroes, gipsies, foreigners, or persons born in England'

Some years following Dr Johnson and Boswell's visit to Mull, the minister Dugald Campbell carried out a census of his parishioners. Among the 3,002 persons in his parish, there were 'No Jews, negroes, gipsies, foreigners, or persons born in England, Ireland, or the colonies.' He continued: 'No people are more attached to their native country [...] and it is only necessity that obliges them to leave it.'

On Mull one often comes across small deserted villages. Roofless houses, but with solid stone walls, lie in beautiful, lonely places. Once, the island had a population of 10,000. The casual visitor might be led to believe that nobody would leave here of his or her own free will, as the Rev. Campbell had declared. The guidebooks on these areas are thus inclined to equate the ruins with *the Clearances,* the forced evacuations. There can be no doubt that some of the people of Mull were forced from their homes. However, many of the villages were abandoned in more recent times and the inhabitants left voluntarily—to seek work and education, and to live their lives in warmer, more hospitable places. In short, to become more comfortable.

In 1970, the population was down to only 2,000 souls. Then something happened in the years that followed. Even although the migration continued, immigration was greater. Today there are 3,000 people living on Mull. No persons born in England, Ireland or the colonies, Campbell wrote. Is that so? A local joke says that 'there are more Englishmen living on Mull than in England.' Mull attracts many incomers because the island is near the mainland and offers good ferry connections. Today, one in four inhabitants is English: as were Mr. and Mrs. Morley, and their chow-chow Winston, whom I met in 2007. I stayed with them in Achaban House, a bed and breakfast near the ferry quay of Fionnphort on Mull. The over-middle-aged couple had, as did many other fellow Englishmen, sold all they owned to realise an old, romantic dream: to move to an island and start a new life. I wondered to myself how long they would cope. Managing a B&B business is no ordinary pensioners' life; the lights went out late at night, and as dawn came, they were already in full swing frying eggs and bacon.

The rural watchdog

I asked Anja Grosse-Uhlmann, a German who lives on the isle of Iona just west of Mull, about attitudes to incomers like herself. 'Well, many pensioners come here, and they are often better off than the locals. This angers people, because ordinary small houses are sold for 200,000 to 300,000 pounds. The consequences are that the sons and daughters of the local folks can't afford to buy a house. So now and again you find these anti-English sentiments. On the other hand,' said Grosse-Uhlmann, 'the incomers do contribute to the community.'

The question is: What will happen to the islands when a large percentage of the population originates from England? The tourists come to experience the island culture and way of life. The music. The Gaelic language. Green pastures, sheep, and Border collies. Pubs where fishermen in long, yellow Dunlop wellies consume stout, after the scampi have been dispatched to Spain on lorries. Peace and hospitality. Shops closed on Sundays. Unlocked doors and bicycles and a lack of criminal behaviour one can only dream about in Glasgow or London.

Some tourists may say, as did Dr Johnson over two hundred years ago, that 'we came thither too late to see what we had expected.' Tourists share a common feature: they have come TOO LATE. After reading the travel journal of Dr Johnson, it seems that tourists have been coming too late for several hundred years. The authentic, the original, has always been there BEFORE they managed to arrive.

Others will point out that the islands are not museum pieces, and the most important issue is their viability. The fact that cultures are in continual flux, that cultures are not destroyed, only changed. The islands will be better places to live thanks to the incomers and the changes they bring. Envy and gossip in small places can hinder creativity and innovation. The most resourceful leave: some argue they are fleeing from the pettiness. So we better wish the incomers welcome and create a society that is more tolerant, where it is easier to be different.

All small, tightly-knit communities have this less-than-charming side. When I approach the topic, ever so gently, the locals clam up. 'We look after each other here,' is the refrain. Up to now I have managed only to get incomers to discuss this issue. But they too tend to emphasise the positive aspects of small community life: 'We help each other out!'

Those incomers who have lived here for a number of years have managed to adapt. Others didn't. Perhaps they arrived on a beautiful day in May, when the cuckoo called and the daisy-covered *machair* merged into white sandy beaches, lapped by a turquoise sea. But then came autumn and winter. Everyday life. It became too stifling. Too much gossip, not necessarily of the nasty type, okay, but the longing to once more feel anonymous grew stronger with every stormy gust. The rural watchdog, invisible in May, now made itself felt, and was on duty day and night. There was not enough space. Or it was too dark. Too much rain, too many

Rubha nan Gall lighthouse, Mull

cancelled ferries, too many power cuts. The shops shut too early and had too few fresh items on their shelves. Not enough street lights, roads too narrow, too few job opportunities. Those contending with such matters moved back to the mainland.

So what exactly is this 'rural watchdog,' or the *bygdedyr*, as the expression created by the Norwegian author Tor Jonsson goes? What does he, or she, look like? The sociologist Andreas Hompland proposes: 'It's a kind of watchdog, good and faithful to those who conform and are well-behaved, but it barks against incomers and snaps at those who are different [...].' 'However,' he continues, 'this creature is soon to become a threatened species.' The question then is: Will it be missed? What will be lost when the *bygdedyr* dies? 'Then many small communities will die with it,' to cite Hompland.

Is this what will happen on islands like Mull and others with many incomers? Will the social control and the solidarity among people, the very glue bonding island communities, dissolve? What happens when incomers bring their own norms and values in their baggage? Will island communities become an 'incidental framework around solitary individuals' when there are sufficient incomers? So far, it appears that individuals on Mull and several other islands depend upon and look after each other, perhaps because they all share life on an island and not a mainland village.

An island isolates those who choose to live there. No roads lead to bigger towns. You are all in the same boat, so to speak, surrounded by water on all sides, with the same external challenges, such as the ferry company CalMac. They cancel departures far too often, according to the islanders. They shouldn't monopolize ferry service: They should have competition! Or some groups share the same goals, such as the collection of funds for the new swimming pool, a cooperative effort between big Mull and wee Iona. The island population had to collect at least 100,000 pounds in private donations in order to learn the art of swimming. All creative ideas were welcome, such as auctioning a book on eBay signed by Prince Charles. After twenty-eight years of effort, the building was completed. Now the children of Mull and Iona can, for the first time, learn to swim without having to travel to Oban and the mainland. The swimming pool, which was opened near the ferry terminal at Craignure, is a symbol of collective action. Proof that the communities of Mull and Iona, for the time being anyway, are much more than a bunch of solitary individuals.

From Tobermory to Ulva

Boswell and Dr Johnson left Tobermory after a few days to go to the holy isle of Iona, just off the Mull coast. They had estimated that the journey would take a couple of days. There were no roads from Tobermory to Iona in 1773, so the son of a Maclean chief, Young Coll, accompanied them. The plan was to stay overnight with a friend of the chief, but on the way Young Coll got the news that their host was on his deathbed. The plan had to be revised as so often happens in the Hebrides.

The travellers were forced to find an emergency solution. Young Coll had access to a wide network, including the chief of the clan MacQuarrie on the little island of Ulva, only a short boat trip from Mull. Ulva was so close that the three-some could just make it out in the dark. However, the wind was not on their side that evening, and their cries for assistance could not reach across the narrow sound between Ulva and Mull. By this time, the exhausted friends were imagining an uncomfortable, cold October night in the open, among bracken and heather. This nightmarish fantasy lasted right up until an anchored Irish ship observed them, sent out a row boat, and took the guests over to their unsuspecting host in Ulva House.

Boswell and Johnson had taken eight hours to travel twelve kilometres from Tobermory to Ulva, if they are to be believed. It's not certain that this really was the case. The maps in the 1700s were very different from those of today. But the terrain was the same: heather, moors, and rocky outcrops, and tall bracken where a machete would have been welcome. By the time they knocked on the door of Ulva House they must have been miserably wet and cold.

The Clan Chief MacQuarrie

Dr Johnson and Boswell are received hospitably by Chief MacQuarrie, but the large mansion of Ulva House is in poor repair. MacQuarrie is about to go broke and is up to his eyeballs in debt. But his worries are not allowed to dampen spirits, and they all enjoy a pleasant evening. The travelling companions find their host to be intelligent and good-mannered, in other words a man of the world. The clan is ancient, says MacQuarrie with pride. Ulva, or Ulfr's island as it was probably named by Norsemen, has been in family ownership for 900 years. The clan has, of course, its own burial place on Iona, like other noble clan chiefs and kings.

Boswell is a collector. He collects customs and traditions as if they were souvenirs. So he is all ears when the chief recounts the old tradition of *mercheta mulierum*, which gave the lairds the right to spend the wedding night with their tenant's newly-wed wives. This tradition still survives but in a much less primitive fashion, MacQuarrie assures his guests. When one of his tenants is about to marry, he presents the chief with a sheep. Or five shillings, if he doesn't have a sheep. Boswell is not impressed by the modern version of the tradition. 'I found that in Ulva, and, I think, nowhere else, is continued the payment of the *mercheta mulierum.'*

The two friends are each given their own elegant bed that night. But the mud floor in the bedroom is wet, and rain pours in through a broken window.

MacQuarrie had to sell the island of Ulva four years after Dr Johnson and Boswell spent the night with him. He was not alone. During the 1800s many landowners and clan chiefs experienced the same fate.

'Uncover red panel'

The following day the small party journeys further as planned, to the island of Inch Kenneth. It lies on the route to Iona, and their guide, Young Coll, has arranged a meeting with a relative, the chief of the clan Maclean, Sir Allan Maclean. They leave early that morning since MacQuarrie has assured them that 'there is nothing worth seeing on Ulva.'

Today this statement seems quite deceptive. However, the two gentlemen were first and foremost collecting exotic customs and were not overly interested in natural surroundings. And perhaps it was not surprising that they trusted Mac-Quarrie: after all, he was the expert on his own island. But could it be that in his preoccupied state of mind, MacQuarrie was starting to take leave of the isle the clan had owned for many hundreds of years? Perhaps, then, it was too painful to show his guests around the island he was about to forfeit.

Contrary to when Dr Johnson and Boswell visited Ulva, one can now call up a motor boat from the other side of the sound. 'To summon the Ulva ferry uncover red panel,' says the homemade notice board on the ferry quay on the Mull side. I push aside a little flap so that the red square is visible. And sure enough, the ferryman Donald Munro on the other side of the sound, a long stone's throw away, gets in his boat and sets course towards Mull.

On Ulva there is a little slipway of cement, and I find myself on the doorstep of the old, white stone house, The Boathouse, which serves 'fresh local oysters, cold white wine and Guinness.' There are also tables outside, side by side with a red telephone kiosk and red gas cylinders. A white and pale brown untidy-looking dog, which obviously belongs to the household, slouches around waiting patiently for titbits from visiting lunch guests. The Boathouse also functions as a mini tourist office, supplying maps, brochures, and books on Ulva.

Just behind The Boathouse there's a sign which lists walks in different directions. Ulva's hills rise to around three hundred metres. Walkers and cyclists should wear walking boots and use off-road tyres, the Ulva website advises. Especially if they want to explore the inner parts of the island. One of the signs points to my favourite coastal walk, The Woodland Walk, which meanders through the grounds of Ulva House, a wood with over-200-year-old ivy-clad trees and mossy stone dykes. Gentle rain falls on the pale green roof sheltering the path. The forest floor is blue, yellow and white. Scottish bluebells, primroses and wild garlic abound.

David Livingstone

Another sign points to 'Livingstone's Cave.' The path leads to the village where David Livingstone's father was born. Dr David-I-Presume-Livingstone: the African explorer, anti-slavery activist, and missionary. But did David Livingstone really discover new places in Africa? The waterfalls, rivers and forests often already had names. African names. But that didn't count for much in Victorian times.

Many years ago I was in Westminster Abbey. Livingstone is buried under the floor of the cathedral. He is in good company with other distinguished persons who have had the honour to be laid to rest there. Several of them have one thing in common: they have travelled to the Hebrides. Dr Samuel Johnson. The artists: John Keats, Lord Tennyson, and William Blake. However, it was the engineer William Telford who left behind the most tangible traces. Roads, bridges, churches, schools, harbours and manses which Telford designed and built are still standing today, as is, for example, the little old church in Ulva.

Embossed on Livingstone's gravestone is a brass plaque:

> Brought by faithful hands
> Over land and sea
> Here rests David Livingstone.
> Missionary. Traveller.
> Philanthropist.
> Born March 19. 1813.
> At Blantyre, Lanarkshire.
> Died May 1. 1873.
> At Chitambo's Village. Ulala.

When he died in Africa, the British authorities wished to give Livingstone 'a proper funeral,' as they put it. They demanded that the villagers hand over the body. After some back and forth, the Africans agreed to send Livingstone's remains to England, but they had pinned a notice on the dead missionary: 'You can have his body, but his heart belongs to Africa.' Literally, as was soon to become clear. His heart lies buried under a *mpundu* tree near the spot where he died, in today's Zambia.

At the time of Livingstone's death, the Hebrides and large parts of Africa had one thing in common: roads and bridges were rare. It took many months to carry Livingstone's body to the coast so that he could embark on his last sea voyage to Westminster. After they had embalmed the corpse and bound it in sailcloth, his faithful friends Chuma and Susi bore him more than 1,500 kilometres before reaching the coast of today's Tanzania. There he was delivered to the British colonial authorities. Livingstone did not reach home until the following year. A long last journey.

Just before one comes to the village where Livingstone's grandparents lived, a path leads to 'Livingstone's Cave.' Here the grandparents were said to have stayed while building their house. The opening of the cave is hidden behind scrub, and someone has built a stone wall. To keep the wind and sheep out? Inside the high-vaulted cave, the earthen floor is riddled with deep holes. Someone is obviously trying to retrieve the cave's archaeological secrets. Human bones and flint tools dating from 5600 BC have been found. Seen from an archaeological perspective, the Livingstone family moved out yesterday. The path continues to the village where David Livingstone's father was born and where the family scraped out an existence. The little place lies in ruins on a green slope beside a stream. In the family house a memorial commemorates the famous explorer.

The kelp industry, the Napoleonic wars and forced evacuation

Those who spend some time on Ulva will find more ruins. Wee deserted villages. Once during the 1800s, over 600 people lived here. 600! Today, Ulva is home to only twenty people. Among others, perhaps the most important reason behind the early population explosion was that families could earn money from kelping. 'Kelp' refers to the various kinds of seaweed used in the kelp industry, but the term also refers to the soda-like substance left in the kelp pits after the seaweed has been burnt to ash. Towards the end of the 1700s and beginning of the 1800s, soda ash was used in the production of, among other things, glass and soap. The collection, burning and export of kelp was the primary means of livelihood on many of the Scottish islands. In the course of one year, 100 tons of ash was exported from Ulva.

The price of kelp sank dramatically after the end of the Napoleonic wars in 1815. Britain ended the trade embargo with the Continent, and imported cheap soda ash from Spain competed favourably with Scottish kelp. The income of ordinary folks on Ulva plummeted. When the potato blight destroyed the harvest of 1846, 'The year the potato went away,' many had huge problems paying their rents to landlords. The minister on Ulva, William Fraser, reported in December 1846 that the situation is 'miserable beyond description [...] I believe that it is beyond the power of many individuals to keep themselves in life till summer. It is a common case for me to have an application from a family of six persons, and who did not taste food, as they say, for two previous days [...] there will be many deaths here soon unless something be done immediately.'

The letter was sent to the board of emergency bodies set up in Glasgow. To begin with, the owner of Ulva, Francis William Clark, did much to help the starving population, writes MacKenzie in a book on Ulva, *As it was. An Ulva boyhood.* He bought and imported flour from the mainland during the first years after 1846. He employed people, primarily to create jobs, and used his own money to pay them. However, the potato crop failed over several years and there was no income from the tenants. Gradually it became clear to Clark that he had two choices: 'I had no alternative but either surrender my property to the people or resume the natural possession of the land.' In a letter dictated by Clark in 1851, it appears that he solved his economic problems in that he 'very reluctantly, resolved to promote the removal of the crofters [...]' The population, originally about 500, was reduced to 150. This diminution was accomplished in five years. Clark did as many other landowners had done before him: he converted his property to sheep pasture and rented the land to the best-paying incoming sheep farmers.

Even though Clark adopted the usual solution to 'overpopulation problems,' he has been singled out as an exceptionally evil-minded landowner. 'Notorious' and 'ruthless' are just some of the characteristics attributed to him. So what determines whether actions are 'evil'? Did Clark's deeds diverge much from those of other landlords carrying out evictions? When victims of evil try to describe what happened to them, they often break into tears when it comes to the details, small actions which may appear insignificant compared with other injustices they experienced. However, these apparently less dramatic details often have something in common: they are exaggerated, humiliating, and unnecessary actions. They signal that the molester derives pleasure from his power, lacks respect for the victim, and goes further than necessary to achieve his goal. A story from Ulva tells of a woman who was fetching water from a well when she saw the landowner Clark coming towards her. She ran fearfully away, leaving her teapot by the well. Clark picked it up and smashed it.

Much later, in 1883, the Napier Commission was established by the government to investigate the situation of the crofters, the Scottish small farmers who rented the land they cultivated. The commission travelled around in the Highlands, the Hebrides, Orkney and Shetland and gathered statements from those who dared to witness. Three years later the Napier Report led to land reforms. Gladstone's government had been under massive pressure for a long time from the press, the opposition, and the opinion of the populace, who had seen the worn-out, displaced souls from the Hebrides lying sleeping in parks and alleys in the big cities. Journalist Robert Somers reported that nobody who had seen the 'hundreds of families lying night after night on the cold, damp grass of Glasgow Green, or amid the still more pestilential vapours of the wynds and lanes, and who listened to the barking cough of the infants, as if their little bosoms were about to rend' could doubt that the forced evictions were the cause of this 'Massacre of the Innocents.'

One of the stops of the Napier Commission was Tobermory, where statements were given by a Lachlan MacQuarrie from Ulva, a namesake of the previous chief. He told about Clark's actions on the island thirty years prior. His story was also one of 'excessive and heartless use of force [...]' In another case there was a very sick woman with her daughter living in one of the houses Clark wished to have pulled down. Notwithstanding the critical condition of the woman, he had the roof taken down to a small bit of her bed.

Inch Kenneth

When Dr Johnson and Boswell were rowed over from Ulva to the neighbouring island of Inch Kenneth and landed on this fertile little island, Johnson was in a good mood. For the first time in ages he saw wheel tracks! 'It gave us the same happy feeling,' Boswell wrote, 'as a shipwrecked person has when he discovers footprints!'

Their guide introduced them to the clan chief, Sir Allan Maclean, who lived on the little island with servants and two daughters who had 'polished manners' and 'elegant conversation.' Sir Allan Maclean's ancestors, according to Dr Johnson, had, however, lost much of their property to the powerful, greedy Campbell clan. In spite of this, Maclean had maintained the dignity and authority as befits a true clan chief. Sir Allan also kept newspapers, and Boswell and Johnson threw themselves over the printed matter with enthusiasm after what they considered a lengthy isolation from the civilised world.

The only fly in the ointment for Boswell was that Dr Johnson refused to take as much as a single glass of wine with Sir Allan and himself. According to Johnson, a man changes when he drinks, which is very unfortunate, because drinking affects reason: One of the problems with wine is it makes people mix up words with thoughts! 'I am not convinced by his arguments,' wrote Boswell; '[...] but may it not be answered,' he argues, 'that a man may be altered by it *for the better;* that his spirits may be exhilarated, without the reason being affected?'

Towards the end of the 1700s the middle and upper classes drank wine, not whisky or beer. Dr Johnson and Boswell discuss the changes in drinking habits and reflect on their like-minded peers drinking less than their forebears because they now drink wine and not beer. Do you recall? Beer was so cheap and everybody got drunk every evening! They just swigged it down. It's quite a different story with wine; there's not the same hurry to empty the glass!

Smoking habits had also changed. Dr Johnson explained: 'Smoking has gone out. To be sure, it's a shocking thing, blowing smoke out of our mouths into other people's mouths, eyes and noses, and having the same thing done to us.'

The Mitford family

Today, the house of the clan chief Maclean on Inch Kenneth has been replaced by a large stone house. In the 1800s, the owners built a Victorian house which is still in use as a summer home by the present owner of the island. Close up it is a stately building, but viewed from the sea it appears a gloomy and cursed place, lying deserted and isolated on this little spot west of Mull. Inch Kenneth is often bathed in that special light which blesses the Hebrides when sunlight breaks in broad shafts through black clouds, heavy with rain, gathering over Mull's highest mountain, Ben More, on their way to the mainland.

Some years ago, on the way to the island of Staffa, I asked the skipper of the boat if he knew anything about the history of the big stone house we could see in the distance. 'Are you German?' the skipper asked. I shook my head. 'OK then, I can tell the story.'

Inch Kenneth achieved involuntary celebrity status during World War II. David Mitford, Lord Redesdale, bought the island in 1938. During the war, two of his daughters, Unity and Diana, ended up as Great Britain's most notorious and hated women. One became a close friend of Hitler's; the other married the leader of the British fascist party. 'They were never properly punished,' the skipper said in a somewhat resigned tone. 'That's how it works with the gentry. If it had been one of us, things would have been different.' I became curious about the story and decided to find out more.

The aristocratic Mitford couple had seven children: six daughters and a son. The beautiful and lively daughters were popular in London society, especially for their wild, extravagant parties. In other words, they were not entirely unknown to the press before the scandals began to accumulate.

In 1933, Unity Mitford went to Germany to study Nazi ideology at close quarters, according to the TV documentary *Hitler's British Girl*. She was enthusiastic and stirred by Hitler's speech in Nürnberg. 'The first time I saw him, I knew there was nobody I would rather meet.' Her political sympathies brought her into conflict with other family members, especially her sister Jessica, a declared communist. The two shared a room in the family home, according to biographer Jan Dalley in the documentary, but the room was divided in two by a chalked line. One half was decorated with the hammer and sickle and a portrait of Lenin. The other half was embellished with the swastika and pictures of Hitler. A world war in miniature. Later, this rather childish division was to take a more sinister direction.

Unity had a determined mind-set. She returned to Germany in 1934 and joined a language school in Munich, near the headquarters of the Nazi party. It was not really so difficult to get close to Hitler. She soon discovered that Osteria Bavaria was one of his favourite haunts, according to the biographer David Pryce-Jones in *Hitler's British Girl*. She frequented the place occasionally, and after ten months her persistence was rewarded. Hitler invited her to his table and soon became fascinated by this blond, language student. Her grandfather had been a friend of Richard Wagner, she was conceived in the town of Swastika in Canada, and to top everything she had the Germanic middle name of Valkyrie. Hitler, who according to Jan Dalley was very superstitious, must have thought these connections were signs that Unity had been sent to him. This meeting was anything but coincidental! From then on Unity became a close friend of Hitler and was invited to official occasions and party meetings. Eva Braun sighs heavily over Unity in her diary 10 May, 1935:

> [...] he has now found a replacement for me. She is called Valkyrie, and that's what she looks like, including her legs [...] I, the mistress of the greatest man in Germany and in the world, am sitting here and gazing at the sun through a window.

Unity's sister, Diana, who had been to Nürnberg before with Unity, also returned to Germany. Unity introduced her to Hitler, and Diana also became obsessed with the man and his thoughts. She went back to England with Hitler's friendship secured in her luggage. Her current marriage broke up and in 1936 she married her great love and soul mate, the leader of the British fascist party, the handsome, dashing, Oswald Mosley. The secret wedding was held at the home of the leader of the Nazi propaganda machine, Joseph Goebbels. Adolf Hitler attended as a guest of honour.

In September 1939, Great Britain declared war on Germany. Unity was in Munich at the time. She is astounded, but prepared. Hitler has already told the Mitford sisters that war is inevitable and has asked them to return to England for their own safety. Diana goes, but Unity stays. She had told Diana that if war broke out, she would commit suicide. She cannot bear to see the two countries she loves torn to bits. When war finally erupts she visits *Englischer Garten*, takes a little pistol with a mother-of-pearl stock which Hitler had given her for protection, and shoots herself in the head.

It's a failed suicide attempt. The doctors also think it would be risky to re-move the bullet. Hitler is constantly on the line to the hospital to enquire about her condition, and arranges for the injured, disillusioned woman to be taken to neutral Switzerland. There she is collected by her mother and the youngest sister, Deborah, who take her back to England. She incurs the wrath of all Britain when she declares, during an enormous press meeting at her homecoming in January 1940, 'I'm glad to be in England, even if I'm not on your side.'

The British Secret Service MI5 keeps a close watch on Unity Mitford's activities, and believes she is more Nazi than the Nazis: she should be tried for high treason. Her father, who sits in the House of Lords and knows the Minister of the Interior, intervenes. Unity goes free of imprisonment—even interrogation—probably because of her injury, in spite having supplied Hitler with a list of British people she regards as friends and enemies of Germany. Right up until the breakout of war, Unity held out hope that the two nations would enter into an agreement of co-operation.

Unity's sister Diana, on the other hand, and her husband Oswald Mosley, the fascist leader, were interned in 1940, since they were regarded as a risk to national security. In the archives of MI5 opened in 2002, it is stated that 'Diana Mosley, wife of Sir Oswald Mosley, is reported on the "best authority," that of her family and intimate circle, to be a public danger at the present time. She is said to be far cleverer and more dangerous than her husband and will stick at nothing to achieve her ambitions. She is wildly ambitious.' Diana went to her grave in 2003, unaware that it was her own sister, the radical leftist Nancy, who supplied MI5 this character description of her. Diana's previous father-in-law, Lord Moyne, also informed MI5 of 'the extremely dangerous character' of his former daughter-in-law and that she spoke of 'the destruction of the docks at London and Liverpool' and said that by this means it would be possible 'for England to be starved into submission.' According to BBC News this probably convinced the authorities that it was wise to arrest Diana and Sir Oswald Mosley. The couple were interned separately for a while, before Winston Churchill, who ironically was related to Diana, intervened and improved the conditions of their captivity.

The daughters, Unity and Diana, had brought shame upon the family. But the political divisions also affected the family in other ways. Lady Redesdale had strong Nazi sympathies, whilst the lord ended his flirtation with authoritarian regimes once and for all when the war broke out. He separated from his wife, and suggested that Unity and Lady Redesdale move to the little island they owned in the Hebrides and stay there until the war was over.

During their stay on Inch Kenneth, Unity Mitford became ill in 1948. The thirty-four-year-old was taken to the nearest hospital. A serious meningitis linked to the bullet remaining in her head had stricken her. The notorious society lady died in the coastal town of Oban, far from her family home in England.

Modern pilgrims

It's Easter. I leave the car in the carpark at the little pier at Fionnphort, south on Mull, to take the ferry to the isle of Iona. In the wee village shop they have Serrano ham, parmesan, Indian takeaways, garlic cheese, couscous and fish burgers. On the way to Fionnphort, though, on the narrow roads of Mull, I catch glimpses of pheasant and red deer. Lambs play on the pastures and salmon leap in the rivers. However, these local delicacies are not to be found in the shop. 'We export the Mull lamb and import frozen, cheaper lamb from New Zealand,' the lady behind the counter tells me apologetically. The middle class in the cities, in London and Edinburgh, enjoy gourmet food from the islands, while the islanders themselves have to make do with readymade imported food from the freezer.

Visitors to Iona are not permitted to take their cars. The island is a paradise for walkers, cyclists and sheep. Only the inhabitants can apply to have a vehicle. When I was a child there were none, with one exception: a green van with rounded fenders, and wooden fittings which held the body together. Moss was thriving on the woodwork.

The boat trip across the Sound of Iona with the CalMac ferry MV Loch Buie takes about ten minutes. During Easter there are frequent departures, since this is peak season for pilgrims. Between 100,000 and 200,000 people visit the little island each year.

In the 1800s pilgrims and other visitors were carried over the narrow sound by row boat. One simply sent up a smoke signal if one wanted to cross. Every man on Iona had his own fireplace on the Mull side. The pilgrims lit a fire at the boat place belonging to the one they wished to fetch them, and this blaze was soon answered by a plume of smoke from Iona.

Modern pilgrims travel by bus to Fionnphort, instead of traversing Mull on foot as in the old days. Hordes of people move slowly down the slope towards the ferry, arm in arm, with handbags dangling from thin arms, many with walking sticks and shoes unsuited to the Hebrides. A last pilgrimage, perhaps a journey they have dreamt of for a lifetime, which they now undertake before it's too late.

St. Columba

What are the pilgrims coming to see? Iona, the Holy Island. The year was 563. The legend holds that the monk Columba arrived from Ireland, threw a glance southward, assured himself that the Irish coast was out of sight, and landed on Iona. Columba, or *Columcille* as he is known in Gaelic, was exiled for supporting an uprising against the ruling king of Ireland. That's to say, he supported the rebels through prayer. But Columba was not just any ordinary monk. Early stories tell how he could convert water into wine and other miracles; the supportive prayers of this exceptional monk were in other words very powerful. The king's men lost the battle and 3,000 lives were lost. Columba had qualms of conscience about all the killing and asked for advice from his spiritual counsellor. He told Columba: Leave the land of your birth, save 3,000 lives, and never return.

Iona Catherdral and celtic high crosses, Iona

So it was, according to the legend, that Columba and twelve apostles landed on Iona on the 12th of May 563. They had voyaged in frail vessels, coracles, made of hides. The crew must have been soaked through when the boats scraped the beach on the south side of Iona, today known as the Port of the Coracle. Perhaps it was on a typical Hebridean spring day, shades of blue-green ocean shimmering against white sand.

Columba and his men proceeded to build a simple cloister of rough planks. The monastic order grew and soon became one of the most important seats of religious learning in Europe. Throughout the entire Middle Ages, pilgrims flocked in large numbers to the little island. Then, of course, there were no roads or ferries. A pilgrimage to Iona meant several tough, rainy days of strenuous walking through Mull's barren valleys. Some pilgrims chose instead to sail to the Holy Island. But today's pilgrims still seek the same as those from the Middle Ages: peace, time for prayer and reflection, and the privilege of standing on hallowed ground.

Many present-day visitors stay with the Iona Community. Founded in 1938, it is an ecumenical Christian community working for peace and social justice. Some stay for a longer time, contributing with voluntary work. In return they are given food, a roof over their heads, and a unique opportunity to immerse themselves in spiritual matters. I suspect that the radical Christian community in many ways diverges from the thinking which dominated the earlier cloister on Iona. The Iona Community continually raises issues. About gender and equality. Homosexuality. Poverty. Environmental protection. It challenges us: Boycott Nestlé. Say no to nuclear plants. Buy Fairtrade coffee.

The ferry is about to dock. The grey granite outlines of Iona Abbey fill the view. Nearby lie the ruins of an Augustine nunnery established in the 1200s by Reginald, the son of the great Somerled and the father of Donald, the founder of the Clan Macdonald. The Scottish Reformation in 1560 put an end to the operation of all monasteries. The years went by. The buildings were plundered for wooden materials so very scarce on Iona. The remains rotted, sodden with damp sea air. The roofs caved in. Birds nested in the cracks in the walls, cows and sheep wandered the holy ground. When Dr Johnson and Boswell visited Iona, only ruins remained to witness the influence Iona had exercised for more than 1,000 years. But the charisma of the Holy Island has not disappeared. Quite the opposite. Nearly all books about Iona cite Dr Johnson's humble enthusiasm for the experience: 'That man is little to be envied, whose patriotism would not gain force upon the plain of Marathon, or whose piety would not grow warmer among the ruins of Iona.'

Even the Norwegian Viking king, Magnus Barefoot, was affected by the atmosphere on Iona, and took some time away there during the violent attack on the Hebrides and Orkney Island in 1098. The saga writer Snorri Sturlason tells us:

> King Magnus came with his forces to the Holy Island and gave peace and safety to all men there. It is told that the king opened the door of the little Columb's kirk there but did not go in, but instantly locked the door again, and said that no man should be so bold as to go into that church hereafter; which has been the case ever since. From thence King Magnus sailed to Islay, where he plundered and burnt […]

The ferry Loch Buie pulls into the pier. A little girl in underpants and a white down jacket, with artificial fur lining the hood, has decided that summer has come and is wading thigh-deep in the cold, turquoise water by the beach. The narrow main street is flanked by Victorian stone cottages. The clouds never quite manage to settle down on tiny, flat, green Iona, before they fly hurriedly on to gather on the barren mountaintops of Mull.

The first pier was built in 1850 to receive all the steamships heading towards Iona with hordes of tourists. One of the earliest guides involved in the mass tourism of the times was Thomas Cook, the father of the traveller's cheque. He is still fondly remembered because he established a fund to assist poor islanders on Iona. Prior to the building of the pier, visitors waded ashore, sliding on slippery seaweed or plopping into treacherous underwater holes. The lucky ones were carried ashore on strong shoulders, as was the fortune of Boswell and Dr Johnson when they rowed to Iona from Inch Kenneth on the 19th of October 1773.

Queen Victoria's tour to the Hebrides

There was undoubtedly a desperate need for a pier. The number of tourists really took off after Queen Victoria visited Iona in 1847. The Holy Island was included in a longer trip of the seas around the Hebrides, a kind of island-hopping tour which the Queen describes in her diary, *Our Life in the Highlands*. To my great surprise I was able to borrow a printed copy of the diary, written in the mid-1800s, from the University Library in Oslo. A slightly shabby, green-bound edition. The library also obligingly found a later edition which included the diary from the years after 1861, when her husband and cousin, Prince Albert, died. Both diaries are from her beloved Scotland, and especially from Balmoral Castle which she and Albert had built, but there the similarities end.

The two diaries, written one before and one after her husband's death, are as different as light and shadow. As for the diary up until Albert's death, it's difficult to see it would have been published at all had she not been a queen. It rattles on and on, and the notes from her voyage to the Hebrides are mostly about how seasick she was, and how much it rained. She often chooses to stay on board the yacht and draw, while Prince Albert visits the islands. When they anchor near Iona, Victoria stays on the boat drawing, while Albert is rowed ashore to explore the ruins of the abbey. This may sound as if she is always complaining and moaning about rain and seasickness, but she also shows an ability to find positive aspects in the midst of unforeseen and uncomfortable circumstances. She writes about her subjects and the places they visit in polite and almost admiring tones. However, the diary written during her happy years with Albert is very impersonal and rather anaemic.

Then life takes a sudden turn. Albert dies and she finds herself alone at quite a young age. The opening chapter in the second diary is headed: 'No pleasure, no joy.' The entries completely change in character. She is a widow, she has lost someone she loved dearly, and she grieves deeply. She feels vulnerable, shielded from the world only by silk dresses and jewellery. On one occasion she is scheduled to travel by carriage to Aberdeen to unveil a statue of Prince Albert, on the first anniversary of his death. The opening sentence from her journal entry that day is: 'I was terribly nervous. Longed not to have to go through this fearful ordeal. Prayed for help, and got up earlier.' The carriage arrives at the bridge in Aberdeen where the ceremony is to be held, and she continues: 'I got out trembling; and when I had arrived, there was no one to direct me and to say, as formerly, what was to be done. Oh! It was and is too painful, too dreadful!'

Did she share her grief and anxiety with anybody? She did, after all, dedicate the second diary to her loyal Highlanders and particularly her personal servant and faithful friend, the Scot, John Brown. Did she confide all her worries to Mr. Brown? He must have noticed her grief. It has been suggested that the two had a relationship, and even that they married in secret. She wrote in the diary: 'He is always with me, unless I write the opposite.' The film *Mrs. Brown* revolves around the close relationship between the queen and the Scotsman, but even with this in mind I can't detect any signs of a romantic relationship between the lines when I read the diary.

My opinion of this powerful monarch is conflicted. At the front of the book there are two oval portraits of the queen and the prince consort. She is young and looks like a porcelain doll. A white rim is revealed below her irises, making her eyes appear even rounder, and beneath her nose lie little rosebud lips. Later pictures present a far sterner matron with a double chin, but here she appears delicate and transparent. The prince looks timid and young, with a shadow of moustache on his upper lip. My prejudices regarding marriage in the British royal family are based on an understanding that these unions were more or less practical political arrangements intended to unite nations or families, and involved the wedding of individuals who, in fact, often loved other persons. But this was clearly not the case with Victoria and Albert.

Large demand, little on offer

Iona is a small island with about 130 permanent residents. The smell of coal wafts towards me as the ferry docks. Black smoke is pouring out of a chimney on the main street. They still use coal to heat the houses here. Electricity is expensive on the islands and for the time being they have lots of fresh air to compensate. Heating with coal is now forbidden in Glasgow. But during the 1960s the smog was so bad at times that bus conductors wore masks while walking *in front* of the buses to keep them on the right track. A typical Glaswegian smog joke? 'On a clear day you can see your own furniture.'

Baile Mòr, the big village, consists of a row of granite houses overlooking the Sound of Iona. Some houses are well-kept, others are in a bad state of repair. A building, the Argyll Hotel, is one of two hotels on the island. In front of the Argyll, looking out to sea, is a garden. Guests relax on benches looking over to Mull's pink-flecked granite coast on the far side of the sound. They are enjoying tea with jam and scones, chatting in low tones. In spite of the busloads of tourists, there is always a sense of peace on Iona. The little island has a peculiar ability to absorb masses of Americans, Germans, Australians and Englishmen. The beaches, the benches, the daffodils and the abbey, all the newborn lambs wobbling around now in April—it's as if the noise somehow gets absorbed into the sand, the woodwork, the yellow flowers, and the white wool.

A siren warns us that the gangway is going down. A car drives over the wet, green steel plates. A lady has picked me out in the crowd. I'm renting her house for two weeks but I soon discover that the standard of the house does not match the rent I'm paying. There are few houses on Iona, driving up the costs; the law of the market. I even have to pay extra for electricity, bed linen and towels. In the hall, we stop by a cupboard. 'Here's the electricity meter,' my landlady says, opening the door. 'You have to insert fifty-pence coins or the power goes off.'

When I was a child, this was the norm on the islands. Now, thank goodness, it's old-fashioned and almost gone. There used to be a sudden power cut if you didn't remember to feed the greedy, grey kilowatt metre. Pitch darkness followed. Typically this happened when least expected, for example in the middle of an exciting TV programme or when everyone had sat down for supper. 'Get out the torches or candles!' 'Where on earth are the matches?' 'Has anyone fifty pence?' Everyone searched their pockets and wallets. The nearest neighbour could live a mile away, where we might have to travel to get change for the metre.

We now enter the sitting room. It has not been lovingly furnished. I suspect the landlady of putting in all the furniture she thinks isn't worth keeping. The floor is covered with wall-to-wall flowery carpet. 'Here's the fireplace,' she says. 'You must use coal. It gives you a lovely, warm fire.'

We continue the sightseeing and enter the kitchen. It's cold. Brown scorch marks from cigarette burns on the vinyl floor covering. 'Is this the dishwasher?' I ask optimistically. 'No. You'll have to do the washing up yourself,' says the lady sourly. A very unusual welcome to the Hebrides. That's why I remember her so well.

St. Columba Hotel

If you leave the main street Baile Mòr behind you, pass a SPAR shop and the ruins of the nunnery, and follow the sheep fence up a little slope, you arrive at a tall, ancient stone wall. Behind the wall lie the well-tended vegetable gardens of the Argyll Hotel and the St. Columba Hotel. The hotels cultivate their own vegetables, herbs and flowers. In the mild, frost-free climate, the growing season is long. A gardener in gumboots and overalls is down on all fours weeding away. At this time in April the plants are just awakening.

The white-painted wooden gate in the stone wall surrounding St. Columba hotel leads to a large lawn, just becoming green. Daffodils bloom all along the old wall. Some lunch guests, bathed in Easter sunshine and defying a bitter wind, are enjoying lunch at the wooden tables. White wine and scallops. Bicycles are propped against the hotel's white-painted wood panelling, and the little lobby, which has a stuffy smell of captured sunlight, keeps golf clubs. I have an appointment with Neil Harvey, the hotel's manager.

He is busy in reception. 'Take a seat in the lounge, I'll be with you in a tick,' says Harvey. I find myself a chair in the dusky room. Soon we are both deeply engulfed in our armchairs. 'It's wonderful to sit down for a change,' he smiles, leaning back. 'Almost like being a guest,' he continues, appearing relaxed as he pours us both a cup of tea. Easter is a very busy time. After a long winter hibernation the hotel comes to life, and the ravages of winter become apparent to all. An old house demands a lot of care and attention.

St. Columba Hotel is in danger of losing a star awarded by the Tourist Board. 'They tell us to install telephones in all rooms and are threatening to downgrade us to a two-star hotel if we don't meet their demands. But we don't want to have telephones in every room; we think it's a hopelessly outdated demand. We don't want TVs in the rooms either. We want to be a place where you can retreat and recharge.'

Neil's right. People come to Iona to escape from the hectic modern world. For personal reflection; to concentrate, meditate. Many of the guests are patrons who don't want change, neither intruding telephones nor noisy TV channels. They want to retain the rare privilege of feeling disconnected from the world.

Neil is a combination of businessman, manager, and true idealist. For example, the hotel re-uses cooking oil, converting it to fuel for the hotel's diesel-driven vehicles. The oil costs less than half the price of normal fuel. 'We are actually making biodiesel with recycled cooking oil.' I admit that I've never heard of such a thing. 'Neither had I.' Neil suddenly looks a bit surprised himself.

So is the hotel recognised as an environmentally-friendly establishment? Has it earned itself a green label? Indeed, it has. In Britain, it's not only hotels which aspire to the green image, but also ordinary tourist attractions. Even the abbey is marked as environmentally friendly. The Hebrides have changed in a short time. Environmental protection, preservation, and ecology is 'in.' Sustainable whale safaris. Ecological salmon farming. Huge areas have been converted into bird reserves. Pristine nature has become big business.

Healing hands

I'm on my bike, heading for Iona Abbey to join a 'healing hands service.' The daylight is fading but there are lights in the windows along the little road to the abbey. The streets are deserted this April evening. Once, the Street of the Dead twisted upwards from the Bay of Martyrs by the harbour and ascended to the abbey. It is said that the only thing left of this road is a cobbled remnant that leads from the abbey to the churchyard. The Street of the Dead: where the coffins of prominent persons were borne on strong shoulders to the holy churchyard and laid to rest. Several generations of the Lords of the Isles, the chiefs of the Clan Macdonald, were taken from Islay and buried in the churchyard of Rèilig Odhrain. There are also said to be forty-eight Scottish, four Irish, and eight Norwegian kings resting in the ancient churchyard. The names on the gravestones have been erased long ago.

It's dusk. The shadows slowly engulf the light. I park the bicycle against the stone wall outside the abbey. The daffodils are glowing in the dark as if they have stolen moonbeams. Entering the old door into the brightly lit church, begun in the 1200s, I find a seat in one of the pews. Many of the churchgoers are wearing casual clothes. It's cold. I'm expectant. I want to understand more; the essence of Iona lies in the abbey, the Iona Community, and Christianity.

There are three pews on each side of the aisle, facing each other. Before the arrival of the minister, a woman leads us through the songs we are going to sing during the service. Each pew is given notes with different parts. We now seem to be participating in a kind of choir teaching session, repeating the songs again and again, until finally we remember the melody and text by heart. Our courage grows and we become bolder. The tones resonate among the old stone walls, the voices blending together. We don't know each other but we are creating something beautiful.

Alison from the Iona Community is leading the service tonight. She's reading a list of names from the pulpit. People from all over the world have written names on scraps of paper, names of people in need of a prayer. They have pinned the notes to a cross in old St. Oran's chapel which stands in the churchyard. Some of the names have been sent in a more contemporary form, by postcard or e-mail. And we pray for everybody. Alastair, John, Mona, Kenneth, Tina. Then a psalm: Lord Jesus Christ, lover of all, trail wide the hem of your garment, bring healing, bring peace. New names follow. David, Peter, Joyce, Brian. Lord Jesus Christ, lover of all, trail wide the hem of your garment, bring healing, bring peace. Jolanta, Rob, Mary, Kirsty. Lord Jesus Christ, lover of all, trail wide the hem of your garment, bring healing, bring peace.

It's like being in a trance. Some of those we are sending our prayers to are ill from AIDS; others have lost their family in traffic accidents. Several have drug problems and some have been saved for the Lord. Anonymous people, names from all over the world. Fates we don't know of but whose names have been pinned to a cross in a little chapel on Iona. It's not only people who receive our prayers. We also pray for peace among nations: Iraq, Israel, Palestine, Zimbabwe, Iran and Afghanistan. Lord Jesus Christ, lover of all, trail wide the hem of your garment, bring healing, bring peace. The turmoil of world politics fills the holy space, closing in around all of us who are sitting and shivering this April evening on the little peaceful island of Iona.

Come bring your burdens to God, for Jesus will never say no. The time has come for the blessing. One by one we approach the circle of pillows lying in the aisle. As we kneel, Alison lays a hand on the head of each one and they in turn put a hand on the shoulder of their neighbour. We all read a prayer from the abbey's own prayer book. A prayer for each of the kneeling persons. Again, the trance-like atmosphere. So unfamiliar, even though this is part of my cultural heritage. During this service, for several minutes we give our time and attention to another. Would things be different if everybody gave some time to think of others? A quiet moment in every home, every day, would that make a difference?

The service is over, it's late, but I remain behind in the abbey and chapel for a while to look around. When it's time to leave, the night is dark, the moon hides behind clouds. I'm freezing. There's not a living soul outside the chapel, only the ancient gravestones of the dead. I always feel nervous in churchyards, but this one is special. Here, on Ì Chaluim Chille, as the island is called in Gaelic, lies Shakespeare's MacBeth and the Scottish King Duncan I, whom MacBeth murdered. In the theatre piece, which goes under the name *The Scottish Play,* in fear of the curse which can destroy those who call the piece by its real name, the nobleman Ross asks where the body of the king has disappeared to. The hero Macduff answers that he has been taken to the island of Colme-kill: 'The sacred storehouse of his predecessors, and guardian of their bones.' I bike past the ruins of the nunnery, down the main street, and follow the seashore past Martyr's Bay, where sixty-eight monks were massacred by the Vikings in 806. Blood-soaked robes on white sand. Who was left to bury the martyrs?

Pilgrimage

Richard Sharples is a minister and the warden of the abbey. He is leading the traditional Easter pilgrimage on Iona. Half an hour before departure, only two others have signed on. I have to read an obligatory information brochure to join the walk. 'Are you wearing appropriate footwear? With ankle support? The majority of injuries are ankle sprains. Bring what you need of medicines, for example, inhalers.' I am hereby warned, sign on to the tour, and await the start.

By two o'clock about thirty people have now gathered around St. Martin's Cross, the starting point of the pilgrimage. This ornamental Celtic cross was already here when the Norwegian Vikings attacked Iona the first time in 795. They returned. Again and again. Twice monks were massacred and valuables from the abbey plundered, and once, for good measure, they even burnt down the abbey, according to Irish annals. Finally, the monks took action and evacuated the treasures of the abbey to Ireland. Among them, it is thought, an illuminated, elaborate and very beautiful book, the *Book of Kells.* There is divided opinion about how the four gospels written on vellum ended up in the Irish Abbey of Kells. The dominant theory is that the book was initiated on Iona and completed in Ireland. It soon became apparent that there was no worse place to hide the book, but who could have foreseen that the Vikings would later also raid Kells?

Today's pilgrims are of all ages. Richard repeats the warnings, informing us that they have *some* training in first aid, but if anybody is using an inhaler or the like, they are responsible for this treatment themselves. He's not bringing along anything like that. Of course not. Why should he? My thoughts go to the pilgrimages to Mecca, over huge desert areas in burning sun, and all those who are trampled to death every year. They could really use first aid.

Our group strolls from the Celtic cross and into the chapel dedicated to Saint Oran. Irish Oran who, according to legend, offered to sacrifice himself and be buried alive under the first chapel Columba built on Iona. Why? Because the chapel kept collapsing during the building process, and always at night. Some said the monks were being thwarted by evil powers. The earth had to be cleansed through a Christian consecration. Columba had a dream: The chapel demanded human sacrifice if it was to remain standing. Christianity was young in these parts, so why not play it safe and cultivate old traditions as well? Oran the monk, who was possibly a cousin of Columba, volunteered, and was immured into the obstinate construction. That did the trick. The legend says that after three days, Columba wished to see his face and take a final farewell of his relative. When the face was uncovered, it was found that Oran was still alive. He even insisted that there was no God, hell or eternal life, words so blasphemous, according to the legend, that Columba immediately gave the order for him to be re-buried: 'Earth, earth on Oran's eyes, in case he starts to babble again.' This time Oran's mouth was shut for ever.

In the small chapel from about 1100, which was possibly built as a burial chamber for the Norse-Celtic ruler Somerled, we lean disrespectfully against gravestones mounted on the walls, with our feet equally lacking in reverence for those set into the floor. But there is not much room to move around in these few square metres. The gravestones have been saved from wear and tear caused by beating rain and hail. Slowly my eyes adapt to the darkness. The details in the stonework become visible as the chapel fills with Gore-Tex-clad pilgrims. The gravestones are decorated by stone masons from Iona. They were among the best in Scotland, and exported Celtic crosses and gravestones to the wealthy, to churches, and to abbeys.

Richard Sharples wears shorts, but has removed his cap. Easter Eve is a day of waiting, he says: 'A day when we look back at the dramatic events during Easter week. This is what our pilgrimage will do. We are literally going to walk in a circle, going nowhere in a sense.'

Richard reads from the liturgy about the crucifixion and the days before and after. A woman from the Iona Community steps forward from the crowd, and reads: 'And Mary Magdalene looks back: What could I have done for Him? Nothing—or could I?' The woman reads with empathy, imagining herself as Mary reflecting over her choices, her qualms, her wish to be without guilt.

'Those who come to Iona often want to reflect on their lives,' says Richard, 'so as to see it clearer. Many find themselves at a crossroads and are in a quandary about important choices they have to make; they have a dilemma. Just as those who were close to Jesus during the dramatic days surrounding the Crucifixion.'

He ends with a short prayer and starts to chant: 'Watch, watch and pray, Jesus will keep to his word.' The group follows on, repeating the simple prayer while leaving the chapel. We continue chanting through the small churchyard, out the wooden gate, and follow the narrow tarmac road past the St. Columba Hotel, halting at the arches of the Augustine nunnery from the 1200s. 'We know relatively little about this abbey compared to what we know about the Benedictine abbey of Iona,' Richard says. 'Perhaps it tells us that it was not women who were writing history?'

No, women did not record history. Neither did most men. In the early Middle Ages, it was mostly the monks who commanded the skills of reading and writing, and who wrote and defined history. According to the historian Norman Davies, the accounts written by the monks influence posterity's view of the Vikings. The monks had a negative, biased view of those they viewed as heathen pirates. The monks' version of history went unchallenged by other, more positive sources, Davies continues. The old sagas were mainly written on far-away Iceland and only became generally known in modern times.

There is no doubt that the Vikings showed brutal behaviour in the Hebrides. My personal opinion is that the old sagas from 'far-away Iceland' do not do much to improve this impression. But after the first period with the worst plundering and killings, the Norsemen made their homes as settlers, found ways to make their living by peaceful means, and married into the local population. Slowly and surely the Hebrides, called *Innse Gall,* 'The Islands of the Foreigners,' were occupied by a Gaelic-Norse population. Whether it was this bicultural ethnic mix called *Gall-Ghàidheil,* 'the Scandinavianised-Galls,' or whether it was the Scandinavian-inspired Gaelic warriors led by Norsemen who originated the name, we don't know, according to the researchers Jennings and Kruse. We know little about this cultural melting pot apart from written accounts of violent episodes. The monks showed minimal interest in the settlers' everyday life, trade, and peaceful co-existence.

'We are heading towards the *machair,*' says Richard. *Machair* is a unique ecosystem only found on the west coasts of Scotland and Ireland: ancient raised beaches lying above the present sea level and with a fragile carpet of short grass holding the sand in place. The *machair* is saturated with calcium, inviting millions of daisies, small orchids, clover and buttercups to put down their roots. The machair on Iona also doubles as a golf course. Not by any means exclusive, it shares place with the island's sheep, but the view of the beach and sea beyond is exceptional.

My map tells me that we are at the Bay at the Back of the Ocean. Richard also has his back to the ocean, wondering out loud: 'Was St. Columba really a Christian man who journeyed here to save souls, or was he of noble birth, a fellow with blood on his hands seeking power and influence in a new country?' Think it over. Perhaps both versions are true. 'It's not only Christians who undertake pilgrimages,' continues Richard. 'Muslims, for example, are obliged to a make a journey to Mecca at least once in the course of their lives. They throw stones against a pole to show that they will fight evil. I ask you now to go down to the beach. Take a stone in your hand, feel the weight of it, and reflect on how each of you will contribute to fighting against evil in the world. Through fighting and violence, or by non-violent means? There are no right answers or easy solutions. When you have thought through this question, throw your stone, preferably without putting anybody near you in danger.'

'Watch, watch and pray, Jesus will keep to his word,' the pilgrims hum as they walk towards the beach. The stones are rounded, polished smooth. Some have a greenish tint; Iona is known for its green marble. Others are grey or pinkish. We spread out, bending down, each finding their stone. We all consider Richard's question. Some seem to know already how they are going to tackle evil in the world, and throw at once. I find I have never really pondered so deeply over this question, and hesitate.

As I stand by the shore, I remember an elderly, dignified gentleman I once met in India. His sons ran a beach bar made out of bamboo and palm leaves. It was the monsoon season. Rain and thunderstorms came and went every day and there was hardly a tourist in sight. The elderly philanthropist behind the counter of the bar had plenty of time to share his thoughts with me. 'Every evening as the children were growing up, I told them: "Now, I want you to think of one thing which has made your day more meaningful and beautiful".'

Maybe that's a good way to fight evil, I contemplate, standing on this Scottish beach with a smooth stone in my hand, casting it into the sea.

Everyone has thrown their stone. We wander along the beach and climb over a fence, meeting some local bathing beauties in T-shirts, and with pale, bare legs, paddling in the shallow water. The warm sun caresses our backs as we climb a close-cropped hillock and settle down by a wee, rusty sign informing us that we are pausing by hole number 11. It's time for a rest and some water and biscuits. We stroll on after Sharples has shared Pilate's dilemma: Should he please the masses and crucify an apparently peaceful man? Or should he free Jesus and become unpopular?

The following stretch is marshy and uphill, our shoes getting muddier as we climb. Richard stops and points. We are looking down towards The Hermit's Cell, the home of a lonesome monk. 'As we go down to the cell' says Richard, 'I would like you to proceed without saying a word and observe a couple of minutes' silence down there.'

A couple of minutes pass. 'Was this really a place where the monks retreated to reflect and pray, or was it in fact an enclosure for cows?' asks Richard. The magic fades quickly. *A cow-pen?* He continues: 'The truth is we don't know, but anyway ... This has become an important place for Christians the world over. They come here to experience a quiet, meditative moment. Anyway it's not so important what really lay here—there are many ways to worship God.'

'With God, all things are possible, all things are possible, with God,' the group chants as we head for the last part of the pilgrimage. More marsh, more mud. 'All things are possible,' shouts joyfully a Canadian professor of theology, as he tries to hop over a marshy pit. Mud splashes onto hairy professor legs.

St. Oran's chapel is once more packed with pilgrims. We have come full circle,

Cormorants, Staffa

but perhaps some have gone even further. In one direction or another. That's what brings people here. To be moved, or to move forward themselves.

En route to Staffa

Down by the quay is moored the Isle of Iona, a large wooden boat belonging to Davie Kirkpatrick. There are not many of us now, it's still spring and out of season. Kirkpatrick is taking us to the basalt island of Staffa, a geological wonder north of Iona, before the summer crowds swamp the little island.

Kirkpatrick gives us a hand on board. Some are from South Africa, others from the Netherlands and Spain. Binoculars and cameras dangle from necks. There is not much chance of seeing whales and sharks. Huge basking sharks with their two fins breaking the surface are not an unusual sight, but the water is still too cold. However, there is a good possibility of spying an eagle or two, or of coming upon a seal colony.

Before he loosens the ropes, Kirkpatrick gives us a little quiz. He points to an island lying just outside Mull on the other side of the sound. 'Do you see that wee island over there? Do you know what it's called?' Nobody says a word. I get an uncomfortable feeling about being the show-off in the class, but I respond that the island is Erraid. 'Do you associate Erraid with anything?' is the next question.

Silence. Smarty-pants answers again. 'Robert Louis Stevenson.' Kirkpatrick goes on: 'Has anybody read *Kidnapped* by Stevenson?' Nobody has read it. Except me. I feel I need to offer an explanation. 'I'm a fan of Stevenson. It's a long story ...' At last he starts the motor. The wind force is seven mph. Kirkpatrick has reminded me about a visit to Erraid I made three years ago.

Erraid

Erraid is a small tidal island. When the tidal water flows out of the shallow sound separating Erraid from Mull, it's possible to cross over the sandy surface almost without wetting your feet. But the tide rises dangerously fast in these parts. There is a big difference between high and low tides, so before starting out on this walk, I give careful attention to the tidewater table hanging in the wee shop at Fionnphort and speak to the fishermen on the pier.

Erraid actually lies off the track, but my visit to the island was a literary pilgrimage tracing the footsteps of Robert Louis Stevenson, or 'R.L.S.' as he often signed his letters. When it comes to number of translated publications, Stevenson beats both Charles Dickens and Oscar Wilde. His writing is poetic and precise. One may then ask: What was the author of *Treasure Island* and *The Strange Case of Dr Jekyll and Mr. Hyde* doing on Erraid?

Twenty kilometres southeast of Erraid lies the Torran reef. It's about seven kilometres in length and lies partly submerged. This black reef was reputed to be the most dangerous in British waters during the 1800s. That was before R.L.S.'s father, Thomas Stevenson, led the work to build a lighthouse on the rocks, the greatest technical challenge he was ever to experience as an engineer.

Before the building started, The Northern Lighthouse Board, which ordered the construction of Scottish lighthouses, collected all the petitions which had been sent to the authorities demanding a light on the Torran Rocks. One captain Ticktack, for example, had informed the authorities that he had 'lost Seamen, Wife and Child as well as Ship' and claimed that a lighthouse would have spared him from 'all his subsequent sorrows and losses.' The pressure to build lighthouses around the Scottish coastline often came from shipowners and captains unwilling to risk losing valuable cargo, according to author Bella Bathurst. They had good reason to be concerned. The maps of the sea around Scotland were at best unreliable. In the 1830s two shipwrecks were registered every single day, and between 1854 and 1879, Lloyds of London had noted about 50,000 *registered* shipwrecks. But many vessels disappeared mysteriously, without anybody knowing their fate. That is to say, some knew but did not report it. Wreck-salvaging was a lucrative business for many islanders, and resistance against lighthouses was strong. Thus the threats abounded when in 1790 the founder of the Stevenson dynasty, Robert, began to build lighthouses.

The Northern Lighthouse Board

Over the course of 250 years, up until 1940, eight Stevenson engineers from four generations built ninety-seven lighthouses around the Scottish coast, often under extreme weather conditions. From Muckle Flugga in Shetland, the most northerly point in Scotland, to the most southerly point on the Mull of Galloway. This means that virtually all the lighthouses in the Hebrides, Orkney and Shetland have been designed and built by engineers from this one family.

The first Stevenson engineer was Robert Stevenson, the grandfather of the author Robert Louis Stevenson. In 1790, Robert was an apprentice to his stepfather, Thomas Smith. His stepfather had already designed four lighthouses, among others the one on the Mull of Kintyre. Smith was also the first engineer to be employed by the foundation, which later became known as The Northern Lighthouse Board, NLB. The Board was established following a large increase in marine accidents towards the end of the 1700s. Merchant ships and warships were torn apart, cannons sank to the ocean depths and bales of cotton washed ashore. Thousands of soldiers, merchants and emigrants drowned. A parliamentary committee was established which soon recommended that at *least* four lighthouses must be built on the most dangerous coastal areas of Scotland. In 1786 the recommendation was approved by law. The Board of NLB granted the money and decided where the new lighthouses were to be built. The engineers designed them and led the construction process.

Perhaps the title 'engineer' is a bit misleading, since a formal education in this profession was not available at that time. A few decades earlier, Dr Samuel Johnson had defined the term 'engineer' in his famous dictionary: 'An officer in the army, or fortified place, whose business is to inspect attacks, defences, works.' But things had changed since Johnson's definition. A purely Scottish version of the enlightenment period, the Scottish Enlightenment, inspired the Scottish towns, universities and intellectual elite from the mid-1700s. Philosophers, economists, scientists—all were united in the belief that human beings were not at the mercy of nature, that nature could be tamed, formed, and indeed conquered. And not only nature, but also the structure of society, population growth, poverty, disease, the economic system, and agriculture. These things were not to be regarded as God-given and therefore unalterable. On the contrary, human beings had been endowed with intelligence, by God of course, true enough. But intelligence was, in a way, delegated to humans who could and should utilise it wisely and diligently to improve society.

Scotland was, in other words, emerging from the backwaters following union with England in 1707. Many now realised that the hub of development, for far too long, had been London instead of Edinburgh. It was high time Edinburgh and Glasgow awoke from what some might term a self-pitying hibernation, during which Scottish wounded pride was nursed and cosseted. Scotland had also begun to harvest some of the advantages of the union: access to overseas markets and lucrative colonies. Scots like Adam Smith, David Hume and James Watt, represented each in his own way the spirit of the Enlightenment. Thomas Smith and his stepson Robert Stevenson were part of a new generation which replaced superstition and fatalism with rationality, self-confidence, optimism, and empiricism, coupled with the will to tame and control the environment. The profession of engineering was in the making. And lighthouses fit in well with enlightenment ideals. It was no longer a question of the mercy of God whether or not a ship survived. The crew no longer drowned as a punishment from God: they died because the coast was pitch dark.

When the lighthouse Dubh Artach was about to be built in the coastal waters of Erraid and Iona, it was Thomas Stevenson, the son of Robert and the father of Robert Louis Stevenson, who was in charge of the construction works. The demand for light on the treacherous Torran Rocks gained strength after the American schooner Guy Mannering went down just outside Iona on the last day of December in 1865. It was on its way to New York with cotton and grain when a hurricane hit the Scottish coast. The wind tore the sails to pieces and the captain saw no alternative but to steer the vessel straight towards Machair Bay on Iona, where the golf course lies today. As the ship came into shallow waters, it disintegrated. Around half of the crew were washed onto land, or clung to pieces of wreckage and cotton bales and were hauled ashore by islanders. Seventeen people drowned. Over twenty other vessels sank in the same area in the course of that day and night. Enough was enough.

Dubh Artach

A year and a half after the shipwreck, in June, the first hammer blows from the granite quarry on Erraid could be heard. Enormous blocks of stone were blown out of the grey mounds of rock, measured precisely, and finely honed so that they could be laid stone to stone without much further adjustment when hoisted onto the Torran reef. The lighthouse was to stand on the biggest rock, Dubh Artach.

The building of the lighthouse did not proceed according to plan. It was delayed by bad weather. When the stonemasons finished the year's work in October, they fell far behind the schedule of Thomas Stevenson. Work re-started in April the following year, but once again there was atrocious, depressingly bad weather. By the end of June, weather conditions permitted Stevenson to visit the black reef for one hour. Perhaps that was the reason that Mr. Brebner, the supervisor on the building site, on a fine, late-summer day, made a dangerous decision.

On this calm August day, Brebner and thirteen men set off to Torran to work, and decided to stay the night in the iron hut which had been put up to house the workers. Brebner and his companions were probably relieved that the afternoon was mild and still. One imagines they scanned the sky for signs of bad weather and concluded that it was safe to spend the night on the rock.

During the night a storm blew up which grew into a hurricane. Hebridean weather changes rapidly. The islands are exposed to westerly winds straight off the Atlantic, without the protection that mountains or a large land mass would afford. Brebner and his men spend six days in the iron-clad hut, their only protection from the raging green waves. The sea spray reaches far over the roof of the hut and the men hardly sleep at night. They sit on their beds listening to the masses of water thundering against the floor beneath them, even though the iron hut stands eighteen metres above sea level. They are all fully aware of the forces confronting them. One of the most terrifying moments is when the sea breaks through the iron door in the first floor, foaming around the feet of the marooned men and sweeping away most of their rations.

When, exhausted and thirsty, they finally get back to Erraid, they are met by a furious, terrified engineer, the uncle of R.L.S., who also works with Dubh Artach. Just like a mother who has lost and then found her child, a torrent of anxiety and relief is released. He yells at them.

In the summer of 1870, Robert Louis Stevenson goes to Erraid to visit his father, his plan being to work in the quarry. Thomas still clung to a vain hope that his son would become an engineer like himself, and two of his brothers. It's possible that young Stevenson did a bit and even pretended to be interested in the drawings of the lighthouse. Mostly, however, he took the opportunity to bathe and lie in the sun, wander around the island, write poems, and ponder over his future life. One thing was clear: He hated engineering work, but did not want or dare to disappoint his father. Not yet.

In his notes Robert Louis describes a busy little community on the tidal island of Erraid, where fifty men were in full swing. They had already built a row of granite houses for the lighthouse keepers. Rail tracks led from the granite quarry to the small harbour which had been built to transport the blocks of stone to Dubh Artach. A crane could be pushed along the tracks to dump the building blocks into the sea. There they were bound to the little steamboat which bravely struggled to tow them twenty kilometres out to the Torran reef.

When I visited Erraid, it was 134 years since R.L.S. had spent his summer there. On this April day it's misty and there's drizzle in the air. 'The music of clinking tools,' as R.L.S. described it, fell silent in 1871 when the lighthouse was at last finished. But one thing remains the same: the row of grey stone houses built for the lighthouse keepers is still here. As is the stone pier where the steamboat was moored. But what is this? There's smoke curling up from the chimneys! Erraid was deserted for many years until an idealistic community, the Findhorn Foundation, hired the houses from the Dutchman who bought the island in 1977. According to itself, the foundation 'is a spiritual community, ecovillage and an international centre for holistic learning, helping to unfold a new human consciousness and create a positive and sustainable future.' I don't see one single ideological soul as I stroll past the old row of houses; they are probably all busy getting the vegetable gardens behind the buildings in order, or fixing one of the houses.

There's a path behind the houses leading up to a gate. A white enamel sign with red letters reads: 'Any person omitting to shut and fasten this gate after using it is liable to a penalty of forty shillings.' Even though the currency is now outdated, I don't want to risk anything and close the gates behind me before climbing up the path towards the quarry. The granite blocks lie patiently in the mist. They are not going anywhere. They got left behind and never achieved the honour of being part of the Dubh Artach lighthouse. Maybe they were superfluous, or maybe the iron bolts had spilt them in a way that did not meet the approval of Thomas Stevenson.

The path continues upwards to a rusty signalling tower where the Northern Lighthouse Board could signal to the lighthouse keepers, until the lighthouse was automated in 1971. There's a wonderful view from up here. Or rather, there could have been. On a clear day looking south, I could have seen the Paps of Jura. But at least I can make out Dubh Artach and the waves breaking threateningly over the long reef.

In 1886, many years after R.L.S. visited Erraid, he published the novel *Kidnapped,* inspired by the three weeks he spent on Erraid. On the surface the novel is a suspense story. Case in point, Mark Twain wrote in a letter to R.L.S.: 'My wife keeps re-reading *Kidnapped* and neglecting my works. And I have not blamed her. I do it myself.'

Kidnapped

The main character in the book is the orphaned young boy from the Lowlands of Scotland, David Balfour. His evil uncle first swindles him out of his rightful inheritance, and thereafter proceeds to have Balfour kidnapped and sold as crew to the captain of the ship Covenant. Balfour's bad luck does not end here. The ship runs aground on the Torran reef and sinks. Balfour survives and is washed ashore on the island of Erraid. For some days he lives like Robinson Crusoe, surviving by eating raw shellfish. He is continually wet and cold, but keeps his hopes up by gazing over at Iona Abbey and staring at the smoke arising from the houses. Civilisation is so near, and yet it seems even more meaningless to Balfour considering he might perish on Erraid. On the fourth day, when he is near death from cold and hunger, he spies a sailing vessel on course to Erraid. He had seen the same boat the day before, when two fishermen shouted to him in Gaelic, laughing so much that they almost capsized the boat. Balfour stood there shivering and furious, and was shocked when he saw the boat turn around and set course for Iona. However, now the fishermen clearly had come to their senses and turned back again. They even brought along an 'interpreter.'

The boat lowered her sails but it still seemed doubtful that they were going to rescue the shipwrecked boy. The interpreter was almost dying of laughter and sniggering while he chattered quickly away in Gaelic. Balfour signed to indicate that he did not understand a thing, it 'might have been Greek and Hebrew for me,' but this only irritated the interpreter. Balfour 'began to suspect he thought he was talking English.' Finally, he picked up a word he understood: tide. Suddenly he got it. The interpreter turned to the fishermen with a look that said: I *told* you I speak English! Balfour has no time to lose and runs to the sound separating Erraid from Mull. Sure enough! Now it's easy to cross over the sandy floor. Delirious with joy and relief, he travels across on foot.

Some of R.L.S.'s perception of Celtic culture is articulated through the words and thoughts of the young lowland Scot. Balfour arrives at a house built of stones which has never seen a hammer or chisel. There is turf on the roof. In front of the house, or rather hut, sits an old gentleman smoking a pipe. Balfour remarks to the reader of *Kidnapped*, 'I call him so because of his manners, for his clothes were dropping off his back.' Furthermore, R.L.S., who himself is a lowland Scot from Edinburgh, speaks through Balfour: 'If these are the wild Highlanders, I could wish my own folk wilder.' He walks on and crosses Mull in four days. Today, a road follows the same route as Balfour. It takes under an hour to traverse by car.

Balfour is taken by boat over to the mainland, where he searches for a friend from the shipwreck, the antagonist in the novel, the Highlander, Catholic, and Jacobite, Alan Breck. The action in the book takes place just after the Battle of Culloden in 1746, and the story has many references to the revenge suffered by the clans following the rebellion. One of the fundamental themes in the novel is precisely the tensions and conflicts between the Scottish Highlanders and Lowlanders, personified in the meeting between the rationalist Balfour and the romantic Breck.

Strolling down the path from the signal tower on Erraid I pass the quarry, making sure that the gate is properly closed. It's raining softly. The tide is rising in the channels and streams the sea has carved out in the sea floor. Thinking of Balfour's fate, I pick up speed. As I return over the sound to Mull, the tide comes silently and swiftly in.

The Ross of Mull and pink granite

Mr. Kirkpatrick, the skipper, steers the boat along the pink granite coast of the Ross of Mull, the long arm of land forming a peninsula southwest on Mull. This stretch of coast changes colour according to the weather, the granite taking on the orange tones of the sunset, then changing to pale pink in the white light of day. Kirkpatrick's voice on the loudspeaker: 'There was a granite quarry here in the old days. The granite from the Ross of Mull was of very high quality and was used, among other things, in building the Town Hall in Manchester, and Liverpool

The Ross of Mull seen from Iona

harbour. It was also exported abroad.' The scars left by extracting the granite are still plainly visible, and from the boat I can make out grooves left by the wedges once carefully and patiently hammered into the stone, until it broke off cleanly in straight-edged blocks.

Why is the granite pink? The stone blushes with a ruddy hue due to potassium in the feldspar it contains. The attractive granite was readily worked and polished, and became enormously popular in Victorian times. Some granite blocks became pillars supporting Blackfriars Bridge and the Holborn Viaduct in London. Others were destined for more distinguished futures. When Queen Victoria lost her Prince Consort, Albert, in 1861, she decreed that a monument to him should be raised in Kensington Gardens in London. It was to be a granite obelisk. A stone block weighing seven hundred tons from the granite quarry on Mull was thought at first to be worthy of the honour. However, no obelisk for Albert ever materialised, at least not made from *that* particular stone block, which was found to have several defects. The project was abandoned. How on earth this monster stone was to be transported to London was another matter. Could it have been towed? What if it had struck a rock and dragged the boat down? The rejected would-be obelisk stone is still lying in the deserted quarry today, and is known as the Prince's Stone.

In London, it was decided to ditch the obelisk idea in favour of organising a competition: Who could design the best memorial? A gothic look-alike temple won the day. It was over fifty metres tall with a gilded statue of Albert under the vaulted roof. After Queen Victoria laid the foundation stone in 1863, nine years passed before the Albert Memorial was finally completed. Grotesque, or a work of genius? Nevertheless, there it stands in Kensington Gardens, and in spite of the fiasco regarding the obelisk, granite from Mull finally found its way to the Albert Memorial. To those planning a walk in this park: Look closely at the pillars of the monument and send a thought to the deserted quarry on Mull.

Hebridean Princess

A stately black-and-white veteran edition of a Caledonian MacBrayne ferry, outlined against the dark cliffs of Mull's west coast, comes into view as the boat moves out into open waters on the way to Staffa. 'There goes the Hebridean Princess,' Kirkpatrick tells us. He's seriously beginning to sound like a guide on a charter tour. The boat was previously named Columba, and is a Cinderella story of a perfectly ordinary car ferry which became worthy of a queen. The boat was built in 1964 and was the first generation of CalMac ferries to transport cars to the Hebrides. This was before the roll-on-roll-off, or Ro-Ro ferries made their debut during the 1970s. Columba and two other sister boats acquired the affectionate nickname 'the fat ladies,' because of their broad hull which accommodated the cars. On their return journey, the ferries carried cattle and sheep to mainland markets. These rounded, voluminous ladies also had another special feature. They were all equipped with external water-sprinkling systems in case it should become necessary to remove radioactive pollution. The Cold War had arrived in the Hebrides.

Caledonian MacBrayne sold Columba in 1989, and now she has been transformed into this beautiful five-star cruise ship, the Hebridean Princess, with a rounded bow, a red funnel, and a low hull compared to the present-day monster ferries. The Hebridean Princess is a stylish lady reminiscent of MacBrayne's mail boats from Victorian times. The deck and railings are wooden, and the lacquered interior bears little resemblance to today's ferries, with their synthetic carpets, Respatex, and steel fittings. The ratio between crew and passengers is about 1:1. When Queen Elizabeth II celebrated her eightieth birthday, the court booked the Hebridean Princess for a week. About 150 years after Queen Victoria sailed to the Hebrides, her great-great-grandchild decided to follow in her footsteps.

Basalt columns on Staffa

As we approach Staffa, I recognise the square, slightly sloping silhouette of the little island. The name is of Norse origin: Stavey, the island of staves, or columns. The volcanic basalt columns reminded the Vikings of the vertical staves which supported the roofs of their longhouses.

Basalt columns

A large white bird with a pale yellow head, bigger than a seagull, glides past. Suddenly it dives perpendicularly at high speed towards a fish only it can see. A gannet on a day trip, maybe from the Outer Hebrides eighty kilometres west, or even from St. Kilda, 140 kilometres further west in the Atlantic. Small puffins fly speedily, skimming the matt green sea and characteristically flapping their wings. The closer we get to Staffa, the more we see of these busy, seemingly purposeful creatures. 'It's too early yet to see puffins on land. They haven't started nesting yet,' says Kirkpatrick. 'Puffins like people,' he assures us. 'If you're patient, they'll come right up to you. People protect them from the gulls, who want to eat them. They're only safe on the sea where they can dive.'

On the 13th of August 1772, the year before Dr Johnson and Boswell travelled to the Hebrides, Staffa was 'discovered' by the botanist, scientist, and adventurer Joseph Banks, who was underway on a new expedition, this time to Iceland. When he landed on Staffa on that summer day he was astounded by the rock formations. The island was composed entirely of perpendicularly-edged columns. Some had five edges, some six, and a few even eight. Some columns were short but of different heights, forming smooth convenient steps. Others were long, fusing together to form cliff walls. The pillars could also take rounded shapes, as if a giant had taken a fistful of columns when they were still warm and pliable and squeezed them to resemble cockle shells.

Banks was right in his supposition that the columns were lava formations. Staffa was born out of volcanic eruptions sixty million years ago. The lava cooled down slowly and split up into erect columns, following the same principles as when parched earth cracks into six-sided shapes.

Banks discovered Staffa in the same sense that David Livingstone 'discovered' the Victoria Falls. But he made Staffa known to the world, attracting visitors from far and wide. The island had, of course, been discovered a long time ago. When Banks made his visit in 1772, he found a lonesome shepherd there, according to the writer Ann MacKenzie. Banks had put up his tent to shelter for the night, but the shepherd had insisted, hospitably but firmly: Spend the night with me, sleep in my house! Banks accepted. As was common in the islands, the hut was constructed of stone, with a roof of grass and earth. The entrance was barely one metre high, so Banks had to double up to get inside the simple hut. The shepherd sang Gaelic songs the whole night long, although Banks was unable to understand a single word. The following day he was itching intensely all over his body: fleas! A whole colony of them. He made a mild complaint to his host. The shepherd stood up, extremely offended: Not at all! It was Banks who had brought these vermin to his island! Would it not have been better if he had left them behind in England?

Fingal's Cave

Our boat, Isle of Iona, puts in to the cement quay on the east side of Staffa. As usual, Kirkpatrick gives a helping hand to all needing assistance. The path soon splits in two, one going up a steep iron ladder to the plateau where the puffins are nesting and where Banks stayed the night with the shepherd. The other path goes along the rock wall to Fingal's Cave, an impressive oceanic cavern. The path is rather narrow and at intervals spindly iron railings are bolted to the rock. Some of the basalt columns rising out of the sea have a white layer of barnacles. Others are pale green, covered by soft, slimy seaweeds. The columns on land are grey and black, at times coloured orange by lichen which thrives on volcanic rock.

Soon I'm standing at the entrance to Fingal's Cave, twenty metres high and seventy-five metres deep. The biggest basalt cave in the world. The path leads further into the darkened cavern, reminiscent of a cathedral from the Middle Ages. The vaulted roof rises over a deep channel of clear, restless seawater. The waves are sucked into the cave, throwing themselves violently against the cave wall, frustrated that they can't reach any further. The path along the cave wall is slippery. The flimsy railing is more of a psychological support than a real one.

Following Joseph Bank's description of Staffa, the interest in this remarkable island increased enormously. Admittedly, Banks was not unknown. His reputation was already well established among the academic elite of Europe. In 1768, four years before he visited Staffa, he had sailed around the world with Captain

Staffa

Cook. The voyage was organised by the prestigious Royal Society of London for the Improvement of Natural Knowledge. Known as the Royal Society, this oldest academic society in the world was established in 1660. Captain Cook's task was to chart the South Pacific to gain leverage in the struggle for world dominance among European nations. Cook's expedition on the ship Endeavour sailed around the globe to South America, Tahiti, New Zealand, Australia and Java. But the expedition also had another purpose in mind.

The plague of the seas

Captain Cook, Joseph Banks and the entire crew of the Endeavour were involved in a gigantic medical experiment. The quest to eradicate 'the plague of the seas,' the dreaded scurvy. The disease did not only affect sailors of course; folk in the Scottish islands were also well acquainted with this strange affliction, and knew that it could be treated with scurvy grass which grew along the shoreline.

Scurvy had not been a serious problem before the European superpowers embarked on longer voyages lasting weeks to months over the Pacific Ocean, writes Professor Jonathan Lamb. The deadly potential of scurvy was brutally brought to public notice when the British sent a squadron to raid Spanish ships in the Pacific in the mid-1700s. Only 700 seamen out of the original crew of 2,000 survived the voyage. The rest died mainly of scurvy. The chaplain on board, Richard Walter, describes the various stages of the feared disease:

[The skin...] black as ink, ulcers, difficult respiration, rictus of the limbs, teeth falling out and, perhaps most revolting of all, a strange plethora of gum tissue sprouting out of the mouth, which immediately rotted and lent the victim's breath an abominable odour.

He also described strange sensory and psychological effects. The victims appeared to become oversensitive to taste, smell and noise, as if the usual barriers between their external surroundings and their senses disappeared, completely overwhelming the sufferer. The noise of a pistol shot was enough to kill a man in the last stages of the disease, Walter observed. If sufferers got hold of the fruit they craved, they gobbled it up 'with emotions of the most voluptuous luxury.' The least setback brought the previously tough seamen to the verge of tears, and they were overcome with an intense, all-encompassing longing to return home. This particularly strong homesickness and vulnerability to adversity became known as 'scurvy melancholy.' However, documentation of the symptoms did not immediately lead to an understanding of how to prevent them.

Lamb writes that all the British expeditions launched towards the end of the 1700s were used to test out prophylactics for this disease, which caused both bone and tissue to disintegrate. There were many widely different theories as to the cause. Perhaps too much salt in the food. Too much oxygen in the body? Fat skimmed from cooking vessels, perhaps. Bad air. Too thick blood, too much sugar. In 1753, James Lind demonstrated that lemons were effective in treating the disease. So far, so good. But *what* was it about citrus fruit that could both prevent and treat scurvy? And how could one prevent scurvy at sea? Tons of oranges would be rotten long before the ships reached the Pacific. The big expeditions carried what was thought to be a prophylactic mix of vinegar, mustard, soup, wheat, pickled cabbage, concentrated fruit juice and malt. Cook was convinced that malt was indeed the cure. Woe betide those of the crew who didn't take their daily dose of malt.

Posterity has hailed Cook as the one who eradicated scurvy at sea. But as Professor Lamb writes, we now know that malt is not effective. It contains very little vitamin C, the essential vitamin preventing scurvy. Nevertheless, in spite of the misunderstood effect of malt, Cook did have less mortality on board than other expeditions. He must have been doing something right. Perhaps the answer lay in the fruit juice carried aboard the Endeavour. But unfortunately the juice had been boiled, destroying most of the vitamin content. Then what *was* the reason behind the lower mortality on the Endeavour? According to Lamb, the captain had forbidden the addition of fat scoured from the huge cooking pots to the food. Without being aware of it, this was the only thing he had done which could reduce the risk of scurvy. Warm, salty fat formed compounds with the copper in the pots which in turn prevented the absorption of vitamins in the body. However, others also had done the same regarding the use of this fat but without the same effect. The real reason behind the reduced risk of scurvy on Cook's ship remains a mystery to this day.

Children of the Romantic Age

When Joseph Banks visited Staffa, he had already seen much of the world. Nevertheless he was overwhelmed by the basalt columns. In an article in the then current issue of *Scots Magazine*, he is quoted as describing Staffa as one of the most impressive natural phenomena ever, and that the Giant's Causeway in Ireland, and Stonehenge in England, pale in comparison to this island.

This exuberant praise of Staffa from a man of Bank's reputation did not go unnoticed. The rumours spread and the celebrities of the time flocked to the basalt island. For some reason, many of them were poets, writers and painters. Or perhaps this was not coincidental? The Hebrides appealed to the inclination at the time for wild and untouched nature. From the end of the 1700s, Staffa became a 'been there, done that' destination for the rich and famous, a magnet for the children of the Romantic Age.

The cultural elite praised Staffa and Fingal's Cave in their own specific ways: John Keats and William Wordsworth in poetic verse, for instance. But not everything was wonderful. Too many tourists, in Wordsworth's opinion. In 1883! In verse he complains how they feel harassed; they hurry along, unable to contemplate what they are experiencing. Some years previously, Felix Mendelssohn had composed *The Hebrides Overture*, often called Fingal's Cave, in which the orchestra reproduces the sound of the waves booming within the cavern. But then the Gaelic name for Fingal's Cave is as usual far more poetical than the English: *Uamh-Binn*, 'The Cave of Melody.' The young composer was seasick most of the time, so it's not sure how much he actually remembered from the voyage.

The British painter J.M.W. Turner also visited Staffa to illustrate the poems of one of the greatest authors of the time, Sir Walter Scott.

The man behind *Ivanhoe* was perhaps the writer who above all inspired the romantic view of the Scottish Highlands through books such as *Rob Roy* and *Waverly*. In more recent times he has also been given the doubtful honour of reviving the Scottish kilt, and turning tartan patterns into national symbols. Clans which did not have their own specific tartan, invented one. Robert Stevenson, the lighthouse engineer, was an acquaintance of Walter Scott and had invited him on a round trip of the Scottish lighthouses. He certainly did not approve of the new tartan image Scotland was beginning to acquire (and still has). Stevenson remarked in a letter to Scott that he had noted the writer's endless fascination for all things related to the Jacobites and Bonnie Prince Charlie. The Highlanders were re-made as picturesque, noble and wild creatures, who could be observed from a safe distance from the windows of the newly-built hunting lodges.

The list of notables who have trudged over the basalt staves on the way to Fingal's Cave does not end with Sir Walter Scott. Robert Louis Stevenson, of course, visited the island on his way to Erraid, and Staffa featured in one of Jules Verne's many maritime novels, *The Green Ray*. Even the African explorer David Livingstone went to Staffa *en route* to Ulva in 1864, hoping to find remaining relatives. But it was Queen Victoria's journey to Staffa and the Hebrides in 1847 which led to the steamboats, now sailing daily from Oban to Staffa and Iona, being filled to the brim by seasick, smog-impregnated townsfolk.

Tiree – the land beneath the waves

From the summit of Staffa, I can make out a sunlit, flat island, encircled by white shell sand beaches, pitching like a raft on the Atlantic. Tiree is like a Caribbean island, which once upon a time separated from the rest of the archipelago and sailed off northwards. Relatives of my mother are buried on Tiree. My grandparents lie side by side in the graveyard, resting under a carpet of wildflowers and grazing sheep, the gravestones leaning lopsidedly to the east: William MacDonald and Jeana MacDonald. Today yet another relative will be laid to rest, and our family is memorialising him by visiting his favourite places around the island, such as Tiree's second highest mountain, Ben Hough—if it deserves to be called that—rising 119 metres above sea level. Grey cement bunkers from World War II disintegrate slowly on the summit. The Royal Air Force had a base on Tiree from 1941. Their main brief was to sink Nazi submarines before they managed to torpedo the convoys of merchant ships *en route* to the USA. Usually the submarines beat them to it.

One of the reasons for the RAF choosing Tiree was that it already had a small civilian airport located on The Reef, a flat area on the eastern side of the island. The RAF improved and enlarged it using a workforce of prisoners from Scottish jails. It's not clear what the prisoners thought was worse: staying in their mainland jails or in the damp, cold barracks on Tiree, which like the rest of the Hebrides in wartime, was denoted a 'restricted area.'

The airport, the planes and the 2,000 deployed soldiers had all, in fact, been predicted. John MacLean, or Iain mac Eachainn Bhàin in Gaelic, lived in the 1800s. He was known for his prophetic abilities or, as is said in these parts, he had the 'second sight.' He predicted that 'a great war is coming soon, such as the world has never seen.' Thousands would fall in a day and many would be suffocated by a white smoke. Huge birds, pronounced John MacLean to those who would listen, would arise from The Reef, steered by people with noses like pigs. Narrow vessels of iron would travel under the Atlantic, sending shoals of slender silver fish which would sink big ships on the surface. And in an unnamed country, the earth would be soaked with blood from which red flowers would spring forth. Then, for a while, there would be peace but the dark days would return when the arrows

Beach at Hough, Tiree

of death rained from the heavens. Tiree would also witness great changes when armed men would come to the island and live in strange houses.

Now clairvoyants were a natural part of island culture. People experienced that their predictions often came true, so there was no reason to doubt their abilities. In the Hebrides, folk did not feel any contradiction between their deeply-held religious convictions and a belief in second sight. However, missionaries and other travellers from the reformed church frowned upon such practices. Were these not papal tendencies, reminiscent in fact of a Catholic past? Some individuals still possess these special abilities to this day. George MacPherson from the Isle of Skye, an expert on traditions, maintains that there is probably one person in each generation who has the gift of second sight. Sometimes the ability will skip a generation. It is by no means something to aspire to, as it can be very disturbing to always know what will happen in the future.

The traveller Martin Martin relates the phenomenon from his journey to St. Kilda in 1695. One day the islanders had a vision: They saw a man with a grey jacket and kilt floating head-down in the sea. A bird was pecking him in the neck. The islanders followed the body with their eyes for about fifteen minutes until it drifted out of sight. Not long after, one of those observing fell in the sea himself and was drowned. Soon after he was also seen floating head-down, again with a bird pecking at his neck.

Not surprisingly it's windy on the top of Ben Hough. It's nearly always windy on Tiree and there are few sheltered spots to be found. On the other hand, the islanders are proud of the fact that they top the British weather charts regarding the number of hours of sun. The island is so flat that the passing clouds ignore it, leaving it to bask in sunshine. The wind also keeps at bay the dreadful hordes of midges that swarm during the summer.

A red plastic bottle is passed around by my relatives and all the adults take a swig of whisky. This ritual is totally different from that of another relative who died some years ago. He was a native of Tiree and, as prescribed by tradition, was borne to the grave by a procession of men only. The women stayed behind preparing the food and drink for the memorial get-together. But the rituals, both of times gone by and today, share one thing in common: Whisky was and still is a necessary ingredient of funerals.

The arrival of the potato

About 800 people live on Tiree. The name is derived from the Gaelic *Tir-Iodh* or 'the land of grain.' This was the grain centre of the Hebrides, and it also supplied the abbey on Iona with barley. The soil here is mixed with calcium-containing sand, resulting in particularly fertile soil.

In the 1700s the cultivation of barley gave way to the potato. A patch of earth

Black house, Balevullin, Tiree

94

with potatoes could feed four times the number of mouths as a corresponding area of barley. This was one of the factors that led to rapid population growth on the islands in the 1800s. The potato soon became the staple ingredient in the diet. The historian James Hunter writes about a little boy who was asked what he ate for his three meals a day. The answer was the same for each meal: mashed potatoes. 'And what else?' asked the curious questioner. 'What else?' answered the boy. 'A spoon!'

However, it wasn't quite as meagre in all households. The meals often included milk and fish. Vegetables were unknown apart from turnips. The only foods remotely resembling a vegetable were dulse and watercress.

The potato had the advantage of not being the most demanding of plants. It tolerated stormy and damp conditions better than oats and barley, and also provided vital vitamin C to protect the inhabitants from scurvy. The potatoes were grown in so-called 'lazy beds,' parallel strips of ridge and furrow. The outlines of these old beds are still imprinted on the landscapes of the Highlands and islands, and are best seen when the sun lies low on the horizon. One can make out the ancient overgrown furrows stretching from the fields and up the steep hillsides. However, Hunter and others have rightly pointed out that the English word 'lazy bed' is a totally misleading and derogatory term. Those who cultivated the land in this way were anything but lazy. The potato beds were dug by hand and thoroughly fertilised with both seaweed and manure that were carried from the shore and byre in large baskets. Lazy?

The struggle against emigration

As mentioned, population growth exploded on Tiree and the rest of the Hebrides in the 1800s. Potatoes were able to feed many more than grain, and the protection afforded by smallpox vaccination meant the disease took fewer lives on the islands. Ironically, overpopulation was also a result of efforts by landowners who over a period of years *prevented* people from emigrating.

During the 1700s islanders were already, by both planned and voluntary means, leaving for America and other colonies. Landowners became increasingly concerned that they were losing their best workers to the colonies. Who would now harvest the valuable seaweed, kelp, and work for almost nothing? And the authorities? What *they* worried about was the dwindling recruitment base for the army and navy. Who was going to fight against Napoleon if the best men decided instead to make their futures in Australia or North America? The breach had to be stopped! Landowners and politicians joined forces to plug the hole.

The campaign against emigration was co-ordinated by the Highland Society of Edinburgh, according to James Hunter. Its membership included landowners whose wealth stemmed from the extraction of alkali from seaweed, and commercial lawyers connected to the industry. The group co-operated with the British government's chief law officer in Scotland, who was a close friend and colleague of many in the 'kelping lobby.' The campaign was presented with a humanitarian logic it was difficult to argue against. 'The emigrants' said the landowners 'were victims; first, of shippers who were packing America-bound vessels with more emigrants than those vessels could safely carry; they were victims, second, of their own "false hopes" of a continent where [...] only disappointment awaited the average settler.' Ha! The poor things thought they would be better off there!

In 1803 the Passenger Vessels Act was passed. It had virtuous packaging. Presuming to act in the best interests of passengers, the law drastically reduced the number of people emigrant vessels could carry. Ticket prices tripled and ordinary folks could no longer afford the voyage. However, there was no doubt that conditions on board were still terrible, at least for the poorest who sailed on the most notorious vessels. There was no privacy, no toilets. In heavy seas, the lower deck was flooded with excrement, urine and vomit. Thousands of emigrants from the Highlands and islands died of typhoid fever, cholera, and measles.

American author Herman Melville, the man behind *Moby Dick*, described conditions on one of those ships in the novel *Redburn: His First Voyage:*

> How, then, with the friendless emigrants, stowed away like bales of cotton and packed like slaves in a slave ship; confined in a place that, during storm time, must be closed against both light and air; who can do no cooking, nor warm so much as a cup of water, for the drenching seas would instantly flood the fire in their exposed galley on deck? We had not been at sea one week, when to hold your head down the hatchway was like holding it down a suddenly opened cesspool.

Later, when the mood had changed among landowners, they couldn't get the people out fast enough, and even *paid* their passage, the law was conveniently amended, in 1826. By then, however, Tiree and other islands were already overpopulated.

A'bhliadhna a dh'fhalbh am buntàta:
The year the potato went away

The 1841 census registered 4,391 inhabitants in Tiree, the highest population ever noted on the island. Therefore, Tiree was most severely affected by the blight in 1846, 'the year the potato went away.' The crop failure was caused by a species of fungus which emigrated from America to mainland Europe, then travelled over the sea to Ireland and further on to Western Scotland. *Phytophthora infestans* turned potatoes into black, foul-smelling soggy lumps. If the fungus had appeared a hundred years earlier, when the corn was swaying in the fields, nobody would have noticed the potato disease, never mind being directly affected by it. But now the potato had become the staple food, supplemented by some fish and a minimal amount of meat. The potato crop failed in Ireland, the Hebrides and the Scottish Highlands over several years. Tiree was no exception, and people were starving and needed emergency food from the towns to survive.

It's somewhat revealing to read Queen Victoria's diary from 1847. As she was sailing among the Hebridean islands in the Royal yacht, newspapers were printing grim warnings of impending catastrophic starvation. She barely mentions it in her diary. In Ireland, just south of the Hebrides, thousands of people were dying. The figures vary between 200,000 to 1,500,000. Jim Donnelly of the BBC reckons that about one million Irish died of starvation and disease between 1846 and 1851, and that around two million emigrated in less than ten years.

The death toll in Ireland was, irrespective of differing estimates, extremely high. In contrast, in Scotland it was minimal. What explained this difference? And why did the Irish continue to die of starvation and epidemics, considering that Ireland, from 1847, imported enough corn to feed the population, provided it had been correctly distributed? And why was Ireland allowed to export grain in the middle of a famine? Donnelly focuses on three reasons why the authorities in London allowed the people in Ireland to die. The first was the current economic doctrine of *laissez-faire*, an extreme form of market liberalism which held there should be minimal interference by the state in private affairs. Thus the authorities thought it inappropriate to forbid the export of corn. The soup kitchens which provided around three million people with one meal a day were stopped after operating for only six months. People could become lazy and dependent on emergency rations. It was also seen as an unnecessary and artificial interference in the economic system to assist people in emigrating.

Yet another perception preventing the authorities from taking adequate action to deal with the emergency was a Protestant conviction that the famine was a punishment from God. Indeed, the whole Irish catastrophe was direct evidence that the Almighty thought the Irish system of farming functioned very poorly in comparison to the big, well-organised farms of England. In other words, the Lord acted, albeit brutally but effectively.

The third ideology preventing an appropriate response to the emergency, according to Donnelly, was a moral argument with racist and religious overtones. There was something about the Irish Catholic character which had caused the country to suffer this crisis. The Irish were rebellious, dirty, and totally unable to manage themselves. Well then, London thought, let them learn to stand on their own two feet and stop begging! If you were lucky, you could work and live under the strict discipline of the dreaded workhouse, and you could receive wages according to your efforts in cutting stone or other types of hard work. This was what was needed to counteract laziness, this unfortunate national characteristic of the Irish.

When the potato blight reached Scotland, it had totally different consequences from those experienced in Ireland. The clan chiefs still held a degree of ownership in the Hebrides. True enough, they had gradually moved away from the ancient tradition of caring for their clansmen, towards perceiving clan lands as their own and behaving as any landowner would. Nevertheless, when the crisis hit, the old clan loyalty awoke once more, at least in the hearts of some of the chiefs. Several of them spent fortunes buying grain which they distributed among the starving.

Slum or Patagonia

In contrast to most other islands in the Hebrides, the mass emigration from Tiree was not due to people being evicted from their homes. It was not necessary to force people to leave; many were desperate to escape from the island. They usually had two choices. They could go to the mainland, for example to Glasgow, which at that time was rapidly expanding. The problem with Glasgow was exactly that: it was growing so fast it was unable to absorb all those flocking in from the farming districts. Large slum areas developed as the city grew, where tuberculosis and other potentially fatal diseases thrived. The second choice for the people of Tiree was to emigrate. Many left for Canada, and as immigrants still do today, they settled in the same areas and married among their own folk. It was not quite *comme il faut* to marry an Englishman or Irishman.

There was also a time when many went to Patagonia in Argentina and to Chile. The huge sheep farms in the southern point of America needed herders. The wages were good, and gradually several immigrants bought large areas of land and themselves became sheep farmers. Paradoxically, the folk from the Hebrides became responsible in part for ousting the native population of Patagonia for exactly the same reason they themselves had been evicted: the establishment of sheep farms. The ousted became the ousters, and participated in 'the white gold rush.' The herding was carried out on horseback. A grandfather of a member of the museum committee on Tiree immigrated to Patagonia in the 1800s. Some years later he owned a farm of several thousand acres. His brother, still in Tiree, received a letter: 'It's time you came here; you can earn six times more as a shepherd in Patagonia than in Tiree—but bring a good sheepdog!'

Every small farm which has sheep on the island also has a Border collie. When the black and white sheepdog is not herding sheep, it's busy herding everything else which moves: cars, cyclists and footballs. Since the collies are not tethered and there are no fences surrounding the houses, they can be a real bother for passers-by. They run alongside bicycles, barking loudly, threatening to get caught up in the spokes. Or they run fearlessly alongside the car while the driver frantically tries to avoid running over the dog, which is trying its best to herd the car into the flock. Meeting a border collie is like going into close combat with an ancient instinct yet to adapt to the discovery of the wheel.

Foster children

In several books on the Hebrides I have come across stories of children from disadvantaged homes on the mainland being fostered on the islands. Scotland has a long tradition of placing children in foster homes instead of institutions. From the 1800s it was often Christian organisations which took responsibility for giving a new start in life to children whose parents were abusive, poor, or addicted to alcohol. The children were placed far away from Glasgow where the majority originated. So many children from the Lowlands were fostered on Iona that English displaced Gaelic in the playground, according to MacArthur. During a census of pupils in 1896, there were forty-one children from Iona, while thirty-three were foster children from Glasgow.

Jane MacCallum from Balevullin, on the west coast of Tiree, grew up with the old farming system called crofting. But she can also tell another story: She was one of many foster children who were placed in homes on Tiree. She was only two years old when she arrived on the island on the 9th of April 1938. She still does not know where she comes from, or why her mother left her. She was brought up by Mr. and Mrs. Kennedy in Balevullin; and their two sons, Neil and Donald, became her brothers. 'I was really a baby when I came, and I don't think I had many words, so I learned Gaelic, and that was my first language in school.'

We are seated in the sitting room. The door is wide open, and the threshold leads right out onto the green *machair* which slopes down to the white shell sand of Balevullin beach. There I glimpse the bright-coloured sails of the surfers riding the waves. The sounds of crying seagulls and barking dogs float through the door. The floor is covered with well-worn linoleum, but Jane is busy fixing other parts of the house and sits opposite me on the sofa in her painting clothes. She lights a cigarette and speaks with a deep, hoarse voice.

'I grew up on this croft. I've always liked it and still love this life. Even though I'm getting older and it's getting harder for me to run the croft now. I love the animals, the cows. Sheep too, but I don't have sheep myself.'

Jane MacCallum belongs to a generation of islanders which is slowly disappearing. She has lived through the times without tractors, piped water and electricity, before flight connections or frequent ferry crossings. 'The years went on, happy, happy years, the truth *must* be told,' she says, as if she is expecting resistance. Or is it just a manner of speech? The truth *must* be told.

She inherited the house we are sitting in from her foster parents and brothers. As she grew up, she realized that her background did not make any difference. This was her home, and the Kennedy family were 'my folk and still are my folk.'

However, the authorities had a different view. When Jane was about fifteen, they took her back to the mainland. She had not been officially adopted by the family, the only one she knew, and spent eleven months in a home run by the

Scaranish, Tiree

Salvation Army. 'This was completely against my own wishes,' says Jane. 'We had a lot of schooling, but the way we were treated, all the restrictions, it wasn't right for teenage girls, but again, that's just my opinion.'

Again this phrase which I've heard in the other islands: 'It's just my opinion.' Even when commenting on one's own experiences. The manner of speech softens strong opinions, adamant conclusions and criticism of others. A way of expressing oneself which facilitates living together in small, tightly-knit communities and avoiding aggressive, open confrontation. Moderation. A modesty which can be exploited and misunderstood by incomers used to expressing their opinions loudly and clearly in committees and meetings, where issues concerning the future of the small local communities are discussed. Both committees and a self-assertive manner of speech are unknown among older people on the islands.

The teenager Jane MacCallum was not forgotten by her family on Tiree, and they fought to get her back. After three court hearings she returned to Balevullin. 'The authorities did not want me to return. They didn't want any of the children fostered on Tiree to go back there. I don't know why. But as you get older, you think about such things. And was this not unkind to those families who had fostered those children?'

We return to the opening theme of our conversation. Crofting as a way of life. 'When I came here as a wee girl, we only had five cows. They had to be milked by hand. The spring ploughing was done with a horse, and if you were sowing corn, you used two horses. Neil ploughed, my father sowed, and I carried the corn seed to him in a bucket. It was the same when we planted potatoes; the soil was turned by the plough.' They got manure from the cows and seaweed which they fetched in barrows from the beach. 'We went out in the moonlight to spread the seaweed or muck with forks.' For a moment I fantasise: Maybe this was a kind of ritual? Fertilising by moonlight, a vestige of the Celtic druids? Born out of a belief that seeds would germinate more quickly if they were fertilised by the light of the moon? For the sake of clarity and to confirm my epiphany, I ask: 'Why did you fertilise by moonlight?' 'Because we had to collect the manure and seaweed during daylight. And in the afternoon the cows had to be milked. So we had to work at night as well.'

Jane harvested seaweed as late as the 1950s, 'the tangles,' as she calls tangle weed. She carefully broke the long leaves from the stems, which she laid out to dry on stones. The stiff stems dried throughout the winter: 'But you had to be careful. If it was a wet winter, they got soggy and wet, so you had to look after them.' The first time she collected seaweed for money was during the winter season of 1956, when she gathered three tons. That amounted to fifteen pounds in May the following year. 'That was a lot of money.'

'We have to be honest,' she says, as if she is about to divulge a big secret. I lean forward, all ears: 'Tiree has improved in many ways. Some will say we had slavery before, when you think of the lives we lived, but I still think it was a healthy way of life. We were out in the fresh air, everybody was satisfied, and we were more than willing to help our neighbours. And when you came home, you were ready for your meal whether it was a rich meal or a poor meal. Everybody was in the same boat; there was little money but people were so very, very happy.'

I say goodbye to Jane MacCallum while thinking that perhaps both versions are true. It was better before, and it's better now.

Skerryvore

The village of Hynish lies southwest on Tiree. The road ends among old stone-built workers' houses converted into a museum, a short tower, and a stone pier. Fifteen kilometres out to sea, waves break over a rock, barely discernible through the mist. Although it can be difficult to make out in daylight, there it stands, Skerryvore Lighthouse.

When an employee of the Northern Lighthouse Board acquired a list of the damage Skerryvore rock had caused, he saw that at least thirty ships had sunk between 1804 and 1844. But he pointed out that the rock had caused much more havoc than that. Many vessels sank without anybody knowing what had happened to them. The shipowners had to give up trying to find even a vestige of a sail. The lost ships were listed in the vaguely-termed 'lost at sea' register. Yet another indication of the rock's notorious behaviour was that fishermen from Tiree often visited the rock after a storm to salvage wreckage, a profitable business. When the lighthouse engineer Robert Stevenson explored Tiree, he found that the price of land on the west side where the wreckage was washed ashore was much higher than other places on the island.

The pressure on the NLB to build a lighthouse on Skerryvore was indeed nothing new, according to the author of the book on the Stevenson dynasty, Bella Bathhurst. But some became very quiet when the proposal to build a lighthouse and secure the rock once and for all was mentioned. The seamen who were most at risk said nothing. Neither did the fishermen and islanders on Tiree. The latter had economic motives for anticipating more shipwrecks. The salvaged materials provided valuable timber for roofs, wood for furniture, rope to hold down the roofing, and diverse useful items according to the cargo of each ship. The islanders were also in league with the seamen in their deep conviction that a lighthouse would impede the will of God. If He had not wished that the rock should lie just as it was, He would not have put it there in the first place. And if He had wanted it to be visible, well, He would have placed a lighthouse there Himself!

Skerryvore is the highest point of a ten-kilometre-long reef, most of which is submerged, even at low tide. Robert Stevenson visited the rock in 1834 to make an assessment. Was it at all possible to build a lighthouse in this godforsaken, windy and dangerous place? Yes, Robert concluded, and oddly enough wrote that the project would be much cheaper and easier to construct than the Bell Rock Lighthouse in the North Sea. As Bella Bathhurst writes: 'It was a strange judgement, not least since the North Sea rarely matched the ferocity of the Atlantic storms. Also, the area around the Bell Rock was well surveyed in comparison to the waters around the west coast and the Hebrides.'

It was Robert's son, Alan Stevenson, who was given the job of building Skerryvore. By then, Alan had for several years co-operated with the Fresnel brothers, Leonor and Augustin, in Paris. The brothers specialized in developing lenses, including lighthouse lenses. The cooperation between the Stevenson and Fresnel families began in 1820, when Robert visited French lighthouses during a study tour. Augustin Fresnel was then already far ahead of his time; he was working on intensifying light beams by placing reflectors behind the light source and prisms in front. Alan continued the alliance with Augustin and adapted the lenses to the Scottish lighthouses. Thanks to work with Alan's brother David Stevenson, the Scottish lenses were further developed to give the strongest light the world had ever seen.

The project to erect Skerryvore began in 1838. Tiree lacked everything that could support the construction of a lighthouse: stone, timber, stone masons and fuel. Alan noted that the locals had used up all the peat on the island to make whisky, and had to row or sail to other islands to get firewood to keep warm and

The 'Skerryvore' band

cook food. It wasn't quite true that Tiree did not have stone. The stone masons began by hewing blocks of black granite, but soon discovered it was a difficult material to work with. Alan knew that the granite from the island of Mull was a much more suitable stone, and although it was a challenge to transport this rock all the way from the neighbouring island, Alan had no choice. Thus the lower part of Skerryvore is made of black granite from Tiree and the rest of the tower is of pale granite from Mull.

The construction of the tower itself was a challenge. It was too risky simply to copy a lighthouse erected on the North Sea. An Atlantic hurricane could hurl waves with a pressure of almost three tons per square foot at the base of a foolhardy lighthouse trying to prove its strength. In comparison, the highest recorded challenge faced by the Bell Rock on the east coast was one and a half tons. The Skerryvore Lighthouse had to withstand monster waves. Bathhurst comments that posterity has proven Alan's calculations to be correct. The dome of the tower, forty-two metres above sea level, was at times continuously overwashed by waves.

However, what distinguished Skerryvore from other lighthouses was its unique shape. Alan was at heart an aesthetic. He had chosen a simple, almost severe style to please himself and others. From a base twelve metres in breadth, the tower rises, narrowing to five metres in circumference. His nephew Robert Louis Stevenson labelled it 'the noblest of all extant deep-sea lights.'

In the summer of 1842, the tower itself was completed. It remained to put in place the lantern and the Fresnel lens. The rotating light from Skerryvore could be seen all the way from Barra, almost sixty kilometres away in the Outer Hebrides. Alan recommended that lighthouse keepers on Skerryvore should be paid ten pounds extra per year, in view of the exceptional disadvantages of living on a rock where one could hardly stretch one's legs. They would risk being cut off from their families for several months during the winter storms. The only way they could contact land, that is, Tiree, was by light signals to the tower at Hynish. As Alan had rightly predicted, the lighthouse keepers had a very demanding existence. When the lantern was to be installed in the tower, the weather became so bad that the workers had to wait on Skerryvore for seven weeks, until a boat from Hynish on Tiree could rescue them. The stranded men could live with their ragged clothing, but the craving for tobacco was worse than anything.

Skerryvore was not automated until 1994. Today the land station is a museum dedicated to the history of the lighthouse. If one goes up a little hill to the signal tower behind the museum, one can just make out the lighthouse. A narrow, dark needle points heavenwards, a fitting monument to the man who never quite achieved his dreams, Alan Stevenson.

Eigg—the island that bought itself

The ferry to Eigg leaves from the little fishing village of Mallaig on the west coast of Scotland, a few hours' journey north of Oban. Mallaig is an important departure point for the Caledonian MacBrayne ferries, although much smaller versions than the big vessels which set forth from Oban. Mallaig's ferries go to the huge island of Skye, and the 'small isles' Rum, Eigg, Canna and Muck.

Only the permanent inhabitants of Eigg, around seventy, are permitted to drive a car. Others must walk, cycle, or hike on the island, which invests in eco-tourism. I'm standing on the pier watching a Norwegian fishing boat, when a man kindly offers to heave my baggage into a pickup, one of the two cars going on board.

The little CalMac ferry takes about one and a half hours to reach Eigg. The island is mostly known for being the first in the Hebrides where the population actually went ahead and bought back their own local community from a private owner. They joined forces with the local authorities and a nature conservation organisation and made an acceptable offer. This buy-out, as it was called, happened in 1997. However, the process leading up to it was an obstacle race, with remarkable challenges along the way: burnt vintage cars, fraudsters, and fake millionaires.

Kenny and Sheena Keen, who rent out Sandavore Farm where I'm staying, are waiting on the pier. Sandavore is one of the oldest buildings on the island. The house is first mentioned in the 1600s and was Eigg's original inn and pub.

The Sgurr, Eigg

The story goes that in 1609 the central authorities issued an order, the Statutes of Iona. The aim was to weaken the power of the clan chiefs over the west coast and western isles, and to consolidate Scotland into a single nation. One of the new laws forbade clan chiefs from entertaining guests with food and drink according to the old tradition. They were no longer permitted to hold court with big feasts, bards, casks of wine, and whole-roasted oxen. Instead, they were obliged to establish places to stay the night and which served food and drink: 'inns,' such as Sandavore.

'We don't have rules like that here.'

Kenny shows me the shop at the pier. 'By the way, it's open every day, also on Sundays,' he says. 'And on Monday, even though it's the 1st of May. We don't have rules like that here.' He sounds proud. The opening times are the first concrete evidence that the people of Eigg are in charge, but also reflect the multicultural population. There were not many true natives of Eigg left when the islanders bought the island. If there had been, it's unlikely the shop would be open on Sundays.

But the opening times and attitudes towards the day of rest are not the only contrasts to other Hebridean islands. I get myself a bike and breathlessly struggle my way up a small tarmac road rising steeply from the harbour, through lush woods on the sheltered side of Eigg. Pine trees throw shadows, chestnuts are flowering and the beaches are green. Up, up, up. Mr. and Mrs. Keen have driven ahead and are waiting for me by an old red postbox. The road forks in two. To the left, a rough muddy farm track leads to Sandavore Farm, a traditional blackhouse with double stone walls, filled, insulated and drained with stones, gravel, or sand. The walls are one and a half metres thick; the windowsills are almost as deep.

When I was on Eigg the island still had problems with electricity supply. The plan was to become virtually energy self-sufficient, using water, sun and wind energy in the near future. But for the time being, many of the houses depended on humming diesel generators. We're leaning over the built-in, diesel-smelling monster. 'It's a bit temperamental,' says Sheena. 'But if the light goes, usually the heating works, and the other way around.' 'Just ring if it botches,' adds Kenny. It must have slipped his mind that the mobile network on the island is also 'temperamental.' 'But you can't use any electric gear that takes more than 500 watts. So no hair dryers,' warns Sheena, 'but PCs and chargers are fine.'

The house is completely modernised inside, with tile flooring and an enormous bath. There's a smell of damp in the lounge. In the old days, the fireplace was in the middle of the floor. It was never allowed to go out; the smoke and heat did not disappear up a chimney but instead filled the room, the warmth drawing the damp out of the walls. Now, in the days of panel ovens and electricity restrictions, the damp hasn't time to leave the walls before yet another Hebridean shower decides to make a detour over Eigg and saturate the walls of old Sandavore Farm.

'The case of Eigg'

In June 1997, the journalist Warren Hoge in the *New York Times* reported the following to his American readers: 'Island Tenants Triumph: They're the Lairds Now.'

The tiny island of Eigg made headlines all over the world when the inhabitants bought the island. The battle to buy Eigg revealed to everyone that Scotland differed from other European countries with regard to its system of land ownership. The purchase of Eigg, and not least the process leading up to it, created a huge stir in the heart of parliament and the government. 'The case of Eigg' clearly showed what could happen when local communities were sold on the open market like properties in a Monopoly game.

Large areas of Scotland were, and still are, in the hands of a few owners: conservation organisations, oil companies, Arabic sheiks and aristocrats. Until the land reform of 2003, privately-owned properties were run on feudal-like principals. The throne was formally at the top of the hierarchy, but rich landowners bought and administered land which they in turn hired out to 'tenants.' Within this system, tenants had always to ask permission from the landowner to carry out the smallest of changes to the site they rented. Consent had to be sought to put up a fence or cut down a tree. But that wasn't the worst of it. Folk who had rented the same house for generations could risk getting a few weeks' notice to move if a new owner decided to tear down their home. A landlord could simply throw out a family who had fallen out of favour. Those who complained about poor infrastructure, or showed a lack of respect by failing to open the gate for expensive cars swishing by in a cloud of dust, were either very courageous or extremely foolhardy.

It was precisely conditions such as these that the people of Eigg had had their fill of. That's not to say that all lairds failed to treat their tenants properly or administer their property responsibly. Many did. However, Eigg had had more than a reasonable share of unpredictable landlords who came and went, but never lived on the island themselves. When the residents bought the island, many were living in run-down camper vans, or houses where the rainwater leaked in causing large blisters beneath damp wallpaper. Eigg had been under neglectful administration for too many years, ever since the 20th Chief of Clanranald, a branch of the Clan MacDonald, sold the island in 1827.

Singing Sands and a meeting with a descendant

If you cycle to the northwest coast of Eigg, the road ends at a white two-storey house. This is Cleadale, or *Cliadal*, the Old Norse name for 'The pastures by the cliff.' And indeed, the name is bang on. A wall of black basalt encloses Cleadale, the cliff rising dark and steeply upwards from luscious pastures. According to the brochure, *The Geology of Eigg,* the cliffs are continually crumbling, and on a calm day one can even hear it happening.

The path down to the beach, called the Singing Sands, leads from Cleadale Farm. Now, as usual, the English name is less poetic than the Gaelic *Traigh na Bigil*, The whispering sands. The dry quartz grains of sand ring clear like crystal, singing, and the beach hums softly as I tread gently on its surface. The place name is associated with a Celtic myth: whispering voices, those of drowned seamen speaking to their women. 'Weep for us no longer, we are in the land beneath the waves. All the tears you shed after the time of mourning become drops of blood. If you do not cease to cry,' pleaded the voices on Traigh na Bigil, 'we will drown once more. In blood.'

There are cliffs here too. Throughout the years the waves have cast themselves against and caressed the soft red-brown sandstone, carving out arches and caverns and piercing stones on the beach with perfectly rounded holes.

I don't have the Singing Sands to myself; an elderly man, who introduces himself as Michael Butler, is taking his daily walk. Some days later we will share a cup of tea in my little kitchen in Sandavore. Michael's great-grandfather was Dr Hugh MacPherson: surgeon, professor in Hebrew, theology, and Greek—and the first private laird on Eigg. MacPherson bought Eigg from the clan chief Ranald MacDonald for the sum of 15,000 pounds in 1827. The clan chief was, as were many others, obliged to sell land to rid himself of debts acquired in gambling or other excesses in London or Edinburgh.

An issue of the *Rough Guide* describes Hugh MacPherson's behaviour during the Clearances as follows: 'Only on Eigg was some compassion shown.' I share this remark with MacPherson's great-grandchild. He seems relieved as he leans back in the chair in the little kitchen. The light filters in through the window set deep into the thick stone wall. 'What I'm saying is that he wasn't as bad as the others. He was a laird,' says Michael. 'And the norms for how you should treat people have changed, haven't they?'

In spite of a certain amount of understanding for the crofters' plight, MacPherson nevertheless followed the same pattern as many other landlords, including those on the neighbouring islands of Rum, Canna and Muck. He rented out some of Eigg's grazing lands to a farmer from the Lowlands wanting to start commercial sheep farming. The farmer offered to pay higher rent if the land was cleared of people. The villages of upper and lower Grulin below the rocky massive Sgurr, the landmark on Eigg, were cleared of people and livestock. The smallholders had a deadline of November 1852 to leave their homes. Eleven of the fourteen families boarded a vessel bound for Nova Scotia in Canada. New Scotland. They were received, starving, thin and dressed in rags, by shocked, head-shaking Canadian authorities.

Michael Butler was nine years old the first time he spent a summer on Eigg in 1931. Theoretically, the island could have been his if his great-grandfather had not sold Eigg out of the family in 1895.

A round dance of buying and selling

One of the most peaceful and stable periods on Eigg was when Sir Walter Runciman owned the island from 1920 to the 1960s. He was a member of the British parliament and a representative of the Liberal party which at that time enjoyed considerable support. He was elected in 1899, winning against the conservative candidate, a gentleman by the name of Winston Churchill. 'Don't worry, I don't think this is the last the country has heard of either of us,' Runciman told his political rival.

Runciman was a landlord genuinely interested in Eigg and had ambitious plans for the island: the population would become self-sustaining regarding food, the houses were to be maintained, and the school building renovated. A residence for a doctor would be built and also a post office and a shop in the middle of the island. The only problem for the cottagers was that the patches of land they rented from the landlord, the crofts, were too small to generate enough income to pay the rent. This meant they also had to work for the landlord to supplement their income. Of course the whole idea behind the crofting system was that the allotted acreage of farmland could not generate any surplus: the cottagers were obliged to labour for the landlord to meet their rent. So now the people on Eigg worked for the new owner. Thus the old interdependency continued as before, but in spite of this, Sir Walter Runciman is remembered as a laird who made the island blossom.

However, Runciman caused even more blooming. In 1927 he built a beautiful house in the Italianate style which still stands today. From their Lodge, the Runciman family could view Sgurr mountain from the dinner table. True enough, the landowner's big white residence, with a flat roof, rounded small-paned windows, balconies, and a large terrace, did not quite fit in on Eigg. Palm trees lined the driveway, giving visitors the impression of driving into an Italian film set. And the garden. Oh, the garden! One summer evening I visited the overgrown garden, wandering among the plants which had survived Runciman. Mediterranean memorials which defied the westerly winds. Magnolia. Eucalyptus. Fuchsia. Rhododendron. Strawberry trees with scarlet balls. Roses on the rampage, ecstatically stretching their thorny arms much further than previously permitted, reaching out over lawns once cut with nail-scissor precision.

The Runciman family put Eigg on the market in 1966. As they packed their possessions, stability, the very trademark of the family, left, along with all the suitcases and boxes loaded on the awaiting boat. A Welsh farmer, an elderly gentleman who never intended to live on Eigg, bought the island for 66,000 pounds. The plan was to conjure up prime beef from the pastures. Soon a big herd of heavy, meaty English Hereford cattle was to be seen lumbering around. The poor beasts, used to the gentle, rolling English countryside, were no doubt shocked and surprised on meeting the green, but by no means gently-rolling, pastures of Eigg. The cows failed to thrive, and many died of disease brought on by the damp, harsh surroundings. The combination of Eigg and Hereford cows was not profitable. Five years later the island was for sale again, and once more the islanders waited apprehensively. Who would they have to put up with next?

In 1971 they got their answer. One Mr. Farnham-Smith, the head of an English charity fund, the Anglyn Trust, bought the island for 120,000 pounds. The plan was to use Eigg as 'an adventure school for handicapped boys.' However, it soon became clear that these boys were not so handicapped after all. They were 'difficult' children from rich families, boys who had become troublemakers in private schools. It would seem any plans to develop Eigg were conversely proportional to the means available to invest in the island.

Schellenberg buys Eigg

When Yorkshireman Keith Schellenberg, ex-Olympic bobsled driver, sports car enthusiast, vegetarian and businessman, bought Eigg from the Anglyn Trust in 1975, the island had been on the property market three times in less than ten years. This time, however, the people were optimistic because the new owner had money.

And capital was a decisive factor in the development of Eigg. Many lacked electric lighting, piped water, bathrooms and toilets. And most smallholders would soon be pensioners. So Schellenberg and his money were more than welcome on Eigg.

There was a promising start. The tourists returned. Like Runciman, Schellenberg also had a vision: Eigg was to become sustainable. The population increased to sixty persons and the school could now boast of twelve pupils. Workers were recruited through newspaper advertisements.

One of those answering an advert was Camille Dressler. Originally from France, she had come to Eigg in the beginning of the 1980s together with her husband, an artist. The couple had sent a letter to Schellenberg. They offered to work for him in return for renting a house at a cheap rate. The deal was clinched, but the pair got a surprise the evening they arrived on Eigg. Their new home was a tiny hut, lit by gas lamps. The miserable conditions were an omen of much worse times ahead.

Many of those who came to Eigg to work for Schellenberg had interpreted the contract as giving them the right to stay on the island if they so wished. Buy a site, or rent a house, do it up and get a long-term let. They were wrong. From Schellenberg's point of view, the more attractive the contract was, the more the market value of the property fell. The whole affair became a downward spiral, leading to ruined buildings and insecure people; it generated feelings amounting to hatred.

The paradox was that there were ample public funds available to support maintenance of housing. But the authorities in charge of district development funding had one clear condition: the applicant had to either own the house or have an extended rental agreement. They wanted to avoid improving houses which held a risk of private landowners evicting the tenants and selling the house on the private market for considerable profit. So Camille Dressler and her family soon ended up like many others—moving into a caravan.

I met Dressler when I stayed on Eigg. I just managed to have a chat with her before she went off to a music festival on the neighbouring island of Rum. We walked briskly along the narrow road which runs over the flat plateau right across Eigg, in the direction of her house at Laig, northwest on Eigg, sheltered by the cliffs of Beinn Bhuidhe.

I turned up the recorder, worrying that the wind would drown our voices, and scribbled in my notebook as we walked. Camille pointed out a small building to the right. It had green-painted corrugated iron walls and a faded red, built-in postbox. The sign on the postbox informed us that post would be collected one hour before departure of the ferry. This was the old shop-cum-post office, the building which Schellenberg refused to improve because of its picturesque appeal, according to Dressler. Mairi Kirk ran the shop. She asked Schellenberg for permission to modernise it; she wanted to put in water and a WC, electricity for lighting and a refrigerator. It wasn't as if he had to pay for all this, but she needed an extended rental contract and his permission to access sources for economic support. But Schellenberg liked the old-fashioned *look*, the nostalgic feeling one got when stepping over the threshold of a grocery shop like this one. His guests, visiting him during the short summer months, also thought the wee shop was quaint in its touchingly dilapidated state. Mairi Kirk was told that if she wished to change anything, she was to contact his lawyer.

After four years, Kirk's lawyer had still not managed to get an answer from Schellenberg. Mairi Kirk had to resign and forget about lighting, heating and a WC. This was in the 1980s. 'Mairi had two small children,' said Camille. We had stopped for a close look at the old shop, now home to a little local museum. 'She had to change their nappies in the shop and then she wiped and washed herself as best she could before slicing cheese for the customers. Not very hygienic.' If only the rich holiday-making friends of Schellenberg had known. On the other hand, they probably got their supplies from the mainland; they were not dependent on cheese from the wee shop, as all the permanent residents were. 'So you can imagine how much better it was when we got the shop at the pier, with a freezer, fridge and everything,' Camille Dressler said as we hurried on.

The struggle between the islanders and Schellenberg intensified as frustrations grew. The idea of 'a free Eigg' developed in 1990. At first as a utopic fantasy in the minds of four people who had observed the fate of Eigg from the sidelines, and who established a foundation with one single aim: to buy Eigg and give the islanders independence. It was an entirely new concept, a third and unexpected solution to the never-ending political quarrel about what was best: private or public land-ownership? It was soon evident that the road to independence was going to be just as long and bumpy as the roads on Eigg itself. And there was nothing then which indicated that seven years on the island was to make headlines as far off as Australia.

Eigg for sale—again

In 1994, the original initiative-takers pulled out of the foundation and gave over the management to the people of Eigg. The Isle of Eigg Heritage Trust, which they now called themselves, allied itself with the Scottish Wildlife Trust and the Highland Regional Council. The three groups shared a common goal: to buy Eigg. Schellenberg made his opinion of the whole concept very clear indeed. He declared to the BBC that he could not support such a communistic and childish takeover bid, writes Alastair McIntosh, the founder of the original initiative for Eigg's independence and the author of *Soil and Soul*.

Some years later, this childish, revolutionary idea was put to the test in the commercial property market. But the wheels of time grind slowly. It was not until 1992 that Eigg went up for sale again, after Schellenberg was forced to sell the island in a divorce settlement. Eigg Heritage Trust was more than optimistic. Although lacking money, it enjoyed massive moral support, and its members were working on the financial case. But the closing deadline for offers was drawing near, and on the 10th of July 1992 the news exploded in the national newspaper, the *Scotsman:* Schellenberg had bought Eigg—again!

'No one was really surprised,' wrote Camille Dressler dryly in the book *Eigg: The Story of an Island*. As Schellenberg had told the reporter from the *Scotsman*, he could well do without the responsibility that came with being a laird, but the truth was there were no other bidders who shared his philosophy on owning an island. He could well be right about that. In the meantime, the people had to put up with Schellenberg: again.

'Burnt Eigg Rolls'

One early January morning in 1994, when an inhabitant of Eigg was on her way to work, she saw black smoke rising up into the winter sky down by the pier. When she got closer, she saw dying flames licking a burnt-out wreck. It soon became clear to everyone that Schellenberg's 1927 Rolls Royce had driven its last journey on Eigg. The newspapers, of course, couldn't contain themselves. 'Burnt Eigg Rolls,' reported the *Sun*. It's unlikely that Schellenberg laughed at the double *entendre*. The next day, he arrived on the island accompanied by police from the mainland. He was angry. No, he was furious. Like some people become when they're afraid. And Schellenberg was seriously afraid. He believed that the attack on his vintage car was a well-organised conspiracy on the part of island locals, and he portrayed them in the press as cannabis-smoking hippies and communists. The English incomers, of whom he was actually one, had compromised and destroyed the Hebridean culture and had incited people to revolution. 'He called us, among other things, the Red Army,' Camille recalled as we took our stroll, leaning into the wind.

Schellenberg's remarks had only one effect: to strengthen the bond between the incomers and the island's original inhabitants. They sent an open letter to Schellenberg which was printed in the *West Highland Free Press* in January, saying:

> [...] The island has a small but united population of local families and incomers who are between them struggling to develop a community with a long-term future against the apparent wishes of an owner who seems to want us to live in primitive conditions to satisfy his nostalgia for the 1920s.

Schellenberg saw the fire as a direct attack on his person. 'It is a very worrying climate,' he told the *Independent*. 'It was once the laird's factor who went about burning people out. Now it seems it's okay to burn out the laird himself.'

A German artist by the name of Maruma

In 1995, rumours circulated that Schellenberg had sold Eigg. According to these rumours he was experiencing financial problems, in part due to his divorce from his third wife. Schellenberg denied the rumours, but turned up on Eigg nevertheless and packed his bags.

He had indeed sold Eigg! To a German with the *nom d'art* Maruma. He had been given the name by a guru who had read the moniker in a dirty puddle in Abu Dhabi, according to McIntosh. 'Marlin Eckhart,' as he was actually named, was a professor and a painter, and it was said he had made it big and become rich by selling his artwork. The agreement to buy Eigg, according to the rumours, had been written on a napkin during a dinner party late one night in the Lodge. The people of Eigg were in shock. What were they supposed to make of a laird from Stuttgart whose work involved igniting the canvas, thereby establishing a telepathic connection between his own imagination and the elements, and the element of fire in particular? What kind of a laird was Maruma? And what did he know about owning an island in the Hebrides?

Like so often before, it started off painlessly. Maruma said, for example, that he was willing to pay to remove all the rusty, derelict cars that had piled up in farmyards and gardens. He also wanted to build a new ferry pier and buy a boat that the island's residents could use. Absolutely free. In an interview with the *Scotsman* after a few hours on the island, he said:

> I love this island. When I went to the cave, I knew this was the right place to be. The cave is the island's soul, because this is where it has been hurt. That's what the Maoris believe—the cave is special. It is like the birth canal of a woman ... the uterus. All the pain is there and yet all the energy is there too. Do you understand?

Massacre Cave

The cave to which Maruma referred is called 'Massacre Cave.' The entrance is so insignificant that it is difficult to find. A narrow chink in the rock. Slippery green algae grow on the pale stones by the entrance. You have to crawl on all fours to explore the passage. 'Take a lantern if you want to explore this cave,' says the brochure from the Scottish Wildlife Trust. I don't want to crawl into the darkness. I know that there's a place inside where the narrow crevice widens into a large space. A shelter from the past. A safe hiding place. Right until disaster struck Eigg's population one winter day at the end of the 1500s.

Uamh Fhraing, literally, the 'Cave of Frances,' or Massacre Cave, was the scene of only a single crime in an entire cycle of bloody acts of revenge between

Graveyard, Eigg

the Clan MacDonald, who owned Eigg, and the Clan MacLeod. It is never easy to say where such a cycle begins, and there are differing versions of the episodes of violence, depending on which clan is relating the story. There is a tendency for the stories to contradict each other when it comes to who did what, and when the atrocities, or the acts of heroism—depending on how you look at them—took place. Many of the tales have been handed down orally. That doesn't mean they are any less true than written accounts, as war propaganda lies anyway, but it is difficult to know how many victims each misdeed involved. The clans perhaps boasted of more victims than they actually had on their conscience. Incidents that took place several hundred years ago, therefore, have to be taken with a pinch of salt.

The feud that led to the massacre on Eigg is said to have kicked off after a grave insult against the MacLeods by members of Clanranald, one of the branches of the Clan Donald. The offending statements came during a gathering of clan chiefs on the island of Mull. The Clan MacLeod was derided for having a dirty pedigree: there was Norwegian blood in their veins! This was a slap in the face. The name of the first chief, Ljótr, or Leòd in Gaelic, was of Norse origin, as were the names of his two sons who were the first to bear the name of MacLeod: Torquil and Tormod.

But the escalation of the conflict started in earnest when a storm forced a ship carrying men of Clan Donald to land on the island of Harris in the Outer Hebrides. The MacLeods did not welcome the castaways. They saw fit to behead every single one of the soaking wet sailors, fix their heads to a rope and give them as a gift to the governor of Harris. Such a savage act naturally demanded revenge.

Soon a boatload of MacLeod men was captured off an island in MacDonald territory, and all thirty-six were thrown into a dungeon where they remained until they starved to death.

Later, when a boatload of MacLeods was forced to seek shelter close to Eigg, they decided not to go ashore. History had shown how badly it could go if you asked for help from the MacDonalds. Instead, they moored by Castle Island, a small islet just off Eigg. The men helped themselves to a couple of cattle at pasture and harassed the girls who had been looking after them. That's at least what the MacDonald version says, while the MacLeods hold that the castaways were denied hospitality. It is, however, the Clan Donald's version that recurs in most sources, and attacking the girls from Eigg was not something the MacLeods should have done. To kill and cook the cattle might have been all right, but to harass or rape the girls was beyond forgiveness.

The MacLeods were tucking into their dinner when the MacDonalds of Eigg attacked, killing them all except for their two leaders, for whom another punishment was intended. The arms and legs of these last remaining were broken, and some versions say they were castrated. Then they were put on a boat with no oars or sail, and sent on a final, fatal voyage. Or so the MacDonalds thought. But the boat drifted with the currents and the wind back to Dunvegan on Skye, the castle and seat of the Clan MacLeod. There a furious chief swore to take vengeance on the murderers. A group of boats soon set sail from Skye, ready for 'Operation Eigg.'

The MacDonalds probably didn't know that the boat with the battered MacLeods had drifted back to Skye, and that the clan chief now knew the details of the story. But it still stands to reason that the population of Eigg must have been on the lookout for retaliatory attacks. When the sails of the MacLeods' boats appeared outlined against the winter sky, the people of Eigg knew what lay in store for them, unless they hid in the cave that was their traditional and perfect hiding place. It was right down by the sea. The narrow entrance was hidden behind a waterfall. No living person would guess that there, behind the raging water and through a low, narrow tunnel, the passage widened into a large chamber with space for several hundred people. Or for 395 people, as hid in this case on a winter's day in 1577.

The men of Clan MacLeod searched Eigg for three days. The small villages lay empty. The livestock were there, of course, but otherwise there was not a living being in sight. Except, as in all tales of atrocities in the Hebrides, for an old lady. She was a tough cookie, and when this enraged gang tried to force her to tell them where the people had gone, she is said to have answered: 'If it comes through my knee, it can't be helped, but it shall not come through my mouth.' This answer, her stubbornness and courage could have been taken straight from an Icelandic saga. They burnt her house and destroyed her harvest. 'Ha!' she mocked them, showing no respect. She could seek shelter under the rocks: those were her home. Besides, there was always a splendid meal to be had of seafood down at Laig Bay, where there were all the shellfish she could wish for. The furious MacLeods combed the sand for shells and threw them away. The old hag laughed; she still had the seaweed to eat, not to mention the delicious cress by the well at Hulin. The MacLeods gave up the search; the whole population must have fled to another island, they reasoned. They went to their boats with a strong sense of having been completely duped and cast off. Then a shout was heard from one of the boats. A finger pointed towards the southern point of Eigg, at a figure outlined against the fresh white snow that had fallen that night.

The MacDonalds had sought refuge for three days in the safe but damp and dark cave, when they decided to send out a scout to see if it was prudent to head back home. If they had waited another hour or two, the cycle of violence might have ended. And if there hadn't been snow that very night, this and other massacres might have been avoided. But just as the MacLeods' boats rounded the point on the southern side of Eigg, they saw the scout. And he saw them.

The tracks in the snow led the men from Skye, thirsty for revenge, straight to the waterfall. They immediately saw how everything fitted together. Perhaps they held a conference at the cave opening. It was clear to see there was only space for one man at a time to pass through the narrow passage, and furthermore he would have to crawl on all fours. So they could forget sending in an assault force. Also, if they crawled into the cave, they would all be cut down somewhere inside the tunnel, one by one. No, that was not a good plan. A bright spark soon found the solution. Someone was tasked with redirecting the water course. Others fetched twigs and heather and anything flammable was put in a huge pile inside the cave opening. The easiest thing was to suffocate the MacDonalds. With smoke.

The story goes that the clan chief agonised about exterminating the entire island population. Perhaps he was struck with some form of compassion or a feeling of Old Testament-style justice. To wipe them all out, the children and elderly too, was far beyond an eye for an eye. He left the decision to God and to chance. If the wind blew towards the cave at day's end, the bonfire would be lit. If the wind blew away from the cave, the refugees would be set free. A breeze from the south grew in strength, sealing the fate of the people of Eigg.

In Victorian times, tourists flocked to the mass grave on Eigg, plundering it for souvenirs. Skulls found their way to polished desks in London or behind glass display cases in museums. In 1846, the geologist Hugh Miller wrote the following:

> [...] we come upon heaps of human bones grouped together [...] They are of a brownish, earthy hue, here and there tinged with green; the skulls, with the exception of a few broken fragments, have disappeared; for travellers in the Hebrides have of late years been numerous and curious; and many a museum [...] exhibits a grinning skull, its memorial of the Massacre at Eigg. We find, too, further marks of visitors in the single bones separated from the heaps

and scattered over the area; but enough still remains to show, in the general disposition of the remains, that the hapless islanders died under the walls in families, each little group separated by a few feet from the others. [...] And beneath every heap we find, at the depth [...] of a few inches, the remains of the straw-bed upon which the family had lain [...].

In 1979, the last skull in the cave to date was found by a boy holidaying on Eigg. The skull belonged to a child aged five or six.

Creditors

In spite of his eccentric behaviour, the new owner, Maruma, was making a good impression, especially on the older inhabitants of Eigg. He personally visited every individual on the island to introduce himself. No previous owner of Eigg had ever done that. If they did drop in, it was without knocking, and they would go to lift the lid of the pots to check whether the simmering contents, for example a rabbit, had been poached from their estate. No, previous lairds, including Schellenberg, used to summon them all to the Lodge when they wanted to announce what plans they had made for Eigg.

But there was still something odd about Maruma, writes McIntosh. He didn't look rich, walking around in his jeans, bright red shirt, and black beret. He didn't look like a laird or a millionaire. The journalists clearly didn't think so either. The German magazine *Stern* soon revealed that he was unknown in the art world, and that he was not a professor either. All that was certain was that he was in massive debt, and that German legal authorities were trying to auction off all of his allegedly valuable paintings to cover his obligations. The pictures were worthless.

People on Eigg would soon realise that the new laird was a big, broken, swizz. The fate of Eigg reached all the way to parliament and international newspaper editors. The pressure for land reform in Scotland was increasing in strength. TV crews from Japan, France and New Zealand helicoptered in to report on the absurd situation.

It wasn't political reform that led to Eigg ending up back on the market the year after Maruma had bought it. It was down to Maruma's creditor, a German businessman in Hong Kong. He simply wanted to get his money back. A property company by the name of Vladi Private Islands was given the job of selling Eigg. As Vladi, the company's owner, told the *Scotsman* quite precisely in 1996, 'Scottish islands are the Van Goghs on the international island market, masterpieces of mother nature.' He then continued to tell newspaper readers enthusiastically that buying an island is like owning a miniature world, surrounded by water on all sides, where you can be king, where you can enjoy the peace of a private life with friends and family.

I looked up the Vladi Private Islands' website. The property ads had one thing in common: it was difficult, if not impossible, to find out whether the islands were inhabited, or whether they were in Italy, Canada or Norway. It was much easier to find out whether the island was populated by rabbits than how many people lived there.

In any case, in 1996, Eigg was back on the property market. The Eigg Trust worked hard and effectively, in collaboration with local authorities and the Scottish Wildlife Trust. They mobilised Eigg Music Aid, with famous musicians holding concerts to raise money. In November, an anonymous wealthy lady from England felt sympathy for their cause. She donated a significant sum of money, and the SWT mobilised its sister organisations to make contributions towards the purchase. This time they wouldn't be caught napping by some millionaire, with or without money.

The Eigg Heritage Trust can't believe its ears, makes a bid and receives a gift from Talisker

In January 1997, the Eigg Trust received the incredible news that a representative of the opera singer Luciano Pavarotti had expressed his interest in buying Eigg for two million pounds, far over the asking price, reportedly to build a centre for 3,000 students of classical music! According to Camille Dressler, the local authorities nearly fell off their chairs. With a great deal of diplomacy the authorities explained that the lack of facilities on Eigg, which had a population of around seventy people, might present problems when it came to accommodating thousands of first-rate musicians.

It soon transpired that Pavarotti probably didn't have a clue where Eigg was, never mind the intention to buy the island, and that he didn't know about the supposed bidding organisation which called itself the 'Pavarotti Foundation.' The apparent representative of the tenor was exposed as another of Maruma's creditors. The entire media circus around Pavarotti was solely a ruse to raise the price of Eigg.

That was it for Maruma's main creditor. Eigg was his by default, and he took the legal route to get his money back. On the 4th of April 1997, his solicitors accepted the offer from the Isle of Eigg Heritage Trust to buy the island for 1.5 million pounds. The official takeover was set for the 12th of June. The island was turned upside down in preparation for the big celebration. A great influx was expected of friends, supporters, relatives and journalists. The Talisker Distillery on Skye, founded by the MacAskill brothers from Eigg, donated ninety bottles of twenty-five-year-old malt whisky. Eigg celebrated the abolition of its feudal system for three whole days and nights.

'What has changed most in Eigg?' I asked Michael Butler as we stood and looked across the sea from the Singing Sands. 'The people who live here now own the island. That's changed their entire attitude. They don't moan about Schel-

Blackface sheep

lenberg anymore. They're happier.' As if speaking to himself and to his memories—which are perhaps like the paths on Eigg, some clear and easily accessible, others overgrown, hidden behind tall, greedy bracken blocking out the sun—he added: 'And the strange thing about Schellenberg is that people say he was nice to visitors, but he never invited *us* to the Lodge, even if we were descendants of one of the owners. It's not that it really *mattered*. It was just strange that he didn't. We didn't feel we belonged to the island when he was here.'

Exodus from Rum

The ferry, MV Lochnevis, sails from Eigg to Rum and carries up to sixteen cars. But cars cannot be driven on Rum without special permission. Rum. With steep mountains: the Rum Cuillin. And around a thousand red deer, many of which are part of a large research project. How are their numbers affected, for example, if they're left alone? Which individuals survive? Which succumb, and why? When Scottish Natural Heritage bought the island for a song in 1957, it was on the condition that they managed the island as a national park and maintained the castle. The island was otherwise quite uninhabited because of the Clearances.

On Whitsunday in 1825, the families on Rum were given notice. Chief Maclean of Coll ordered them to leave their homes within one year. The forced eviction had already been carefully planned: Maclean offered to pay their passage if they wished to immigrate to Cape Breton in Canada. The whole of Rum was to be emptied of people. As soon as possible. Around 400 inhabitants were to make way for 8,000 sheep and one herdsman from the mainland. Maclean had finally found the solution: sheep farming was far more profitable than the pitiful income he wrested in rent from his poor clansmen on Rum. No, he would do like the other lairds: get rid of the dead meat. One of his herdsmen, John MacMaister, would much later describe the exodus from Rum that summer in 1826. The event certainly etched itself into his mind and stayed there for the rest of his life. Like a traumatic wound constantly being opened, completely involuntarily, just as fresh each time and without the soothing cocoon the memory usually spins around unpleasant incidents:

> [...] the people of the island were carried off in one mass, for ever, from the sea-girt spot where they had been born and bred, and where the bones of their forefathers were laid in the ancient graveyard of Kilmory. The wild out-cries of the men, and the heart-breaking wails of the women and their children, filled all the air between the mountainous shores of the bay.

On the 11th of July 1826, 300 people from Rum boarded ships with the frivolous names 'Dove of Harmony' and 'Highland Lad.' Only a handful of inhabitants were allowed, with some reluctance, to stay on Rum. The voyage to Canada took thirty-seven days. When the emigrants went ashore on the other side of the Atlantic in late August, it was too late for them to sow a harvest to sustain them through a snow-covered Canadian winter.

Nobody knows how many people from Rum arrived in Canada alive, but documents from the Nova Scotian authorities state that the Harmony arrived in Canada again the next year with more Scots on board. The passenger lists showed that 200 emigrants had joined the ship in Scotland. During the voyage, eighteen people were committed to a watery grave from the dirty, overcrowded vessel. Furthermore, on arrival twenty-two passengers had measles, then considered a deadly illness.

Those permitted to stay on Rum eventually had to leave. After two years, in 1828, most followed in the wake of their neighbours and friends over the Atlantic to Canada, aboard the St Lawrence. The ship would soon feature in one of the famous maritime novels of the time, *Redburn*. As a young man, the author, Herman Melville, had been berthed on the same St Lawrence that carried the former residents of Rum. His voyage, the miserable conditions on board, and the extremely brutal crew inspired him to write *Redburn*. Two years later he would publish another seafaring novel that would become much more well-known: *Moby Dick*.

John Bullough and George Bullough

When the Englishman John Bullough bought Rum in 1888, there were 6,000 sheep grazing on the island. The number of inhabitants had risen again to around 100 souls. The residents had two things in common: they all worked on the farm, and none were born on Rum.

Bullough was one of the richest men in Britain. The new laird knew Rum well. He had paid for hunting rights there for a number of years. The 600 deer that the earlier owners had imported were clearly thriving and breeding quickly in their new barren and moist habitat. When Rum was advertised for sale in the *Times*, John Bullough knew what kind of a place he was making an offer on, unlike many others who bought property in the Hebrides.

Bullough didn't have a chance to make much of an impact on his recently acquired Highland dream. He died three years after buying the island, only fifty-three years old, leaving Rum and half of his fortune to his son George. George Bullough was twenty-one years old when he was told to come back from the round-the-world sail upon which he had embarked. Or had he been sent away? According to rumours, he had shown a bit too much interest in his young step-mother, and his father thought it best to send him to the other side of the planet, thus redirecting the tall, young George's attentions.

While his father and grandfather had built up a fortune through hard work, industrial inventions and patents, George would soon turn out to have an unusual talent for spending money. One of his first major investments was a 210-foot-long steam-engine schooner. Of course, George Bullough saw no reason to settle down when he inherited his fortune, and he set off on new round-the-world cruises on his yacht, Rhouma. This vessel took him and his friends to South Africa, Japan, Australia, China, Burma and the USA. But George Bullough also had ambitions to make another journey. A social-climbing trip. Straight up into the British aristocracy.

The Boer War

Few things work as well as a war when it comes to shaking up a society's power structure. Moves are planned, chess pieces are repositioned, some people win, while others make mistakes and are swept off the board. For George Bullough, the Boer War, in which British colonial power fought against the Dutch-descended Boers for gold and diamond rights in South Africa, would be a springboard to the British upper class.

George, Rhouma, and a crew of forty set sail for South Africa in December 1899. The ship served as a hospital vessel for wounded soldiers in a war in which the author and doctor Arthur Conan Doyle had also signed up as a volunteer. Both these men would later be knighted for their war efforts.

Originally, Doyle wanted to serve as a soldier. He had written a lot about war but now it was time to experience life on the front at first hand, he announced to his disbelieving family. But the forty-year-old author of the Sherlock Holmes series had eaten and drunk well for far too long, together with people like Oscar Wilde and the escapologist Houdini. He had already acquired an extensive belly and was unsurprisingly rejected as unfit for active service when he signed up as a soldier for the Boer War.

His friendship with Houdini would incidentally turn sour due to Doyle's enthusiasm for spiritualism. It went especially bad after a séance in which Houdini participated and Doyle's wife, as medium, passed on messages from Houdini's late mother. Houdini's scepticism was more than confirmed when the written greeting came in English, since his mother actually knew only German. It turned even more dubious when his mother, through Lady Doyle of course, drew a cross at the top of the letter. Houdini's mother was Jewish and would never have dreamt of drawing a Christian cross if she were trying to communicate a message to her son, thought Houdini.

Anyway, life had been good to Doyle and he didn't become a soldier. Instead, he put his medical education from the University of Edinburgh to use, and found work as a field doctor in South Africa. And his knowledge as a doctor would certainly be useful, although in a different way from what he had expected. Many more British died from typhoid fever than from the enemy's bullets during the war in South Africa.

Sir George Bullough

In 1901, the hospital ship Rhouma sailed north again on course for Rum. Precisely why George Bullough left South Africa in the middle of the war is unknown. Perhaps he thought he had done his bit for his country. Perhaps he foresaw that the British were going to win. They had struck the Boers (and black Africans too, even if little appeared about them at that time) at their weakest point: women and children. The British set up concentration camps, cordoning off large areas with barbed wire, and the Boers' (and black Africans') women and children died in those camps from fatigue, illness and malnutrition. It was an effective way in which to crush the Boer guerrillas' fighting morale.

As thanks for his patriotic deeds in the Boer War, George Bullough was made Sir George Bullough, for having lent the government 50,000 pounds, and for having made available the Rhouma. Arthur Conan Doyle was also knighted for his services. It was rumoured that King Edward VII was an enthusiastic fan of Sherlock Holmes, and that he hoped a knighthood would encourage Doyle to write more stories about the consummate detective he had thrown into the waterfall in *The Final Problem*. Doyle, on the other hand, wanted to be freed from Sherlock. The detective was holding him back, he was blocking the path to serious authorship, thought Doyle. When Sherlock Holmes fell into the Swiss waterfall and was effectively killed off by Doyle, 20,000 fans cancelled their subscriptions to *Strand Magazine*, publishers of the series. It isn't easy to say who was more pleased, the editor of the *Strand* or Edward VII, when Holmes reappeared in the magazine in the story *The Return of Sherlock Holmes*.

Not everybody was knighted for their efforts in the Boer War, even if it was rumoured that the war correspondent Winston Churchill might receive the Victoria Cross for the courage he had shown when his escort was attacked by the Boers. Fifty years would pass before he could call himself Sir Winston Churchill.

When the schooner's engines had built up steam and the yacht puffed out of Table Bay in Cape Town, the vessel had British officers on board. They were on their way to a well-deserved convalescence on an island they had barely heard of, and would be the first guests at George Bullough's new home, Rhum Castle. The grandson of a man who had worn wooden clogs his whole life could welcome the wounded officers to a two-storey castle of imported red sandstone, with towers and French windows, an Edwardian mansion grander by far than his father's humble hunting lodge.

The Luddites

The castle was built with old money, capital that Bullough's father and grandfather had earned during the Industrial Revolution. Like many other revolutions, this one had blood on its hands too.

George's grandfather James Bullough, the one who wore clogs his whole life, was born in 1799. When he started weaving as a seven-year-old, there was perhaps not much to distinguish him from other young boys in his home town. Except that he was born with two key qualities: creative ability and a mind open to change.

As a young weaver in a cotton mill, he saw the Industrial Revolution hit with full force. Steam-driven monsters, the mechanised looms replaced the hand looms. Weavers who worked by hand lost their jobs. The new looms soon became a threat, a thief stealing bread and potatoes off the plates of large families. Many workers were already on starvation wages.

The weavers became desperate. Northern English factories were wrecked, one after another, by gangs going by the name of 'Luddites.' They were reportedly led by a self-appointed leader, General Ned Ludd, and they waged war on the machines. It is now doubtful whether their general actually existed, but nobody in their right mind could question the presence of Luddites there in flesh and blood. The new looms and knitting machines were smashed in fury and desperation. In some cases the factory owners were injured or killed. More often though, soldiers shot into the crowds and killed the protesters. Everyone saw that the riots had to stop. The government had to intervene, the Luddites had to be punished.

The fear that the French Revolution might spread to England set the scene for parliament to introduce the death penalty for machine-breaking. According to Karly Walters from the University of Birmingham, it wasn't the *physical* destruction in itself that parliament was afraid of. No, the arson and damage were a threat to *property rights*, the very foundation of the British state. Government simply couldn't allow people to take things into their own hands in this revolutionary manner. And who could guarantee that other new-fangled French ideas wouldn't drift across the Channel like dandelion seeds? Slogans like 'liberty, equality and fraternity,' not to mention ideas about the separation between church and state, or, as some whispered, God forbid, the abolition of the monarchy, and republicanism!

Only a few members of parliament defended the workers and spoke out against harsh penalties. The poet Lord Byron gave a long speech in the House of Lords in 1812 in which he stated:

> Are we aware of our obligations to a mob! It is the mob that labour in your fields, and serve in your houses—that man your navy, and recruit your army—that have enabled you to defy all the world—and can also defy you when neglect and calamity have driven them to despair. You may call the people a mob, but do not forget that a mob too often speaks the sentiments of the people.

Even a poet of his stature could touch neither the hearts nor the minds of the Lords. In 1812, parliament decided that the death penalty could be imposed on those who broke textile machinery. That year, when a mill near Manchester was set on fire, twelve men were arrested by the police, suspected of arson. Four of those arrested were sentenced to death according to the newly passed Frame Breaking Act which Lord Byron had found so reprehensible. The family of one of the condemned, Abraham Charlston, appealed to the authorities requesting that he be released. The boy was twelve years old. Spectators reported that he cried for his mother as he was being taken to the gallows. His was only one of the many death sentences handed down on weavers in the years that followed. The lucky ones were deported to the colonies. For life.

No, James Bullough was not one of the Luddites. Quite the opposite: he came up with inventions to improve the automated looms, with the result that he was chased away from his hometown by furious weavers afraid of unemployment. In the 1850s, he joined a company that made machines for the textile industry. Soon his son John Bullough also joined the company. These two generations would have one thing in common with Sir George Bullough: a particular fascination for new inventions. And it was these inventions by John and James that laid the entire foundation for the fortune of their heir, George.

Kinloch Castle

Three hundred workers were needed to build Kinloch Castle on Rum. The red blocks of sandstone were transported to the island on small, flat-hulled steamboats. The vessels were unrivalled for supplying places without proper harbours. Like

Rum, for example. They simply sailed into the bay at high tide, unloaded at low tide, and sailed off, lightened of all cargo, when high tide lifted the boat back up.

Sir George was thoroughly characteristic of his time. His hunting estate and castle were in the heart of the Celtic lands, and what could be more natural than for his employees to dress up like real Scots. At least like Englishmen thought Scots should look. The workers who built the castle were paid an extra shilling a week to wear kilts. It is also said that the laird of the castle paid them extra to smoke cigarettes, because the smoke kept the dreaded Rum midges at bay. That may make it sound like this insect is an especially aggressive, flesh-eating variant of the Scottish midge. And those who have stayed on Rum in the middle of the summer can confirm this is correct. In his childhood memoirs from Rum, Archie Cameron writes of a clan chief who, long ago, supposedly punished one of his subjects by stripping his clothes and tethering him to the ground with ropes and wooden pegs. The chief's wife eventually took pity on the naked man but it was too late. The swarms of the almost invisible insects had taken their fill so energetically that the man died of the bites.

The factor

Archie Cameron, who passed away a few years ago, was the last living person from Rum who could remember the time from before the First World War. His book describes well the skewed power relationships between ordinary people and 'the rest.' His parents worked for the Bullough family, but that didn't help much when Archie fell out with the island's factor. Without asking the factor for permission, Archie and a friend had borrowed a boat to go fishing. The factor, who was an especially power-hungry example of the species, gave Archie a fine of one pound. That was equal to half a month's pay, and Archie wrote a letter to Sir George Bullough to protest the fine. The complaint never reached him. Bullough's secretary sent the letter back to the factor, who promptly docked Archie's pay and increased the penalty: he was given a month to leave Rum. With no chance to appeal, Archie Cameron had to vacate the only place he knew, leaving his mother, father and six brothers and sisters. It was 1920 and Archie was seventeen.

In his book, *Bare Feet and Tackety Boots*, all artillery is set on factors as an occupational group: men who demanded rent on behalf of the lairds, fined poachers, and banished those who didn't behave satisfactorily. They were prosecutor, judge, and appeal court all rolled into one. When the history of the Clearances is written, it is often the factors who are accorded the blame for injustices, while the lairds get off scot-free. Cameron writes that the 'curse of the Highlands was midges and factors, and the worse was the factor.' But as Tom Atkinson writes in the foreword to *Bare Feet*, it was always the proprietor who held ultimate responsibility when his factor threw families out of their homes and set fire to their roofs, or committed other atrocities. The same goes for Rum, too: it was the laird Sir George Bullough who employed the factor.

Lady Bullough: Divorce, rumours and scandals

Rum soon became known as 'the forbidden island.' It was only guests of Sir George and his wife, Lady Bullough, who were welcome. Others were chased away. Not by the laird and his wife themselves, of course. The Rum estate had around 100 employees in the hectic periods when the Bullough couple and their guests took over the castle for a few weeks every autumn during hunting season.

Lady Bullough was of French origin. Her family was descended from Napoleon Bonaparte's sister, at least according to Lady Bullough, and why would she lie? Her ancestors lost everything when they fled to England in 1791 to escape the carnage that accompanied the French Revolution. Or perhaps it should be seen like this: they at least held on to their lives, unlike many other French aristocrats.

When the impoverished French aristocrat Monica Lily first met Sir George Bullough, she was already married. In the court case that dissolved the marriage between Monica and her first husband, Sir George was cited as the one responsible for the break-up. The divorce was finalised in May 1903, and Monica and George's wedding was celebrated at Kinloch Castle in June of that same year.

It was rumoured that she had been the lover of the Prince of Wales, who had become King Edward VII when his mother, Queen Victoria, died in 1901. In that case, Monica Lily would have been one of several women who made the marriage between Edward and Alexandra of Denmark somewhat crowded. Another lover, Alice Keppel, was even invited to the king's deathbed in 1910. Perhaps it would have been some consolation to Edward and Alice if they had known that, in a way, they would meet again. Their respective great-great-grandchildren would also become lovers: Prince Charles and Camilla Parker Bowles.

It is said that today's monarchy is threatened by all the scandals connected to members of the Royal Family. Even the queen stumbled slightly when Diana, Princess of Wales died. But aren't they just following in the footsteps of their forebears? Widowed Queen Victoria, dressed in black, managed to acquire the nickname 'Mrs. Brown.' The family's scandals have also shown a tendency to emigrate, like Edward VII's daughter, who became Queen Maud of Norway and would get entangled by rumour-mongering. And if you think that the members of today's Royal Family engage in especially sensational acts, what size of headline font would *The Sun* or the *Daily Mirror* have found suitable for Henry VIII or Richard III?

A morning at Kinloch Castle

So what was life on Rum like during Sir George Bullough's regime? Let me try to reconstruct a day. The guests, who had maybe been drinking wine and smoking cigars long into the night, were awakened by bagpipes at eight o' clock. They may have pulled a pillow over their heads to block out the screeching. What a barbarous din! Hadn't they gone there to enjoy the silence? But some early birds sat up, leaning against their soft down pillows to listen. They really were a long way from home; this was pretty exotic, no doubt about it!

It was difficult to get back to sleep after having been wrenched out of it by the pipes, so they might as well get up. That day they were going hunting, the reason for visiting George and Monica Bullough in the first place. Some of the guests would have had throbbing headaches, if we are to believe one of the guests, a certain Harry Hinton:

> [...] we sat round the table drinking until two in the morning. I did this for two nights and then got up and went to bed as dinner was over. I never met such a set of sportsmen and they rarely killed anything [...].

A few then staggered out of bed, putting on their silk dressing gowns, and ditto slippers, to go to the bathroom. Perhaps a shower could get rid of stale perfume or the smell of cigars, but how were they supposed to attack this water-spouting monster in the bathroom? Who had seen anything like it before? Confound George and his fascination for new-fangled gadgets!

The brass taps sent warm water to showerheads placed at different heights on the walls. The streams were aimed at different parts of the body. In other words, if they managed to understand the intricate system of pipes, they could direct the streams wherever they wanted. A conventional choice was, of course, to turn on a tap that brought the water down onto your head from above. Another showerhead persuaded the water to shape itself into a gorgeous, massaging ribbon around the neck. Ah, that helped with the headache! Or they could turn on the so-called 'spray,' which sent needle-like drops through the air like heat-seeking missiles. The daring, or the unknowing, turned on 'the jet' and received a column of water directly into their crotch.

After having mastered the hypermodern shower, it was critical to get dressed in the right outfit. Maybe the guest had to borrow a few items of clothing, because the previous day had been unusually wet even for Rum, and the clothes brought up from London were still hanging to dry. Then they pulled on some breeches and a Rum tweed jacket before going down to breakfast. And what a breakfast! They could help themselves to fruit from the heated greenhouses in the garden: apricots, grapes, figs, strawberries! This was something to write home about. Indeed, their host had even changed the island's name and printed his own stamps that said 'Rhum.' With an 'h.' Maybe George Bullough had changed the name because he was fed up with inebriated guests' jokes and allusions to the drink by the same name. 'Ha, ha, do you get the joke, Sir George?' But who knows? One old gravestone in the churchyard does actually say 'Rhum.'

Deer and alligators

After breakfast the horses were fetched from the stables and waited patiently by their 'ghillies,' from the Gaelic word for 'boy,' and equivalent to the notion of 'boy' in the colonies. The ghillies tracked down animals and transported the game, or sat at the oars on fishing trips. The party moved slowly up towards the mountains with Old Norse names: Trollaval, Hallival, Askival, Ruisval. If they were really lucky, they went home with three deer over their horses' backs. And if a novice in the group shot his (or her) first deer, they would have a handful of blood from the dead creature smeared on their face, to their disgust (or delight). Naturally, this ritual led to considerable fuss, especially from those who had invested in a tweed outfit for the occasion. But as Archie Cameron remarks in his memoir, if they just let the deer blood dry, they could brush it off like powder.

Not everyone wanted to go hunting, though. Maybe some stayed at the castle, where there was plenty to do. A round of golf on the course, or why not squash or bowling? They could also go for a stroll, preferably with a midge net over their face, and admire the gardens: the Italian garden and the rose garden. Or what about the Japanese one, then? There was also a certain entertainment value in visiting the heated ponds where turtles swam. Sometimes these may have ended up in the French chef's soup in the castle kitchen. The story goes that one of the turtles unfortunately swallowed a diamond ring. The ring fell into the pool by accident and the greedy animal thereby sealed its own and all the other turtles' fate. They were rowed out and released straight into the sea, an especially unfit place for these tropical creatures. It didn't go so well for the alligators either, at least not when they reached adult size or escaped their cages. In either case, they would be shot so that they didn't disturb the guests.

Dinner at Kinloch Castle

Before dinner, there was perhaps table music and drinks. Sir George had purchased a so-called 'orchestrion' that Queen Victoria had reportedly ordered for Balmoral Castle. But then she died in 1901 and would never use it, so Sir George, with his fascination for all technical gadgets, bought the instrument. It was very popular and modern when it was installed at Kinloch Castle, but it soon had to concede first place to the much smaller and more practical gramophone which appeared around the First World War.

So before they went into the dining room, Bullough's guests stood there, prob-ably speechless with wonder and terror, watching the rolls of perforated paper slowly turn in the orchestrion. The notes from Wagner's Lohengrin, apparently from a fully-populated orchestra, resounded off the walls. Bass drums, snare drums, cymbals and triangles lifted the music towards an enthusiastic crescendo. The mood was really given a boost thanks to this musical monster. Soon the men offered the ladies their arm and proceeded, eager and laughing, into the dining room furnished with tables and chairs from the yacht Rhouma. And what tastes better than venison, deer you've shot yourself? True, it had been dressed out and cooked by the servants, but still.

After dinner, the men and the women departed separately. The men retired to the smoking room. Perhaps they took a round of pool—that went down well—or they played cards or roulette. Maybe they discussed politics, such as the revelations about King Leopold's enterprises in the Congo Free State. The outrages made even the British get worked up, although they were hardly above reproach themselves when it came to misconduct in Africa. Some of the gentlemen had just come home from the other side of the Atlantic, where they had read the interview with the American, Mark Twain, in the Boston Daily Globe. Maybe they brought out the newspaper, the men in the smoking room peering over each other's shoulders to read the columns in which Twain launched his assault on the Belgian king:

I have seen photographs of the natives with their hands cut off because they did not bring in the requited amount of rubber. If Leopold had only killed them outright it would not be so bad; but to cut off their hands and leave them helpless to die in misery—that is not forgivable.

It was not just the human rights advocate and opponent of slavery Mark Twain who got involved. Brits such as Sir Arthur Conan Doyle had also become engaged, shocked by the accounts from British missionaries. And some of the gentlemen in the smoking room might have read Joseph Conrad's Heart of Darkness. But there were also other political affairs that affected Britain more directly, like the war between Japan and Russia. The British supported Japan; in fact Sir George Bullough had again sent Rhouma to distant seas to play a role in another war taking place far from Britain. This time his yacht would host the delegations participating in peace negotiations in 1905. In gratitude for his help, the Japanese emperor sent a couple of incense holders and an enormous monkey-eating eagle, all in bronze, to Sir George, who placed them in his castle on Rum.

The ladies, on the other hand, retired to the afternoon warmth of the pastel-coloured drawing room. Out of the French windows they could watch the changing colours across Loch Scresort. A door led out onto the glass veranda, where hum-mingbirds quivered in the air above tropical plants. Until the birds unfortunately froze to death—the climate wasn't exactly right for hummingbirds. So as not to bother the ladies with the time, the large wall clock had only one hand. The minutes didn't count at Kinloch Castle. At least not for the guests. Perhaps the ladies chatted about the day's hunt, or discussed, blushing with outrage or excitement, Sigmund Freud's latest book, in which he claimed that the *child* was a sexual being, indeed that sexuality was a driving force for *all* people. Which must mean this also included them! Maybe Lady Bullough agreed with his theories; it is said that she was quite broad-minded, even that it is she who is pictured naked on an animal skin in a painting on the first floor.

A ball at Kinloch Castle

Some evenings a ball was held at the castle. But why did the musicians have to play behind a curtain in the gallery? And why were the drinks served through an opening in the wall? Both things were put in place to prevent the servants from seeing what was going on in the ballroom. Furthermore, the windows were placed high up on the wall, so nobody outside in the dark could sneak around and peep into the lit room. Such devices certainly got the imagination going. The air was thick with rumours. Did Sir George have other interests than his wife? Was he more interested in men? And, we may wonder, why are these stories so persistent that the castle's guide still recounts them? Might the answer lie in the American journalist Walcott's long drawn-out sigh in the magazine *Vanity Fair*: 'Why are British sex scandals so much better than ours?'

If Sir George wasn't a family man in the usual sense while he was alive, he was at least a family man in matters of death. He moved his father from his grave in England to the west side of Rum, where only ruins were left after the villagers had been thrown out of their homes seventy years earlier. His stone coffin was lodged firmly in a solid rock wall, until an outspoken guest apparently pointed out to George that the tiles in the entranceway leading into the mausoleum were reminiscent of a public toilet at Waterloo Station. It is possible that after that, George wasn't able to visit the grave without his thoughts digressing to urinals and sweaty train passengers. He moved his father's stone casket once more, and the old grave was blown up with a good dose of dynamite. This time, Sir George had built a Greek-inspired temple in Doric style, with a view out to sea. Now John Bullough rests there, together with his son George, and his daughter-in-law Monica.

The circle is closed

Today Kinloch Castle is open to the public. Wide open, you might say, in stark contrast to when the island and the castle were closed even to sailors wanting to fill up their fresh water tanks. During my tour of the castle, I feel like I am gradually getting an insight into the private life of the Bullough couple.

The large hall on the ground floor is filled with memories from journeys in another era, when Rhouma took George and his friends to other continents 100 years ago. On the floor lies a lion pelt, complete with head. The animal bares its teeth; its fake pink tongue and gums have never tasted flesh from the savannah. A leopard skin festoons the Steinway grand piano, hiding scratches from a wild party. The leopard's paws grip round the polished corners of the piano. Alongside stands the bronze eagle from the grateful Japanese emperor. Two large portraits of George and Monica Bullough look down from the first floor. He is wearing a kilt of Rum tweed, and while he is fierce and dressed for the wilds, Lady Bullough is delicate and ready for the ballroom. A beautiful woman with a distant smile. Her pearl necklace drops down to her navel, and the cut of her soft brown velvet dress reveals her white neck and upper bosom.

The castle is frozen in time. It appears almost as it was left in 1957, when it was sold to the state, together with the rest of Rum, at far below market price, to what is today Scottish Natural Heritage. It is as if Lady Bullough, who had by then been a widow for eighteen years, got up one day from her four-poster bed, which reportedly belonged to Marie Antoinette, took a shower, got dressed, and cast a glance out the French windows before nodding to herself. She had decided. Kinloch Castle and the island of Rum would be sold to someone who would protect nature on the island, and hopefully the castle too, if that were possible. Perfume and wine bottles could stay. As could the boots of her husband, George. They remained by the fireplace in his bedroom, waiting patiently for him to stick his feet back into them and be off to another deer hunt in the hills.

In 2009, the population of 'the forbidden island' voted: Did they want to take over parts of the island from SNH? They voted yes. Now, for the first time, they can buy their own houses and plan for the future. Old plots, those once left by crofters forced to emigrate, will be apportioned and cultivated again. The circle has been closed.

From Mallaig to Skye

The Isle of Skye, or *An t-Eilean Sgitheanach* as it is called much more lyrically in Gaelic, is the largest island of the Inner Hebrides. The original meaning of the name is as obscure as the mountains shrouded by the heavy mist that often rests above the second-largest island of the Hebrides. But Munro, who travelled to Skye in 1549, claimed that the Gaelic name meant 'winged isle.' Yes, Skye has wings, promontories stretching out in every direction. All these headlands have names of Norse origin: Waternish, Trotternish, Duirinish, Minginish. So what do they mean? There is some uncertainty, but how about 'water point,' 'Trond's point,'

Grey seal

'animal point' and 'main point?' And is the name Skye itself also of Norse origin? In Icelandic sagas, Skye is called *Skyd*, or variants of this moniker, 'the cloudy isle.' There are certainly heavy clouds above Skye too.

The ferry to Skye also leaves from the small, busy fishing harbour of Mallaig. On the other side of the sound, Sleat, or *Slettr* in Old Norse, makes up the southern portion of Skye. A lush prelude to the Black Cuillin, a chain of rough, ragged, dark peaks which cut their way sharply through the mist. There are twenty so-called 'Munros' in the Cuillin, mountains 3,000 feet high or more. The Munros are named after the mountaineer Sir Hugh Munro, who mapped the Scottish mountains at the end of the 1800s and published a list of peaks over 3,000 feet: or about 915 metres above sea level. Now, maybe that height doesn't sound very impressive compared with mountains in other European countries, but these mountains don't arise from an Alpine plateau; they protrude upwards from sea level. And when the crumbly volcanic slopes get wet, the porous substrate becomes lethally slippery. Furthermore, the sea mist can quickly cover all paths, all cairns, all cliff-edges. During a trip I made to Skye in 2009, yet another climber had been killed. And one more had been seriously injured.

East of the jagged summits, Skye also boasts mountains of another kind: the Red Cuillin. Unlike their threatening lava-black sisters, these peaks are made of friendly red granite. From a distance, the round rusty-brown peaks appear silhouetted against the cloud layer, and grey strips of gravel run down the slopes like petrified streams.

Loch Coruisk

The black and white CalMac ferry that goes to Skye, MV Coruisk, foams into
Mallaig before slowing down and docking neatly at the pier. There most of the
passengers wait in hill walking boots, with telescopic walking sticks and giant
rucksacks. 'The Islands afford few pleasures, except to the hardy sportsman,' Dr
Johnson warned in 1773. And further: 'To the southern inhabitants of Scotland,
the state of the mountains and the islands is equally unknown with that of Borneo
or Sumatra. Of both they have only heard a little, and guess the rest. They are
strangers to the language and the manners [...].'

Much has changed since Dr Johnson went to Skye. One edition of the *Rough
Guide* travel books also warns visitors, but that's where the similarities with Dr
Johnson end. The problem now is rather that *far too many* people have heard about
Skye: since the opening of the Skye Bridge the island has been busier than ever,
and at the height of summer the road system often begins to bottleneck with coach
tours, minibuses, and caravans.

Ferrymen in helmets and yellow high-visibility vests tie the hawsers. The
cars on the deck rev up their engines and drive ashore, before those of us waiting
in a tidy queue are waved aboard. Not much of a queue though; there aren't many
cars today. There's been a fatal accident on the narrow, winding road to Mallaig.
Again. Those who had booked tickets for this last ferry this evening are stuck in
long tailbacks and won't make it in time. The Coruisk leaves Mallaig almost empty,
on course for Armadale on Sleat.

The ferry is named after Loch Coruisk, a deep inland loch from the ice age,
surrounded by the Cuillin. One of the earliest paintings of the loch dates from
1831 when the artist J.M.W. Turner travelled around Scotland to create illustra-
tions for Sir Walter Scott. It's been said that he almost fell to his death from one of
the crags as he painted. The clear, deep loch would soon become a destination for
national romantic artists and Victorian climbers. The loch's force of attraction has
not diminished over the years, drawing people from across the world. It would,
therefore, be a major exaggeration to say that I was alone the first time I visited
Loch Coruisk. A small boat heading to the outlet where the loch runs out towards
the sea was fully loaded with other people who also wanted to see the dark water
in the wild, empty landscape. The result was, of course, that the loch was neither
wild nor empty. It was teeming with Italians under umbrellas, South Africans in
khaki, and Japanese with binoculars. What's more, it was a warm, clear day with
neither a cloud nor a swirling patch of mist to help make the landscape appear more
dramatic. If it hadn't been that Coruisk was so wrapped in legend, I wouldn't have
given the place another chance.

The second time I was practically alone. The loch lay there, deep and shining. The peaks of the Cuillin were wrapped in soft, thick mist, and a cold breeze

brushed against me from the mountain passes down to the loch. No trees muffled the sound of footsteps, the slopes were steep and harsh, and no fish rippled the water. Only a gull or two swept across the loch before turning back out to sea. The water was clear and apparently bottomless, and what looked from a distance like white beaches were actually pale pebbled shallows. This was indeed Turner and Scott's Coruisk, the one they had admired 200 years ago.

'Cuillin for sale'

In the spring of 2000, the news broke: the twenty-ninth chief of Clan MacLeod, John, announced that he would be selling the Cuillin range. The price tag was ten million pounds, no less. The money would go towards repairing Dunvegan Castle, the MacLeods' seat on Skye for more than 800 years. The plan was also to build a large hotel to house some of the 150,000 tourists who pour in annually. The castle was in such a bad state, John MacLeod of MacLeod told the *New York Times*, that visitors had to use umbrellas in the bedrooms.

The Scottish nation, natural conservation organisations, and the Crown Estate, which until then had taken for granted that the mountains were public property, were more than incredulous when they heard the proposal from Dunvegan. Sell the Cuillin? On the private market? But MacLeod referred to old documents issued by the Scottish monarchy in the 1400s and 1600s. They clearly showed that the mountains belonged to the MacLeods and the yellowed papers were so legally sound that the state did not take the case to court. But, objected many, this was a moral case, not a legal one. 'These mountains are bigger than one person, bigger even than one nation,' according to Bill Birkett, one of Britain's most distinguished mountaineers and author of books on the outdoors. 'Their spirit and soul lie within all the people that love and respect the freedom of wild places,' he wrote in a letter to the local newspaper based on Skye, the *West Highland Free Press*.

When it was made clear that MacLeod couldn't be prevented from selling the Cuillin, the attacks came flooding from conservationist and outdoor organisations: this was nothing but blackmail! MacLeod was betting that either an organisation or the state would be forced to cough up, to prevent a private property speculator from snapping up Britain's most famous mountains, as if buying a painting from Christie's.

For three years, the matter reverberated among newspapers, climbers, island residents and lawyers. A mysterious person turned up as a potential buyer, at least according to John MacLeod of MacLeod. The solicitors of the anonymous millionaire had sensibly enough written a list of sixty-six questions about the purchase. You could say that they were expecting some kind of liability linked to this unique plot. But nobody could find out who this buyer was. MacLeod would not answer the *New York Times*' questions about the suspicious interested party, and many wondered whether he actually existed. Fictitious buyers had, of course, been a trick used in the sale of Eigg too. They could be useful for so many things: pushing up the price and forcing the state into making a purchase.

It all ended up with the clan chief performing an about-turn in 2002. The Cuillin would be donated to the nation. A gift from the chief of Clan MacLeod to Scotland. In return, Dunvegan Castle would be transferred to a charitable trust. The cost of repairs, which had risen from seven to ten million in three years because the roof had deteriorated so fast, would be paid by the trust. For many, this was yet another con; the people would be given a gift that already belonged to them in exchange for footing the bill for a roof that was leaking more than ever. A bad deal, according to the critics. The feelings expressed in letters to newspaper editors and in general conversation had historical roots: a long-standing resentment from the time when clan chiefs sold outright land understood to be the collective property of the clan. Others saw the decision as a practical solution contributing to the conservation of two of Skye's greatest gifts.

Dunvegan Castle, at the heart of the conflict, stands tall atop the sea cliffs by the small village of Dunvegan, unperturbed by all the trouble. Dr Johnson spent the night in the Castle and wrote in his travel journal:

> Dunvegan [...], which is the principal seat of MacLeod, is partly old and partly modern; it is built upon the rock, and looks upon the water. It [is] supposed to have been a Norwegian fortress, when the Danes were masters of the Islands. It [...] might have easily been made habitable, were there not an ominous tradition in the family, that the owner shall not long outlive the reparation. The grandfather of the present laird, in defiance of prediction, began the work, but desisted in a little time, and applied his money to worse uses.

If John MacLeod, the clan chief who wanted to sell the Cuillin, was aware of this 'ominous tradition,' at least he did not take heed of the old curse. He died shortly afterwards, in 2007, and was buried within the walls of Kilmuir Kirk at Dunvegan, alongside several generations of clan chiefs. Ironically enough, the small kirk has no roof, thanks to the Reformation, but the raindrops probably no longer bother the clan chief who wanted to sell Skye's soul.

MacLeod's Tables

There are more mountains on Skye connected to the MacLeods. A pair of striking hills northwest of Dunvegan appear as if the peaks had been levelled with a cheese slicer: MacLeod's Tables.

One of the most powerful chiefs of the Clan MacLeod, Alasdair Crotach, 'the Humpbacked,' ruled in the 1500s. The story goes that Alasdair was once a guest at a royal banquet in the Palace of Holyroodhouse in Edinburgh, the official residence of the Scottish monarchy. During the banquet, Alasdair was asked if he had experienced similar hospitality on Skye. This was hardly a question, as Alasdair Crotach himself could see, but rather a subtle way of humiliating the Highland chieftain. Look what we've got in the Lowlands, you haven't got anything like it on the islands! But Alasdair didn't hang his head and blush. No, now he would arrange a much classier party that would impress the blasé visitors from Edinburgh. The sarcastic, inquisitorial man from the banquet was later invited to Skye and escorted up to the top of Healabhal Mhòr, the lower of the two flat-topped mountains near Dunvegan. The starry sky made a sparkling ceiling. The place was set for a party, just as Alasdair Crotach had promised. Torches threw light and shadow over a wonderful banquet, and the clansmen holding the torches were much more valuable than any candelabra. So said Alasdair MacLeod.

Sleat

The CalMac ferry Coruisk docks at the Armadale ferry landing on the southern part of the island, nicknamed 'the Garden of Skye.' Here, remains of the original deciduous woodlands thrive, the ancient forest that once covered the island. But despite the grazing of sheep, some of the steadfast trees have survived: hazel, ash, aspen, beech, rowan and oak. Trees that also play an important role in Celtic mythology and culture. The Gaelic alphabet has eighteen letters, which have traditionally been linked to names of trees or plants. A for *ailm*, B for *beith*, C for *coll*: elm, birch, and hazel.

Not far from here, my grandparents used to run the Ardvasar Hotel in the 1940s. They leased the hotel from Lord MacDonald, the father of the current chieftain, who still has a seat on Skye. Of course, it was just after the war, but the tables at the Ardvasar Hotel were laid with white tablecloths and silver cutlery. The bar was only open to men. A single generator supplied the hotel with electricity, since Skye was not connected to the grid. Where there is now a car park, there used to be a barn. My mother, who went to school in Ardvasar, remembers an episode from when the clan chief had a different status and power than today. On the way to school, a young boy met the old chief, Lord MacDonald. The boy had manners, so he greeted him, saying 'good morrrning, Sirrr' with a clear, rolled Highland 'r.' His lordship paid no attention to him, so the boy repeated 'good morrrning, Sirrr.' No reply. It was as if his lordship could neither hear nor see him. The polite boy made a third attempt. 'Good morrrning, Sirrr,' he said, almost shouting, and when the lord didn't even turn his head towards him, the boy shouted in frustration: 'Are ye deif, ye bugger?!' His lordship was not deaf. Before long, he turned up at the school to complain about the boy's behaviour.

Trumpan Church—'Remember the cave on Eigg'

Kildonan Church, a small stone kirk with a thatched roof, is in the northwest of Skye where you can see across to the Outer Hebrides. That is, normally you can see them. But not on this early morning, on the first Sunday of May in 1578. The fog is lying low and thick, but that hasn't prevented the members of the Clan MacLeod's congregation from going to worship this Sunday. The small chapel has no windows, but streaks of light slip through a few openings.

In the bay below the church, eight boats scrape onto the beach. The men from Clan Donald have sailed and rowed from South Uist across the Little Minch, the stretch of sea that separates Skye from the Outer Hebrides. They have one aim: revenge. The year before, all the MacDonalds on the isle of Eigg were massacred in a cave. Babies, infants, the elderly. Men and women. The MacLeods had ruthlessly set fire to a pile of twigs outside the cave and the smoke that filtered into it made no distinction between guilty and innocent. Blessed be their souls. And the MacDonalds from South Uist promised the victims would not be forgotten. They could be ruthless too, if need be.

They walk in silence. The green grass, filled with daisy buds about to bloom, doesn't betray their footsteps as they head for the small church. Song and voices can be heard from within the church walls. Perhaps they hear a baby crying. Maybe some of them think for a moment of their own children, and question whether they are doing the right thing. Or perhaps their hearts are as hard as the steel of their swords. A flame is lit and the fire soon spreads through the thatched roof. The churchgoers hear battle cries outside: 'Remember the cave on Eigg!' They suddenly understand what's happening. One atrocity will be avenged with another. The MacLeods in the church die just as the MacDonalds in the cave died: suffocated by smoke.

When the mission has been carried out, the MacDonalds retreat to their boats. They didn't spot the young woman who escaped the church through an opening in the wall. She's bleeding heavily, one of her breasts having been torn off as she fled through the narrow crevice. She soon meets her own people, the MacLeods of Dunvegan Castle, who have been warned about the attack. She tells them of the tragedy, but they don't manage to get there in time. There isn't a soul alive in the smoking remains. But in the bay below the church, the MacDonalds are busy fleeing. That's easier said than done, because all their boats, apart from one, are stranded on land. The tide is out.

The MacLeods hurry down to the shore, but it soon looks like the MacDonalds will win the battle; there are simply more of them. Suddenly, though, their fighting fortunes take a dramatic turn. The MacLeods have unfurled their magical banner, the silk 'Fairy Flag.' Out of nothing, armed men appear and butcher the MacDonalds. When the fight is over, the bodies are stacked along a wall made of turf, and the winners push the wall down on top of the fallen. The struggle will forever be known as 'the Battle of the Spoiling Dyke.' Only one boat gets away, and the men row westwards for dear life, speeding back towards South Uist. But, writes the storyteller George MacPherson in his book, *Celtic Sea Stories*, the chief of Clan MacLeod summoned a witch, who cast a spell on the vessel: 'May it never reach the Outer Hebrides!' A large wave came from nowhere and smashed the boat to pieces.

And so it came to pass that none of the MacDonalds returned home to Uist. The murder of the MacLeods in the church did not bring the dead of the cave in Eigg back to life. And the death of the MacDonalds, now buried beneath the turf, did nothing to help the families lying in the crumbling, glowing ashes of the church. The events were merely another turn in the cycle of violence between the two clans.

The Fairy Flag—or the Land-waster

The flag that saved the MacLeods, the Fairy Flag, still hangs in Dunvegan Castle, the oldest continuously inhabited castle in Scotland. It was woven in silk between 300 AD and 600 AD. That much has been proven, but then legend takes over. How did the flag end up with the Clan MacLeod? Hugh MacLeod of MacLeod, the thirtieth chief in his line, asks the question in a booklet about Dunvegan Castle. The clan has two explanations: either the flag was given as a gift from the fairy people, or it was either looted or purchased during the Crusades. But the Crusades hadn't begun when the flag was woven, and if we choose to exclude the fairy explanation, the question still remains open: How did the flag which was made sometime in the Middle East end up in Scotland? And what are the origins of the legend that the flag will always lead the clan to victory? MacLeod pilots even took along pictures of the banner for protection during their sorties in the Second World War.

It was the clan's twenty-seventh chief, Sir Reginald MacLeod of MacLeod, who had the threadbare flag mounted in a glass frame. One day he was listening to an expert, a certain Mr. Wace, who had travelled the long distance to Dunvegan from one of the great London museums. The expert said that many things pointed to the flag having been taken to Britain by the Norwegian King Harald Hardrada, whom the Clan MacLeod regard as an early ancestor. The expert from the Victoria and Albert Museum continued on to explain that the Norwegian king had been plundering on his pilgrimage to the Middle East, and had looted the yellow, but now so faded, silk article. One thing backing up this theory, he asserted, was that Harald Hardrada had a banner that, according to Snorri Sturlason's saga about the king, was his most prized possession. Called 'Land-waster,' it was renowned for protecting the king in battle. According to the saga, when King Harald fell in the Battle of Stamford Bridge in 1066, the banner was there in use. The saga says nothing of who saved it and how it may have ended up on Skye. But men from the Hebrides, who were among Harald's soldiers, could well have rescued the flag and held it in safe-keeping until, in one way or another, it ended up with the MacLeods.

Sir Reginald listened politely to the theory about Harald Hardrada and his flag before answering: 'Mr. Wace, you may believe that, but I *know* that it was given to my ancestor by the fairies.'

The decisive meaning of censorship

When Boswell and Dr Johnson were on Skye in 1773, they visited the clan chieftain Sir Alexander MacDonald at Armadale Castle on Sleat in the south of Skye. Dr Johnson delivered poorly-disguised criticism of his host, who had been educated at Eton in England. 'Sir, the Highland chiefs should not be allowed to go farther south than Aberdeen. A strong-minded man [...] may be improved by an English education; but in general, they will be tamed into insignificance.' And Dr Johnson proceeds to inform his host how he would've acted had he been a clan chief: 'Were I in your place, sir, in seven years I would make this an independent island. I would roast oxen whole, and hang out a flag as a signal to the MacDonalds to come and get beef and whisky.' In his own journal, Boswell writes that they tried to communicate some of their enthusiasm to Sir Alexander. At the same time, it shows through in Boswell's account that his companion, Dr Johnson, oversteps the line in his eagerness to restore the old clan system. 'I should not forgive myself,' writes Boswell, 'were I to record all that Dr Johnson's ardour led him to say.' But the truth was that Boswell did write down every sentence, only to censor them from his travelogue, *A Journal of a Tour to the Hebrides*.

Is that not how all travelogues are written? How much bad blood would have been brought about if everything that was discussed and debated along the way were printed? Suppose that I, as the traveller, were to relate everything that's shared with me on my journey. A number of the smaller isles in Scotland have a population of a few tens of people, others several hundred, and some have several thousand. But, more or less, everyone knows everyone else. People, therefore, censor what they say about others, and are careful with whom they share gossip. Open conflict in small places can split the community for generations. That's why the writer, unless it is her intention to create conflict, must allow residents or incidents to remain anonymous if delicate matters are discussed. But in some cases this is impossible. The community is too transparent. Some may not think that what they are telling me might come out in print. It's not always clear what is 'off' or 'on' the record. Neither to them, I expect, nor to me. We might establish an air of confidentiality, an intimacy that encourages us to speak from the heart. It can feel safe, maybe artificially safe, to confide in a stranger who is without self-interest in what happens in a small place.

Portree, Skye

On one of the islands, for example, I asked someone who works for the Royal Society for the Protection of Birds if he had read the books of Ian Mitchell. Mitchell is a journalist and author who has written extremely critical, and often entertaining books, ridiculing the RSPB and other environmental organisations. My man from the RSPB hardened when I mentioned Mitchell's name. Perhaps this was the end of our conversation, I thought. He probably wondered for a moment where I stood on Mitchell's crusade against the RSPB's reputation. If he had asked me, I wouldn't have known what to answer. It isn't just Mitchell who criticises the conservationists for having far too much power in rural Scotland, so there must be some substance in what he writes. 'Spiteful nonsense,' said the RSPB man, glaring at me defiantly. 'He writes that the RSPB's manager on Skye met him in fluffy slippers!' He seemed deeply annoyed. 'She's never even owned any such thing!' He then directed serious accusations against one of Mitchell's relatives, who has apparently come into conflict with the ornithological association. My man from the RSPB alleges that's why Mitchell is out for revenge. He spits out his words. 'He's got an agenda against anyone who wants to protect birds and wildlife.'

After our conversation, I look up Mitchell's book, *Isles of the West,* and he has indeed described the slippers. It's probably not accidental. He finds weak points in those against whom he bears a grudge. But regardless of the fluffy-slipper claim, the question remains nonetheless: Why doesn't the RSPB representative attack the *substance* in Mitchell's critique of environmental organisations? They are, after all, the largest private landowners on many of the islands. Some feel that the organisations live with the deluded aim of protecting the islands against their own inhabitants. In fact, maybe it would be the ideal situation for them if there were no settlements on the islands at all. But the paradox is that many species of bird extinct in England, from whence the majority of donations come, can still be found on the islands of Scotland. And isn't the biodiversity on these islands precisely due to the locals' careful coexistence with, and respect for, their own natural surroundings?

A 'rude speech'

In 1773, when Dr Johnson was weighing down a horse's back on the rough roads of Sleat, he probably passed the place where Sabhal Mòr Ostaig is to be found, Scotland's only dedicated Gaelic college. Teaching is carried out through the medium of Gaelic, and the college offers language and cultural studies at both the undergraduate and postgraduate level. Tuition in Gaelic music and singing is offered as well. What would Dr Johnson have written in his travelogue had he encountered Sabhal Mòr Ostaig in 1773? The well-versed Englishman did not think highly of this Celtic language:

> Of the Earse [Gaelic, i.e. Irish] language, as I understand nothing, I cannot say more than I have been told. It is the rude speech of a barbarous people, who had few thoughts to express [...]. Earse never was a written language, that there is not in the world an Earse manuscript a hundred years old [...]. There can be no polished language without books.

So it's not only the language that gets ripped apart. The intellectual capacity of the Gaelic-speaking islanders isn't much to write home about either (ignoring the fact that Johnson was wrong about it not being a written language). Fortunately, however, there are some exceptions. Johnson describes the select few men with whom he finds it interesting to converse as 'gentlemen': clan chiefs, church ministers, and a few other worthy English-speakers. Dr Johnson is frustrated, on the other hand, by the local population. He receives different answers to his many questions, depending upon whom he asks: 'They have inquired and considered little, and do not always feel their own ignorance.' Not that the islanders lie wilfully—no, it's not that bad. The problem is that they can't see the difference between what is true and what is false. And they have reflected so little on themselves and their lifestyle that they don't understand the questions that Dr Johnson and Boswell pose to them.

Like so many travellers, Dr Johnson has no command of the language of the people about whom he's writing. Not that this disturbs or worries him, especially since the language is in itself unfit for thinking elaborate thoughts. On what basis are his opinions formed then? On their strenuous journey, he and Boswell are constantly being helped by bilingual guides interpreting their questions to the local people. The two gentlemen enquire and dig for cultural customs, traditions and superstitions, and they receive various answers diverging in all directions. Dr Johnson is irritated: 'Good-for-nothings! Can't a man get a straight answer?'

But is he genuinely inquisitive? When Dr Johnson speaks with the chief of Clan Donald about the clan system, Dr Johnson lectures the chief about how he would have acted as leader. The conversation is marked by a complete absence of compassion or curiosity on the part of Dr Johnson, who could have asked the chief about the advantages of changing clan-based society, such as, for example, by cessation of large-scale massacres. Instead, he fires away with a 'whole spit-roast oxen' and 'clean weapons' tirade, adding: 'Sir, I would have a magazine of arms.' Sir Alexander MacDonald answers calmly: 'They would rust.' Dr Johnson: 'Let there be men to keep them clean. Your ancestors did not use to let their arms rust.' Clearly, the nostalgic Englishman, Dr Johnson, came too late to see the proud Highlanders. All that was left, with a few honourable exceptions, as he says himself, were ignorance and poverty.

Dr Johnson was correct in some of his observations. Poverty was increasing. Overpopulation was becoming problematic. And the clan chiefs who used to do everything to support their people would soon do everything to get rid of them.

The Highland Clearances

[O]ne afternoon, as I was returning from my ramble, a strange wailing sound reached my ears at intervals on the breeze from the west. On gaining the top of one of the hills on the south side of the valley, I could see a long and motley procession winding along the road [...] opposite Kilbride, and there the lamentation became loud and long. [...] It was a miscellaneous gathering of at least three generations of crofters. There were old men and women, too feeble to walk, who were placed in carts; the younger members of the community on foot were carrying their bundles of clothes and household effects, while the children, with looks of alarm, walked alongside. [...] The people were on their way to be shipped to Canada. I have often wandered since then over the solitary ground of Suishnish. Not a soul is to be seen there now, but the greener patches of field and the crumbling walls mark where an active and happy community once lived. (Archibald Geikie, *Scottish Reminiscences*, 1904)

It was October 1853. The first snow had fallen. The factor of Lord MacDonald's land had removed all the furniture from the houses of the destitute tenants in Suishnish, in the south of Skye. It made no difference that some were either very old or just babies. Their houses had to be destroyed in case the exiles tried to return. But one man did get back home. He was found the following morning. Frozen stiff, dead by the door to his old house, in ruins, writes the historian Eric Richards in *The Highland Clearances*.

One banished family took refuge in a wretched building that was 'unfit for sheep or pigs,' according to a newspaper of the time, the *Northern Ensign*. Six people shared a bed of straw that separated them from the damp earthen floor. The newspaper went on: 'On Wednesday last the head of the family, William Matheson, a widower, took ill and expired on the following Sunday. His family consisted of an aged mother, 95, and his own four children – John 17, Alex 14, William 11, and Peggy 9. When a brother-in-law of Matheson called on the family, he found Matheson lying dead on the same pallet of straw on which the old woman rested. Her face and arms were the colour of lead. It was clear that she was starving. There also lay Alexander and Peggy, sick. The orphaned children lay stretched out, one on each side of their old grandmother.'

It remained to get rid of the last inhabitants of the area. In January 1854, the factor returned to Suishnish. There was a blizzard. Among those forced out into the storm was Neil MacInnes, his young daughter-in-law, and her baby. The child was four weeks old.

Courage, myths and shame

It takes courage to approach the theme of this national tragedy, the Clearances. Eric Richards has done exactly that, and sheds a varied light on an epoch which is still an open wound in the collective memory of many Scots. There are those alive whose grandparents were jailed in the fight for fair land division. As late as 1998, Scottish landowners considered making a collective apology for the Clearances, and the injustices their forebears were responsible for more than 100 years ago. But, Richards asks: What was behind these forced evictions? Is the explanation really so simple that all landowners were greedy? And were they mostly English, as is often said when the stories are re-told, or were they in fact Scots, even clan chiefs? And if it was the case that people were thrown out just to earn more money, how come that many landowners went broke? And what would have happened to the people in the Highlands and islands if they had continued to live there? Would starvation and poverty not have driven them to emigrate in any case?

It may seem odd to dwell so long on the Clearances and the 1800s, but this period remains very much alive as a source of identity for those in the Highlands and the islands. However, when a pendulum has swung to one extreme, natural forces send it back in the opposite direction. When individuals or a people are so victimised over a long period, it's not always a pretty sight. The feeling of being victimised serves no purpose if it traps us in a net of helpless passivity or eternal self-pity. Now comes the counter reaction. There are limits to how long present-day landowners should ask for forgiveness! And for how many generations can one allow oneself to feel victimised?

'The landowners in the Highlands must stop apologising,' was the headline of an article in the conservative newspaper, the *Daily Telegraph,* in 2001. David Cotton, the factor for a big estate in Sutherland, said: 'The owners are not defending their own rights, rights that should be defended. There is nothing to be ashamed of. After all, the Clearances finished 150 years ago and this is now 2001.' He continues: 'They must stop asking forgiveness for the Clearances and fight against the Scottish authorities' plan to give the small farmers the right to buy salmon rivers.'

One of the flagships of the young Scottish parliament was a new land reform. Land rights must be returned to the people. But those who worked on the salmon rivers, and who administered large assets on behalf of private landowners, were deeply worried about the future of the rivers. They were afraid that Scotland's most viable industry would collapse. They questioned whether small villages were really able to invest six-figure sums, as do the present landowners. And would the rivers be looked after with the same care and respect as before? Or would any small farmer with a fishing rod be permitted to cast his line, baited with, heaven forbid, worms or shrimps or any old bait, when of course only fly fishing is allowed? A person from the conservative party characterised the entire land reform as 'Mugabe in a kilt.' Others held that the law was revenge for previous wrongdoing.

The Napier Commission and the Crofter Act

I am on my way to visit George MacPherson from Glendale, west on Skye. He is related to one of the heroes from the Clearances epoch, John MacPherson, a leader of the Glendale uprising of 1882. The background for the crofters, the small farmers who rented land, taking this unusual step was that they had asked permission to rent a bigger vacant farm. They needed larger grazing areas to survive. But the landlord turned a deaf ear, and instead hired the land out to one of his own employees. Therefore, the crofters took the fork in their own hands, so to speak. They became land occupants and let their cattle loose to graze on the Waterstein sheep farm. The factors came to Skye to talk with the crofters, and asked them to be patient. 'Our forefathers died being patient,' answered the crofters, 'and they gained nothing by that. On the contrary, everything became worse!'

A court order demanding that the interlopers remove their animals was ignored, and when a herder tried to chase away the animals on behalf of the landowner, he was attacked. At the end of the year a warrant was issued for the arrest of more than twenty men whom the authorities deemed guilty of violence. Four policemen were sent to arrest the crofters, but the whole attempt ended with the protectors of the law being assaulted and chased from the area. Some days later, a larger police force arrived from the mainland, but they chose a hasty retreat when they heard that a famers' army was advancing, armed with forks, bale hooks and clubs. This was virtual anarchy.

Up until then the Gladstone government had shown little interest in the crofters' troubles, but the situation on Skye was getting out of hand, writes the historian James Hunter. What if these wild ideas spread to other islands? A government representative sailed to Skye on a navy vessel. He intended to make a deal. If Glendale sent five crofters to court, the authorities would make an offer. Five men, including John MacPherson, volunteered. The Martyrs of Glendale, as they came to be known, were imprisoned for two months. As compensation, the small farmers of Glendale were given a promise: a public commission led by Lord Napier would be established to investigate the crofters' situation.

In May of 1883, the Napier Commission started its long mission, organising public hearings and noting down witness declarations. Skye was the first stop on a long journey to the Hebrides, the Highlands, Orkney and Shetland. A journey through oppression, hunger, sorrow, and violence. And fear. It also became clear, Hunter notes, that the behaviour of the landlords broke with the ancient traditions of Gaelic society in the Hebrides and the Highlands: everybody who belonged to a clan had the right to settle and farm clan lands, so long as they fulfilled their duties towards the clan chief. This right, *dutchas* in Gaelic, had disintegrated. Now the people wanted it back.

The Commission came to a conclusion in 1884. It recommended land reform. But the directive did not go far enough, according to the Highland Land League, an actionist group with several thousand members who organised a strike among the crofters. They simply refused to pay their rents. They occupied ever more land. The actions spread from island to island, and the protesters demanded that parliament give the farmers protection against eviction from their crofts. Such a law would not really be anything new, the Land League pointed out, it would only restore earlier rights.

Prime Minister Gladstone agreed with the arguments put forward, and supported the demand. He also received the backing of male smallholders, who had the vote for the first time, and elected several representatives to parliament. In 1886 the reform was passed, a far more radical version than was proposed by the Napier Commission. The Crofters Act was historical. It provided the smallholders a guarantee against eviction and confiscation of their land, as long as they paid the rent. The property which they rented from the landlord could now be inherited. This increased security meant that they could invest in their houses, and that the improvements would finally benefit themselves and their children.

Seannachaidh George MacPherson

Today a monument honouring 'The Glendale Martyrs' stands by the roadside, just before it sweeps down the green valley with the Scottish-Norwegian name. 'But the authorities were not happy to put it up,' said George MacPherson on the phone, while he was giving directions to his house. 'And we were not allowed to put it where we liked.' Is this painful period really left behind, as the *Daily Telegraph* asks? No, not quite.

But it is not because of the martyrs I'm paying George MacPherson a visit. He is one of Scotland's last *seannachaidhs*. Once, these men were the chiefs' next-in-command, since they knew the clan's rituals and history. MacPherson's house has a red roof, the only one in the valley, he assured me. This could have been useful information if I had arrived by helicopter, but I'm driving and trust more in route directions. The road is narrow, and the sweet smell of purple heather wafts through the open window. At last I come to a gate marked 'private.' Closing the gate behind me, the road curls on round a bend and into the parking space outside MacPherson's house.

George MacPherson wears a kilt, a white shirt, and a tartan tie. Every day, it is rumoured. From the hall we enter the kitchen, carpeted in blue felt. I keep my shoes on after getting a mild reprimand with a smile in another home when I took off my shoes as we do in Norway. Unawares, I had signalled my status as a guest, and that I didn't feel at home.

Mrs. MacPherson is sitting at the kitchen table, talking to a couple of visitors. They are drinking tea. Always tea. In Britain tea is a miracle drink. Tea with milk soothes wounded souls and wounded knees. In the sitting room, the large windows look out towards the far side of the valley, where white, modern houses pop up as sure as snails after the rain, and strain the electricity supply which is not designed to support immigration on such a big scale. The reason the MacPhersons' light bulbs glow more faintly.

Seannachaidh George W. MacPherson, Skye

Before I'm able to start asking George about his role as a *seannachaidh*, there's another pressing issue on his mind. He's not happy with developments in Glendale. It's a paradox that the valley the martyrs fought to keep is now being taken over by incomers. The verdant cleft which runs down to the sea loch, Loch Pooltiel, now even has a nickname: 'Little England.' The label is not of the benevolent type. At best, the islanders have an ambivalent view of the *white settlers*.

When Dr Johnson and Boswell travelled in the Hebrides, they saw the deserted villages. Johnson had this to say about these areas: '[…] in the Hebrides, the loss of an inhabitant leaves a lasting vacuity; for nobody born in any other parts of the world will choose this country for their residence […]'. Glendale is a living contradiction of his words.

The 'white settlers' are mostly townsfolk. They move to Skye to escape the rat race, looking for a different lifestyle, clean air, unlocked doors—and cheap houses.

'The price of houses on the island is being pushed up,' says George MacPherson. Young local families cannot compete with the well-filled wallets of the incomers, who also bring along their urban ways. A paradox, since that was presumably what they were getting away from. In Little England, many of the English settlers voted for street lighting. 'Street lighting,' says MacPherson resignedly. 'What on earth do we need that for?'

We change the subject. How he became a storyteller. 'When I was three years old, my grandfather took me on his lap and told me a story. Then I had to repeat it for him. I did so, but he said: "Oh no, that's not what I said." Grandad told the same story once more. I repeated it several times until he was satisfied. Because the old stories, the great stories, must in no way be changed. They must be kept as they are.'

That is how George MacPherson began his education as a *seannachaidh*, the keeper of the traditions of the MacPherson clan. He learned the stories over a period of seven years. 'When I was ten years old, I told a story for the first time to an audience outside the four walls of the house.' The ancient profession goes back to the times when most people could neither read nor write. Therefore, the tradition of oral history, and the accurate handing-down of stories, was very important.

There was a time when the storytellers' tradition was under threat. As the numbers of illiterates decreased, people boasted: We can read the stories ourselves, thank you very much! But they had underestimated how the story comes alive in the intricate interplay between an engaged storyteller and a sympathetic audience.

Telephone catalogues from Jamaica

George MacPherson in his seventies is still a very busy man. I have a strong sense that I have been given an audience. He often represents Scotland at international conferences in Switzerland, Australia, or New Zealand. Or he participates in oral history festivals, such as the annual international event in Edinburgh.

The theme of this year's festival in Edinburgh is migration: What does it really mean to have a homeland? A relevant question, since there are many more millions of people of Scottish descent in the world than Scots living in the fatherland. During the 250 years' jubilee to mark the birth of the national poet Robert Burns, the Scots decided to celebrate by calling it 'The Year of the Homecoming.' The descendants of Scottish immigrants to Australia, South Africa, Canada, New Zealand, USA or Patagonia returned home, even though most of them had never set foot in Scotland, much less lived there. Some insisted that they were still refugees, that 200 years in Canada was only a pause, that Scotland really was their fatherland. And in any case, their forebears had not *chosen* to leave. They had been thrown out of their homes. The houses they left behind were wretched, of course, and the emigrants were poor, even starved—no-one could deny that. Not everyone was chased away, either. No one said that, and many built a better life. But they never forgot Scotland. The mountains. The white beaches. The mists. The light summer nights. The Gaelic language. The songs and the stories.

In 2008, a centre for the Study of the Scottish Diaspora was established in the University of Edinburgh. The founder, the historian and professor Tom Devine, announced in the opening lecture that he would challenge the school of thought which he called 'The Burn's supper school of history.' This way of thinking romanticised Scottish history and was influenced by Scottish nationalism. All stones were to be turned regarding the Scottish exodus. Was the nation aware, for example, that the Scots were notorious slave owners and slave traders in the West Indies? Devine got support from the Professor Emeritus at Herriot-Watt University, Geoff Palmer, who was himself a descendant of a West Indian mother by the Scots name Lamond. 'I have a Jamaican telephone directory,' said Palmer to the newspaper, *The Guardian,* 'and I would say that about 60% of the names in it are Scottish.' Some got their name from a Scottish father, others when slave owners simply named the African slaves after themselves. 'Most Scots are completely ignorant of this,' continued Palmer, who wondered why no descendants from, for example, Jamaica, were invited to the Homecoming.

Some returning clan members bear the kilt; others recall lines from sentimental Gaelic songs. Sepia-coloured pictures of great-grandparents travel along with them: families with many children outside log cabins in Nova Scotia, or a shepherd on horseback in Patagonia. The descendants flow to Scotland, searching in electronic archives and old church records to find out where their great-great-grandfather's house with the thatched roof lay. Could there still be a ruin lying in some or other deserted valley? Or maybe they could find his name in the passenger list of a vessel which took several months to reach the Gold Rush in Australia? He was lucky to survive, they are probably thinking, when they see the list of names of those who died of measles and typhoid fever during the voyage.

I have tried to trace ancestors myself, and it's no easy task. There are always dozens of people with the same name on the same islands, as was the case with my own great-great-grandfather Angus MacLeod from Lewis in the Outer Hebrides. One reason it is difficult to research ancestors is that surnames were not so important back then. On an island where every second person was a MacLean or Campbell, other methods had to be used to differentiate one person from another. Alastair Sinclair, at the museum in Tiree, explained the system to me: 'People knew who you were by your own name, the name of your father, grandfather and great-grandfather. In this way, you can trace ancestors through seven generations, sometimes up to ten generations!' He gave an example: a man named Iain may be called Iain, Iain Mhor, Lachlan, Iain. It's very unlikely that another Iain will have the same row of ancestral names. One could also differentiate folk by their nicknames, such as 'Hugh with the red hair,' or perhaps adding where he came from. Some are called by the nickname they had as children, such as 'Young Donald,' to differentiate him from his father, also a Donald. 'But Young Donald may well be eighty years old,' he chuckled.

It's not helpful that neither the Anguses nor the others were very accurate about age when reporting date of birth to the national register of the time. Often they made themselves ten years younger. Who wouldn't if they got the chance? So which Donald, Angus or John is *my* great-great, ask frustrated Americans who have come from afar to find their roots.

If they had had a man like MacPherson to advise them, they might have got an answer. In the old days most clan chiefs had their own *seannachaidh*: a combination of a Gaelic historian and master of ceremonies. When a new clan chief was to be installed, the *seannachaidh* recited the entire genealogy of the new leader, all the way back to the founding father of the clan. Who, by the way, often had Norwegian blood in his veins, according to recent DNA studies. In this way, the *seannachaidh* confirmed that the new chief had a legitimate claim to the title. Times have changed. 'I have been the *seannachaidh* of other clans since they no longer had their own,' says George MacPherson. 'There are practically none of us left.'

The Lord Lyon

So what happened to the *seannachaidh*? Everything went wrong for them. In 1608 King James VI, the son of the executed Queen Mary Stuart, wanted to subdue the clan chiefs and show them who was really in charge in Scotland. His ambition, writes the historian Norman Davies, was to leave behind a common religion in a united country governed by one law. He hatched a crafty plot. The chiefs received an invitation from the captain of the king's warship—would they like to come to dinner? Indeed, they would! Just after they came on board, the chiefs were informed that from now on they could consider themselves prisoners. They were taken southwards and spent the winter in a castle in the Lowlands. And they were kept there until they agreed to assemble at Iona and sign statutes which in reality were designed to pulverize the powers of the chiefs. 'The chiefs were forbidden to keep the *seannachaidh*,' says George. But no one could take the stories away from them.

Even though the chiefs no longer hold court, a *seannachaidh* attends the British Royal House. The position of Lord Lyon, King of Arms, dates to the 1300s, if not before. It was always held by an over-*seannachaidh*, who attended the coronation of monarchs, and legitimised the claim of the king or queen to the throne.

Nowadays there is little doubt as to the credentials of those who would aspire to the British throne. The problem faced by those-in-waiting today is whether they will live long enough to actually be crowned. But nevertheless, the Lord Lyon is never idle. He assists the court at official ceremonies. He approves new coats-of-arms and condemns any irregular use of them, and if necessary, he disperses fines. In addition, he has to keep an eye on the genealogy of the Scottish clans and approve new clan chiefs. This is not always an easy job, since some clans have been without a chief since the 1745 rebellion. Now, Mac-this and Mac-that are popping up all over the world, claiming to be the heir of the clan chief and applying for the post of the clan's supreme leader. Then it will be up to Lord Lyon and the court he is in charge of to resolve any conflicts of interest. The over-*seannachaidh* still has to know his clan history.

Professional ethics

What kinds of stories, then, are passed on by the *seannachaidh*, George MacPherson? 'There are three levels,' he says, 'and to become a *seannachaidh* you have to master all three.'

The most challenging, and at the highest level, are the grand stories, the epic tales, the heroic dramas from the mists of time, when a woman reigned in Skye, a queen whom no man could overcome, neither with weapons nor cunning. Queen Sgiath had a bodyguard of amazons, female warriors who attacked any man challenging the ruler. Inevitably, one day the queen was confronted by her superior, the Irish hero Cuchullin, for whom the Cuillin mountain range is named. These creational tales must be repeated word for word and must wander down the generations unchanged.

'When it comes to the other types of stories,' says MacPherson, 'level two, if you want, the facts have to be repeated correctly. But every storyteller can spice it up with his own personal style.' Like the story of Tiel, a Norwegian Viking who was so happy when he was going to marry a local chief's daughter from Glendale that on his wedding day he jumped over the side of the ship and balanced on the oars in pure joy. And drowned—giving his name to Loch Pooltiel, the fjord which laps the sides of Glendale.

At some point during the prolonged education of a *seannachaidh*, it sometimes became evident to the teacher that the pupil would never make the grade to level three. But the student could nonetheless still tell stories at the second level, and thus become a *sgeulaiche*. There was even a third title for those who mastered only the simplest level: a *sgeulach*, who could tell stories meant only to entertain. They were all allowed to function, as long as they kept to their assigned level. 'But folk don't follow these rules any longer,' sighed George MacPherson. 'A *seannachaidh* could have lost his life if he did not obey these rules,' he says. That must have been strong incentive for the storyteller to relate the stories word for word.

Accuracy and professional ethics among storytellers are no longer considered virtues. Perhaps that's why George MacPherson has published the stories in book form, and on a CD as well. If it is no longer possible to trust that they are related as they were originally told, perhaps it's just as well to give in and write them down, or store them electronically.

When he went to this length, George MacPherson broke with an old Celtic tradition which warned: If oral history is written down, part of the soul of both the story and the storyteller will die. In the introduction to one of his books, *Celtic Sea Stories*, George relates that his own father, who was also a storyteller, never allowed the stories to be noted down or recorded. If he suspected that this was happening, he fell silent and remained so until he was sure that the notebook or microphone had been put away. Therefore, MacPherson never reveals the names of those who have given him the stories now printed in his books. Many gave the stories anonymously, as a gift and on one important condition: that the storyteller's name would never be revealed. George has honoured this promise, even though many of the contributors now lie in their graves. Hopefully, with their souls still intact.

The original kilt – the fillimore

As mentioned, George MacPherson wears his kilt every day, and even though this is rather unusual, in recent years many more are now using kilts as everyday wear. It's difficult to interpret this trend as other than an increase of Scottish self-awareness, a new process of nation-building which can also generate nationalistic pride. In my childhood days it was a long walk between white and blue St. Andrew's flags, ones that now so often flutter in Hebridean gardens, small flags tied to sturdy poles.

When the kilt was forbidden after the 1745 rebellion, that 'kilt' bore little resemblance to today's tartan version of this piece of clothing. It simply did not exist. The original kilt, the fillimore, was more like a toga. MacPherson fetches his own fillimore, which he uses on the occasion of the yearly oral history festival. The material feels heavy, but not when he wears it, he insists. We roll out the cloth; it spreads over half the room. A seven-metre long, one-and-a half-metre wide piece of woollen cloth. MacPherson gives me detailed instructions as to how you arrange a fillimore. There must be no more than twelve folds in the length of cloth, soft folds held in place by a belt. In this respect it differs much from the sharp, firmly-pressed pleats of the modern kilt. The rest of the material is draped in an intricate fashion around the chest and shoulders, and is finally fastened, either with the original simple pin made of bone, or a more modern version of silver.

According to MacPherson, the fillimore was much more than an everyday piece of clothing. At night, you could wrap it cosily around you and use it as a sleeping bag: the fillimore is also warm when you're sleeping out in the hills. 'I have done this myself,' he says. 'And if it's a really cold night, you can dip the material in water and wring it out. Then it keeps the heat better. It's the same principle as modern wetsuits: The water insulates and protects against the wind. The fibres swell and the material keeps in the warmth better.'

MacPherson continues to enumerate the endless uses the fillimore can be put to. If two people were travelling together, they could use one fillimore as a blanket, the other as a tent. If you were crossing a river in the time when there were no roads or bridges on Skye, you could cross safely by tying them together to form a long rope. This must have been a strange sight, considering that underclothes were still unknown.

After the battle of Culloden, it was forbidden to wear the fillimore. Forbid a piece of clothing? How could a garment threaten the national state? Few things are so able to provoke conflict as the right to wear a piece of clothing, or the right to refuse to wear a specific garment. Clothes express identity. Pride. Belonging. Loyalty. Protest. Freedom. Clothes can be dangerous. And to forbid someone to clothe themselves as they have always done is a serious encroachment of personal space and self-expression. Of course, it's not only laws that can change how people dress. Ridicule can be just as effective. The engineer, Edmund Burt, described the fillimore in one of his travel letters from North Scotland:

> The common habit of the ordinary Highlanders is far from being acceptable to the eye; with them a small part of the plaid [...] is set in folds girt round the waist to make of it a short petticoat that reaches halfway down the thigh, and the rest is brought over the shoulders and then fastened before, below the neck, often with a fork and sometime with a bodkin, or sharpened piece of stick [...]. In this way of wearing the plaid, they have sometimes nothing else to cover them and are often barefoot; but some I have seen shod with a kind of pumps [...] which being ill-made, the wearer's foot looked something like those of a rough-footed hen or pigeon [...]. These are not only offensive to the sight. but intolerable to the smell of those who are near them [...]. This dress is called the 'quelt'; and for the most part, they wear the petticoat so very short that in a windy day, going up the hill or stooping, the indecency of it is plainly discovered.

We go out into a wind that earlier in the day blew the coffee out of my cup when I made a brave effort to eat breakfast outside. Beside MacPherson's house lies an old blackhouse. When the group of Americans arrive this evening, MacPherson will gather them in a half-circle around the fireplace in the simple stone house and tell them stories: epic stories of how Skye came to be, or stories of true love which ended tragically, or stories with a moral, about the fate of greedy people. We say goodbye. 'Next time,' he says, 'we can go to the places where the stories took place. I often do this.' This is what keeps history alive.

Callanish stone circle, Lewis

A legend says on the seventh day, the day of rest, God discovered he had left jewels still lying in his pocket. So to avoid breaking the Sabbath day, he parted with the precious, beautiful gemstones by opening a window in heaven, and letting them fall into the sea. They arranged themselves neatly in a row in the Atlantic west of Scotland. The Outer Hebrides.

This island chain lies midway between London and Iceland. It takes over five hours to reach them by ferry from Oban. Upon this geographical reality rest both the strength and vulnerability of the islands. Here, it is never overcrowded. Not a single palm grows on the white shell sand beaches or among the dunes, although occasionally a coconut is washed ashore by the Gulf Stream. The only places which are full of people and booked long in advance are the ferries, the holiday cottages, and the bed and breakfasts. Lucky for the local economy, which would otherwise suffer miserably. But in this string of pearls far out in the Atlantic, a quiet change is underway. This is the last stronghold of the Gaelic language and Celtic culture. If one is to believe the pessimists, in a few years only a handful of pockets of both will survive.

The Outer Hebrides is now the last place in Scotland where Gaelic is spoken in the shops, on the bus, and in the playground. The latter bodes well, many will say. But the language is slowly dying out in everyday usage as younger generations move to the mainland at an alarming rate. The place of the church and the 'Sabbath,' as Sunday is called here, is also waning.

Some will say that the changes are for the better. That it's time the church lost its hold on the population. That strong social bonds can mean too much control and lack of freedom. Others maintain that solidarity in local communities still exists, it has merely changed in shape and colour. Neighbours no longer pop into each other's houses at all hours to share the latest gossip, drink tea, and tell stories. But if something bad happens, if somebody falls ill, if the house is damaged in a hurricane, there's always help at hand. It's still true that everybody knows what's happening with everybody else, at least in the smaller places. But where do you draw the line between gossiping and caring?

On the map, the Outer Hebrides look like the bony skeleton of a fish. In the north lies the biggest island, Lewis, forming the head and body. The elongated tail begins with Harris and North Uist, narrowing at Benbecula, South Uist and

The Little Minch

Eriskay, and then making a last 'swish' at Barra and the small islands south. Two hundred kilometres separate the lighthouse at the Butt of Lewis from the blinking lighthouse on tiny, deserted Barra Head.

If you travel the length of the archipelago on bicycle or by car, preferably from south to north with the wind at your back, the journey will take you through eight islands joined by ferries and causeways. The Outer Hebrides are composed of over 200 small and large islands. Most have long been deserted. The ruins now shelter sheep, and seabirds sit on their eggs in peace.

Kisimul and Foster Children

The CalMac ferry MV Clansman slowly approaches Castlebay, the small main township on Barra. A robust stone castle stands on an island a long stone's throw from the little capital. On top of the fort, a flag snaps in the wind: the arms of the Clan MacNeil of Barra. The sea lies like a deep moat surrounding the little fort, which was home to the clan who owned Barra for many hundreds of years.

In the book, *The Crofter and the Laird*, John McPhee tells a story about two clan chiefs, MacNeil from Barra, and a chief from Colonsay in the Inner Hebrides. By coincidence their wives were pregnant at the same time. The clan chiefs agreed, therefore, to foster each other's child, a custom which precluded conflict and created bonds between the clans. The story says nothing about whether the wives were involved in the deal, nor of their opinion on the original switch the two chiefs had agreed upon, perhaps under the influence of a glass too many. The plan was that their wives should give birth on the other clan's island. In other words, when the time came, Mrs. clan chief MacNeil should set sail to Colonsay to give birth, leaving her baby there. And vice versa. The children would then both grow up with foster parents.

This apparently brilliant plan almost ended in tragedy. Perhaps MacNeil of Barra was not aware of his wife's expected date of delivery. Or maybe he was not a practical fellow, or just very inconsiderate of his pregnant wife. When her time came, she climbed down into the open boat at Kisimul. It was freezing. Indeed, it was midwinter. During the voyage her labour pains began, simultaneous with one of those Hebridean storms which frequent the islands at that time of year. The baby, John, was born under open skies, snowflakes melting against the warm, bloody membrane which covered his little newborn body. It would seem that the crew were of a more practical bent than the child's father had ever been. They understood it was urgent to warm the mother and baby. One of the cows on board, intended as a gift, was killed. The guts were pulled out, and the exhausted mother and her blue-cold baby were tucked inside the cavity of the steaming hot carcass. A fortuitous start. John stayed on in Colonsay as planned, but his dramatic birth was to follow him for the rest of his life. He went under the name 'John from the Sea.'

Mussels from the Traigh Mhòr Airport

The ferry docks at the quay in Castlebay. 'Barratlantic Limited. Frozen and Chilled Distribution' it says on the white lorries standing patiently in the queue, waiting for the gangway to be lowered. The Barratlantic fish and shellfish factory is Barra's biggest employer. Haddock, saithe, monkfish, scallops, scampi, mussels and snails find their way to mainland Europe, and there is a 70% chance that the shellfish and fish end up in France or Spain, according to the Barratlantic website.

Right now, then, in one or another Spanish tapas restaurant, a Spaniard is enjoying mussels from Barra. Maybe he asks the waiter where they come from. Let's assume the fellow is a good waiter who prides himself on being able to help his customers. He would do some research and find out that the shells once lay buried deeply in the beach of Traigh Mhòr: the Big Beach. A tidal beach, where the water foams in twice a day, so the mussel harvesters have to be on the lookout, and get into their rusty cars in time to drive to safety, since they work far from dry land. Standing bent over the rake, concentrating on the tedious work of raking for mussels, it's easy to forget both time and tide. Well, shellfish gatherers on a tidal beach are not very unusual, the Spanish waiter might be thinking. But then maybe he sees a picture of Traigh Mhòr, and his gaze falls on windsocks and poles. Very odd, because the poles are just visible sticking up from the surface of the water at high tide. But Traigh Mhòr is more than just a plate of food. The beach is the world's only tidal airport with regular flights.

Twin Otters have three 'runways' they can choose between when landing. Departures vary of course with the phases of the moon. The travel magazine, *Travel and Leisure*, has published a list of airports with the most difficult landing conditions, and which people with flight anxiety should avoid. Barra airport is number six on that list. This is not really a fair designation. Yes, true, the direction of the winds is maybe challenging, but as far as I know there has never been a single serious accident either on Traigh Mhòr or other islands. That is apart from the incident when Prince Charles, on his way to visit his favourite distillery, Laphroaig, crashed his plane on Islay and got stuck in a peat bog. But that was not a regular flight; the prince himself was at the controls.

I have rented a whitewashed cottage right beside the airport. From the house I have a good view over Traigh Mhòr, and arrivals and departures soon become part of the daily entertainment. At first, a faint hum is heard, and then the little Canadian-produced propeller plane can just be made out over the eastern sea. The windsock is bulging; the lights are blinking to warn everybody of the imminent landing. The shell diggers are gone; it is of course strictly forbidden to dig for cockles near the runway during landing and take-off. The sand is hard and compact with splintered mussels. The salt water splashes up from the wheels as the little plane hits the beach. It's impossible to hear whether the passengers are applauding as the Twin Otter rolls towards the arrival hall lying above the belt of dried seaweed where Traigh Mhòr meets land.

One of the shell collectors is Piotr Mrowiec, a seasonal worker from Poland. During winter, he and his wife run a bed and breakfast in their homeland, but in the summer months they live in a caravan on Barra. He gathers while his wife has two part-time jobs, one in the fish factory and the other at the hotel in Castlebay. Piotr is wearing a military jacket over yellow oilskin trousers. He rakes carefully, exposing mussels just under the surface of the sand. A small variety of mussel, *Cardiidae,* Piotr boils with a little salt on the stove in their caravan, since Barratlantic, on the other hand, is more interested in medium- and large-sized mussels. Piotr keeps the shellfish in green nets spread out over a large area, suitably spaced. They are to be collected by a van next day, and the tidal water keeps the creatures alive and fresh throughout the night.

A bit further out on the beach, at the water's edge, an elderly couple is standing, each holding a bucket, their backs bent over their rakes. They don't look up when the Twin Otter takes off. He stands in water far up his Wellingtons; she's digging in the damp sand, wearing a plastic headscarf, just like the one the queen uses when it rains. Mr. and Mrs. Butterfield moved from England thirty-two years ago. 'I like looking for shells, and it also adds to our pension,' says Mrs. Butterfield, still gazing into the sand. And for a moment, I wonder if she is able to right herself from that back-breaking position. 'Also, you can choose yourself how long you want to dig. That's the beauty of it.' Unlike Piotr, she does not like the taste of the delicacies

Mrs. Butterfield collecting shellfish at Traigh Mhòr airport

she's throwing into the bucket. These will also be sold to Barratlantic for export, as it is against the law to sell the shellfish directly to the dealers; they always have to be controlled first. 'Now the beach has a B-classification,' says Mrs. Butterfield, 'but in winter, when it's safer from the poisonous algae, then it goes up to an A.' And probably impossible to stand upright then, I am thinking, wondering what the windsock looks like in January.

Castlebay Bar

Poles and Englishmen. Nothing wrong with incomers, of course. But if you want to find the natives, there are always some in the ancient Castlebay Bar. The bar goes back to 1911, when you could keep your feet dry skipping from one herring boat to another docked in Castlebay harbour. The bar and its surroundings must have seethed with fishermen and herring lassies, girls who every summer flocked in to gut the shiny, fat herrings, and put them layered with salt into waiting barrels. But then the herring migrated to other hunting grounds, around the time when the market for salt herring disappeared. The customers had now developed a taste for fresh fish.

But the old bar is still full of life, especially on Sundays. Music and beer on the Sabbath day? Enough to make good Protestants squirm, but Barra is, after all, a Catholic island. And contrary to Sundays further north on the Outer Hebrides, when just about everything is closed except for the kirk, the pub in Barra is at its liveliest on the day of rest. Folk music floats through the open doors in the warm summer weather.

The Presbyterian Church, which dominated large parts of the Hebrides, condemned important aspects of the Gaelic culture. It was profane; it did not come from God, that was quite obvious! So its musical instruments and traditional folk songs were replaced by psalms, sung without accompaniment. This dour atmosphere was portrayed by Lars von Trier in the film, *Breaking the Waves,* set in part in the Hebrides. Catholicism, on the other hand, had a much more relaxed attitude towards such worldly practices. On Barra, and on the other neighbouring Catholic islands of Eriskay and South Uist, the traditional music has survived extremely well.

Around the table in Castlebay Bar, five elderly gentlemen are enjoying their half-empty pints. Perhaps some of them were weaving among the legs of the adults in this very pub during the herring harvests between the wars. Three have an accordion on their laps, the fourth small set of electric pipes. On the little table one of them has, unawares, laid out a tableau: an empty whisky glass, a tweed 'sixpence' cap, and a walking stick. Not the urban lacquered kind, not at all. This stick is a robust cousin, a trusty companion when the farmer hunts stray sheep among heather hills and peat bogs.

Ceilidhs

I recognise one of the musicians, a senior with chalk-white hair playing the accordion. He is crouching over the red instrument just as he did some days ago in Vatersay, the little neighbouring island which was joined to Barra by a causeway in 1991. Then he was playing in Vatersay Hall during a gathering which was advertised as a *ceilidh*.

All visitors to the Hebrides will sooner or later come across a poster advertising a 'traditional ceilidh.' 'There is a deep-rooted conviction that Hebrideans spent (nay, spend) their evenings congregated around peat fires in selected houses drinking drams and singing Gaelic songs,' wrote the author Finlay J. MacDonald, himself from Harris. 'It was never like that in these parts. Not then. Not now.' Of course people came together before, he continues. Especially before the radio made its appearance in the 1930s, not to mention how TV changed the way people socialised. But they didn't gather to drink and sing. Of course, that could be the case at a wedding, but in everyday life they discussed the news on BBC or from the local paper. Sometimes stories were shared, tales from seamen who had seen more of the world than perhaps was good for them; or stories from people with the second sight, who could foretell death or illness. It was also a common thing to sing while spinning wool or rowing the fishing boats, of course. But was a ceilidh about playing music, singing, and drinking round lumps of burning peat? No, not then, not now.

Maybe MacDonald is right about the myths surrounding ceilidhs, or perhaps he's just talking about the northern, Protestant islands. In any case, I've never felt very enthusiastic about ceilidhs, and it feels almost like blasphemy to admit it. On the contrary, sometimes I feel they can be quite boring, for example, like the one I experienced that June evening at Vatersay Hall.

The chairs were lined up in rows in front of a small stage. The white-haired fellow from the bar sat upright on a hard chair with his accordion on his lap, playing one piece of folk music after another. Many of the onlookers knew him well; he's a living legend, and the father of two of the leading figures in the local and extremely popular band, Vatersay Boys. But in the public ceilidh, the man and his music were transformed into a detached museum piece in a glass case, thereby losing any contextual relevance. The modern ceilidhs present themselves as the real thing: a version of the myth of everyone sitting cosily round the fire, singing and drinking. But when 'culture' is displayed in a museum and enacted on a stage, it means those ways of life are often already on their way out, and resuscitation isn't helpful. I much prefer to listen to the old-timer's tunes over a beer in Castlebay Bar.

Emigration, Barra

Anonymous Alcoholics

It's a warm July evening. The Vatersay Boys are playing in Castlebay. The pub is full of folk, and folk are full of beer. The band starts up around eleven o'clock: two accordions, two bass guitars, drums, and a bagpipe. They are playing on home field. One couple after another eagerly joins the Scottish dancing. Boy and girl. Girl and girl. Others contain themselves and play darts instead. Down at the pier the Clansman CalMac ferry is lit up like a cruise ship in the light summer night.

After the concert, cars rev up. Some are clearly preparing to leave behind rubber on the one-track asphalt roads which run like a lasso around Barra. Some years ago, *The Guardian* newspaper sent a journalist to Barra to report on the issue of drunk driving. An investigation had revealed that Barra, with its 1,200 inhabitants, topped the statistics on alcohol consumption. (And that's something, if I read the newspaper correctly.) Three-quarters of the population admitted that they drank the equivalent of six whiskies 'on an ordinary drinking day.' In the course of four years, *The Guardian* reported, the little island had lost six young lives due to traffic accidents. All had happened at night, without oncoming traffic, because a system had developed for driving under the influence: A scout was sent out to warn drunk drivers about the whereabouts of the only two policemen on the island, who share one car. The journalist soon discovered that it wasn't popular to discuss this issue openly.

A priest who wanted to start an Alcoholics Anonymous group discovered the same thing. The popular priest met with intense resistance from certain individuals in the congregation. When he left Barra, he said it was because of a 'crisis within the church,' and that anyway it was time for new pastures. Many islanders regretted his departure. 'There is a culture of denial here,' one of the young islanders in Castlebay Bar told *The Guardian*. As with the others who had been interviewed, he (if it were a he) wanted to remain anonymous, for, as another person commented: 'Barra is the kind of place where if you put your head above the parapet, you'll be shot.' Stories like this don't exactly put Barra, known as the Hebrides in miniature because it has the best of everything the islands have to offer, in a flattering light. The island with glittering white sands, poppies, and lovesick singing seals, is suddenly turned into Scotland's Twin Peaks. One may wonder where the journalist got his information. Maybe from an incomer? Or a drunken native who had previously stuck his neck out and had it cut off. Perhaps with good reason. It's not always best to listen to those with the loudest and toughest voices if you want to understand a community. But the resistance to the priest's AA initiative reflects my own experience: The slightest implication that there can be problematic aspects of living in small communities is immediately brushed aside. 'We stick together; we look after each other' is the constant refrain.

An Honest Incomer from Glasgow

The only people who are willing to discuss the pros and cons of small communities are incomers: as, for example, restaurant owner Rohail Bari, of Indian origin, from Glasgow. Some years ago his family decided to move from the 'rat race in the property market,' as he put it, to Vatersay across the causeway from Barra. He and his wife run an Indian-inspired restaurant in Castlebay.

Rohail and I have found a table out in the sunshine. The café, set among grey stone Victorian houses on Main Street, looks out to sea. I ask him if he thought it was difficult to settle in at first. The change from Glasgow, with its several millions, must have been difficult? But, No—to begin with it was very, very easy. A real honeymoon. Everything was new; it all seemed magical. 'During that time, we made some mistakes,' says Bari. 'Everybody talked about us. Some think that you come here to hide yourself. It's the exact opposite. When you come here, it's completely transparent. Everything you do is visible.' The honeymoon was over with a bang. Bari regretted the move for a whole year. But slowly, surely, things fell into place. Now Barra is their home, but in a different way than before. Friendships grow bit by bit. Not through the more superficial get-togethers at the pub, but gradually, in a sober state. In any case, it's not the number of friends that count, says Bari, quoting an old saying from his home town: 'You don't need many friends; six people are enough to carry your coffin.'

I ask what advice he would offer newcomers to the island. To begin with, it's best to hold your cards close to your chest, he offers. Don't be too eager; don't expect that you will quickly become part of this society. If you're too impatient, things won't go well. It takes a long time before folk feel they know and trust you; to have confidence in you. But when all is said and done, this is a wonderful place. Okay, there is a bit of gossip, and people can be quite nosy, but if your car breaks down, five or six people will stop and ask if they can help you. Folk are generous and helpful. He cites a book, *The Stornoway Way*, from the Isle of Lewis further north. 'What's the best about living here and what's the worst about living here? The best is that you know everybody and the worst is that you know everybody.'

Vatersay and the brig, Annie Jane

When the little island of Vatersay was connected by a causeway to Barra, it was high time. The population had fallen to sixty-five. Now, in part thanks to the Baris family, the trend has turned, and grown to about 100.

Two sandy beaches slowly eat their way towards the centre, threatening to divide the island in two. Year by year, erosion takes its bite of the green *machair*. The carpet of grass sends roots far down into the sandy soil, desperately trying to hold the island together.

The intense light reflected from the sand dunes almost blinds me. The beach merges into a turquoise sea and looks like a cliché from a tourist brochure of the Maldives. Even the sharks are here. It's not unusual to see the grey, glistening fins of a basking shark, eight to ten metres in length, parting the surface of the sea a few metres from land. But in contrast to the Maldives, these sharks are more interested in plankton than in the shadows of snorkelers in the clear water. Towards the west, a short walk over the *machair*, which now in July is white with daisies, is the beach of Bagh Siar. The contrast between the east and west coast is striking. The western beach is strewn with large rounded boulders. Strong roots of seaweed still hang onto the stones which the Atlantic has cast far up on Bagh Siar. From the high dunes, I look down at the sea—I am standing on a mass grave.

The brig Annie Jane was not like most emigrant vessels. Lloyds had accredited her with the highest standard attainable. The ship had only her maiden voyage behind her when she left Liverpool for Quebec on the 25th of August 1865. The hold was filled with rails and other equipment for the railway under construction in the British colony. The passenger decks were occupied by several hundred Scottish and Irish emigrants, many of them on their way to build the railway. Ironsmiths, carpenters and other workers had brought their entire family with them to settle in the new land, a few years later to become Canada. West of Ireland, the Annie Jane lost two of her masts in a storm, but continued on the voyage until the passengers organised a petition in protest. They demanded that the captain turn back. On the 31st of August the damaged ship limped into Liverpool. After extensive repairs, the Annie Jane once more left the harbour city behind. The calendar showed the 8th of September. Some of the passengers had pulled out from the whole adventure, perhaps losing faith in the captain, who apparently had intended to cross the Atlantic with broken masts.

The ocean was unwilling to co-operate with Annie Jane. On the 12th of September she was once more seriously damaged by heavy seas. Again, the captain wanted to proceed and the passengers protested, demanding that he turn back. This time, the skipper did not give in, on the contrary: 'I won't hesitate to use pistols against the troublemakers!'

The anxious atmosphere on board calmed down as the wind dropped. On the 28th of September they saw the beam from the lighthouse on Barra Head, and could just make out the cliffs of St Kilda. But the weather changes fast. Autumn is a dangerous, unpredictable time in these parts. The wind increased to full storm. The remaining sails were ripped off and disappeared. The lifeboat had been washed overboard long before. Even the captain now admitted that he had to seek safe haven. But it was too late to reach the calmer waters east of Barra. He decided to ground the vessel, and chose the beach of Bagh Siar on the west coast of Vatersay. Annie Jane dug herself into the sand just before midnight, with her bow facing the beach. But the capricious wind grabbed hold of the boat and forced her sideways, turning her against the huge waves and thundering in towards the boulders.

It's said that it only took about fifteen minutes before the whole ship was smashed to pieces. Many of the passengers were imprisoned in the vessel, and were either crushed to death or drowned. Those who had gone up on deck were soon swept overboard. When dawn came, the catastrophic shipwreck revealed itself to the little community of Vatersay. Bodies continued to be washed ashore on Bagh Siar for days on end. Around 350 people lost their lives. Most of them, whole families, lie beneath me in the sand dunes.

Eriskay

The little CalMac ferry MV Loch Bhrusda sails between Barra and Eriskay, or *Eriksey* as it was called under Norwegian occupation. The ferry can carry only a few cars, and drones noisily as it crosses the Sound of Barra. Through the din I realise that something's happening on deck. Together with other passengers I run quickly up the green-painted steps to the green deck under the bridge, where red plastic chairs are lined up, awaiting company. Passengers are hanging over the rails, gesticulating and photographing. A pod of dolphins is playing alongside the boat, the animals gliding in grey, glistening arcs over the surface.

Forty minutes later the Loch Bhrusda docks near a long, dazzling white beach: Coilleag a'Phrionnsa, or the Prince's Beach. In the summer of 1745, the keel of the little frigate Le du Teillay scraped against the sand, and Bonnie Prince Charlie set foot on Scottish soil for the first time. If the prince had met a person with the second sight who could have foretold the catastrophe he would set in motion the following year, and how the attempted coup was to change the history of the Hebrides, perhaps he would have turned right back to the Continent.

From the beach I continue northwards, past a Catholic churchyard with a statue of the Virgin Mary, to the little township of Am Baile. There, the pub Am Politician proudly exhibits a bottle or two of a very special whisky worth between £2,000 and £4,000. Julia Campbell behind the bar shows me an oval bottle without a label, but the writing in relief on the glass tells me that this is a Spey Royal. The bottle from the whisky-producing Speyside district never made it further than Eriskay, and should have been consumed and forgotten long ago. Instead, it ended as a golden memory, due to a fortuitous navigation error during World War II.

SS Politician

On an overcast February morning in 1941, on the island of South Uist north of Eriskay, someone was hammering on unlocked doors. 'Bata mor air an sgeir! Tha bata mor air an sgeir!' the excited voice was shouting in Gaelic. Ship on the rocks! A big ship is on the rocks!

Some days earlier the Politician had sailed from Liverpool with course for Jamaica and New Orleans, according to the writer Roger Hutchinson. The captain had chosen an unusual route. He wanted to steer the beautiful, elegant cargo ship as far northwest as it was possible to go in British waters. The plan was to sail full steam over the Atlantic Ocean to the American coast after they had rounded the Outer Hebrides. In this way the shipowners as well as Captain Worthington and his crew hoped to avoid the threat of torpedoes from German submarines, which had sunk over 200 British merchant ships in a few months. Upon arriving in Kingston, the ship would unload merchandise, everything that was needed in a British colony: soap and medicines, machetes and oil stoves, bathtubs and mirrors, biscuits and tobacco. The goods from Politician would earn much-needed cash for a Great Britain at war. As far as that went, the Politician was no different from other merchant ships at that time. Except, of course, for the contents of hold #5.

The winter of 1940–1941 had seen numerous aggressive air strikes on Scottish cities, during which two whisky storage halls had burned down. That was more than the Secretary of State, Tom Johnston, could tolerate. The Scottish national drink was pouring out into the snow! Or going up in flames, as if the Luftwaffe were flambéing some sort of gigantic dessert. He insisted that bottles of whisky from all over Scotland must be evacuated to the USA. Top-quality whisky was sent by rail by the big distilleries: John Walker & Sons, Haig & Haig, Ballantine's, and many more producers. Malted and blended, in bottles, casks, and cartons. Scotch corresponding to 264,000 bottles was to be sold on the American millionaire market.

The bottles were said to be valued at around £1.3 million in today's currency.

During the night on the 5th of February 1941, a brisk southwesterly wind was blowing on the west coast of Scotland. It was overcast and raining. The usual fixed points, the lighthouses on Barra Head and Skerryvore, were impossible to see, given that they had been painted black during the war. But the compass reading showed that the Politician was on the right course. Well, almost the right course. The wind increased in strength during the night; the sea was rough. At 8:40 in the morning a shout was heard from the bridge. Land ahoy! But the terrain did not match the map. A massive, threatening headland towered on the starboard side. Mr. Swain, the first mate, acted fast. He managed to manoeuvre the ship away from the threat and for a few seconds he thought the Politician was saved. Until he heard a thump. The ship trembled as she hit a submerged rock. The bow rose up for a moment before the entire ship lodged into place with an ominous bang.

The first emergency signals reached the southwest coast of Scotland about eight o'clock. 'Abandoning ship. Making water. Engine-room flooded.' The nearest vessel, a navy ship, requested the position of the Politician, but neither the experienced captain nor anybody else on board could say exactly where they were.

Hold #5

Captain Worthington feared that at any moment the ship might break in two and disappear under the waves. An anxious atmosphere prevailed on board, and through a misunderstanding, twenty-six of the crew thought they had been ordered to abandon ship. No-one knows who shouted the order into the wind, writes Arthur Swinson in the book with the apt title, Scotch on the Rocks. At any rate, one of the lifeboats was lowered into the green waves foaming against the side of the ship. However, if the crew were in danger on board the Politician, they were certainly no less so in the lifeboat. The little boat never stood a chance; the oars were useless against the roiling seas. The crew were extremely lucky when the waves decided to throw them onto land. They had been shipwrecked for the second time in only a few hours.

The people on the little island of Eriskay had kept a keen eye on the further developments of the grounding. And when they saw that the lifeboat with the sailors had capsized, sounds of running feet and shouts in Gaelic were heard. Soon a little sailing boat was launched into the frothing sound, with course for the rocks and the shipwrecked men. Knowledgeable local fishermen brought them safely back to Eriskay. Later that same afternoon, the wind had died down and the crew of the sailboat judged it safe enough to take the shipwrecked crew back to their mother ship. The vessel had now decided not to sink immediately after all, and Captain Worthington finally found out where they had grounded. Politician was lying in the shallow, dangerous sound between the islands of South Uist and Eriskay. At last they could signal their position, and shortly afterwards the lifeboat from Barra lay alongside the Politician. A relieved crew abandoned ship and were lodged in Castlebay on Barra.

Captain Worthington wasted no time after the shipwreck. Following a thorough examination of the ship, he informed the shipping company that both the Politician and the cargo on board could be salvaged. The first rescue operation began some days later. Everything which was still in good condition and not smeared with oil from the tanks below deck was carried away. But there was one type of goods the chief of the salvage operation, Commander Kay, left behind. He did not touch the cargo in hold #5, the evacuated whisky.

Perhaps Kay thought the bottles and oak casks floating around in salt water and oil were destroyed and worthless. But if the commander himself did not bother about the bottles, there were others who did. An employee in the local customs and excise office was well aware that no tax had been paid for the whisky, since it was being exported. Imagine if people helped themselves and drank it, or, even worse, sold it without the state getting a shilling in income! The customs officer was therefore keen to have the ship guarded by a watchman. But Commander Kay blankly refused. It was far too dangerous; the ship could disintegrate completely in the next storm. How could one take a chance like that? The customs officer had to be content with sealing hold #5, hoping that the seal of His Majesty King George VI would have a deterrent effect on the local inhabitants. They might want to have a closer look at the cargo.

The Rescue Operation

For generations, people on the islands had, as a matter of course, believed that everything the sea threw up on the beach was a gift from heavenly powers. And here in the southern part of the Outer Hebrides, where the population was Catholic, wreckage was a gift straight from the Virgin Mary herself. During the war, what with the rationing and so on, items from torpedoed ships were an extra bonus for the isolated island communities, whose inhabitants had no electricity or piped water. And besides—why should one deny oneself what the Virgin Mary herself had sent them? And what right had customs to interfere with Her decisions?

When it came to the Politician, it was also true that both the shipowners and the head of the rescue operation had announced officially that they had abandoned the ship and the oil-soiled cargo. Rumours about what still remained in hold #5 spread like wildfire to the neighbouring islands. Indeed, the rumours even reached the mainland many miles away. Like an enormous regatta, a whole fleet of small fishing boats sailed out to the shipwrecked steamboat, which had already been christened 'Polly.' There was enough for everybody. Below deck, the hold was lit by candlelight and paraffin lamps. Muffled voices in Gaelic could be heard as

Julia Campbell, Am Politician bar, Eriskay

islanders waded clumsily around in the oily seawater. Pull up! Lower! Boxes of whisky of the best makes were firmly tied with a rope before being hauled up on deck. Then they were lowered down to a fellow holding a small sailing boat close in to Polly. The clothing of the nocturnal guests was drenched with oil, but it never occurred to them that the oil stains could be used as proof at trial.

The summer of 1941 was an everlasting party on the Outer Hebrides. What was not consumed at once or given away was carefully hidden. In lobster creels on the bottom of the sea; in rabbit warrens; under the floorboards; or in the peat stacks drying in front of every house. Polly had other things on board too, items left behind by the rescue expedition. Bathtubs and telephones were installed in houses which had neither electricity nor running water. A lucky man found a whole sack of shoes, rowed it to land and trudged all six kilometres to his home before discovering that they were all left-footed. But the best of all was the whisky. As one old lady said: 'It was just like holy water, you never got drunk.' Others maintained that the whisky from Polly could be drunk continually, night and day, without ever getting a headache.

Whisky Galore

The grounding of Politician and the never-ending party in the summer of 1941 might well have become a forgotten chapter in the history of the islands. A memory which gradually faded, as every whisky drinker who had lived through the episode took the story with him to the grave. However, the author, Compton MacKenzie, had made Barra his home in the 1930s, not far from where Polly had lain wrecked and helpless. One night, MacKenzie's driver went to Eriskay, and returned, black as a cormorant, impregnated with oil, but happy as a lark in spring. He gave MacKenzie a present: six bottles of whisky from the Politician. So the rumours about a ship loaded with whisky *were* true!

MacKenzie immediately realised the literary potential of the shipwreck and the salvaging of the whisky. The original story was every bit as good as an imagined one. But the real story had many more serious undertones than the novel, which was soon to be read the world over.

Now Compton MacKenzie already had enough going on. He was very busy with another novel, so it was not before the summer of 1946 that he started to write *Whisky Galore!* the Gaelic for 'lots of whisky.' The novel soon became one of the greatest post-war bestsellers, and the film company Ealing Studios quickly snapped up the film rights.

In the film version of the shipwreck, the SS Cabinet Minister ran aground between the fictional islands of Great and Little Todday, suspiciously similar to Barra and the little neighbouring island of Vatersay. In other words, MacKenzie moved the scene of the shipwreck a little further south from where the original had happened. In the film, the islanders on Great Todday were thirsty. Whisky was rationed due to the war, and when the ferry failed to bring the weekly ration, the islanders fell into a state of depression. No parties, no laughter, neither dances nor weddings without the water of life. But then they got a hint that a ship had run aground—with masses of whisky on board. Under the cover of darkness, three small wooden boats splashing around the SS Cabinet Minister relieved the ship of nailed crates. A cat-and-mouse game ensued with representatives of the authorities, who of course were outwitted at every turn. Parties and weddings could begin again!

The book and the film that followed were a bit too close to the bone for some, who felt they had been more than exposed by Mackenzie's pen. For example, an English incomer, the doctor on Barra. Involuntarily and quite unaware, he was presented as the zealous Captain Paul Wagget, who was doing everything to keep the whisky from falling into the hands of the islanders. The local Catholic priest on Barra, Father John Macmillan, also had his counterpart in the film: Father James MacAllister. It's difficult to say whether the Lord's servant in the film exceeded the original, or the opposite. When the original Macmillan was asked what he thought about the men in his parish who had helped themselves to the whisky, even on the Sunday, he appeared to be greatly surprised by the question. What better day to steal the whisky than on God's own day?

All ends well in the film *Whisky Galore!* At least for those siding with the islanders. They *saved* the whisky, indeed *liberated* it. Anyway, that's how the folks of the Hebrides saw the acquisition of 24,000 bottles of whisky. Others, such as two energetic officers in the Customs Office, branded the islanders as a band of thieves and vandals. Thanks to these representatives of the authorities, nineteen men ended in jail. They were sentenced from twenty days to two months. A detail, the dark underside that Compton MacKenzie had omitted in *Whisky Galore!* And if it had not been for the dedication of these two officers in Customs and Excise, the remaining 48,000 untaxed bottles still lying in the water would not have been blown up by dynamite in 1942. At last, the two zealous officers attained peace in their souls. Mission accomplished, they thought.

Without reason. In the 1980s amateur divers and Donald MacPhee from South Uist retrieved eight bottles from the sandy bottom where Politician lay embedded. Over the years, salt water, oil and other bits and pieces from the sea floor had forced their way through the corks. The labels were long gone but the bottles were still intact. MacPhee wondered whether the undrinkable contents could nevertheless have some value. He sent the bottles to Christie's, the auctioneers, and in 1987 eight bottles from the Politician were sold for £500 to £800 apiece. Since then, the value has increased enormously. The mythical shipwreck has by no means been forgotten by bidders at Christie's auction house.

CalMac from Oban to South Uist

It's April. The CalMac ferry, MV The Sea of the Hebrides, sets sail from Oban, bound for South Uist. Last time I visited the island, I biked over the stone causeway from Eriskay, crossing the sound where the Politician still lies rusting on the ever-shifting sandy sea floor. On the way I paid a visit to Eriskay's ponies, roaming freely among the heather. A good-humoured race which almost disappeared because they were made redundant by tractors. Ponies used to be found extensively on all the islands, but Eriskay's isolation meant that the race did not cross with other breeds. However, that did not mean that the genetic material remained untouched by human hands, so to speak. In the old days, according to the Eriskay Pony Society, women and children were responsible for most of the farm work while the men went fishing. There was no place for aggressive animals which were difficult to tame; they simply had to make way for easy-to-handle individuals. Genetic selection led to a race which is comfortable with people and co-operative. By the early 1970s, there were only twenty or so individuals left of a race which was probably already present in the Hebrides when seafaring pirates, whom the Romans called 'Scotti,' came sailing over the Irish Sea and gave Scotland its name. A rescue operation over the past few decades involving a priest and a stallion, and the latter's sperm cells, has led to the hardy pony race now numbering more than 400 animals.

It's a calm crossing today. The swell is gentle, the weather misty. Soon we pass by beautiful old Lismore Lighthouse. The keeper's accommodation looks like a cluster of white-painted Greek houses. The working shifts were not exactly family friendly. The lighthouse keepers lived on Lismore Island six weeks at a time, then two weeks on land with their families, and right back to a new shift of six weeks.

The ferry enters the Sound of Mull, separating Mull from the mainland. As we sail out into the open sea, heading for South Uist, I make out the silhouette of another lighthouse in the misty landscape on starboard side. It stands in a spectacular position on the most westerly point of mainland Great Britain. Ardnamurchan Point.

The lighthouse is built of granite from Mull. Alan Stevenson took three years to build it in the Egyptian style. Egyptian style? Guidebooks on the west coast of Scotland mention the 'Egyptian style' of the lighthouse, as if it were the most natural thing in the world, with no explanation of how North African architecture found its way to this windy point in Scotland. I search for an explanation in several places and soon find the answer.

Egyptian building style and décor had a renaissance from the end of the 1700s. The British were struck by serious Egyptomania after Nelson's victory over Napoleon in the Battle of the Nile in 1798. Now things start to fall into place. It was not coincidental that Queen Victoria ordered an obelisk from the quarry on Mull for Prince Albert's memorial. Obelisks were a natural choice considering the fashion for all things Egyptian at the time. When the Suez Canal was opened in 1869, Egyptian fever reached new heights in Great Britain. Obelisks, sphinxes, and Cleopatras popped up everywhere. That Alan Stevenson chose to design an Egyptian-inspired lighthouse suddenly makes sense. Also, in many ways Alan shared the same dreams as his nephew, Robert Louis. The difference between R.L.S. and Alan was that Alan, the engineer, never bothered or dared to rebel against his father Robert. The patriarch in the family, Robert regarded it as a personal betrayal if his descendants did not build lighthouses. So, Alan kept quiet. He hid his artistic leanings, in contrast to his nephew. He wrote his poems in secret, and read Dante and Don Quixote when isolated by stormy weather on one or another lighthouse, giving him a spate of relief from building.

He also developed a friendship with the poet William Wordsworth, and through a lengthy exchange of letters the friends discussed literature and poetry. Wordsworth himself said that Alan's recognition was much more important to him than that of others. Alan, on his side, must have been happy and proud when he received small gifts from the famous author: his autograph, a lock of hair, and laurel leaves from his garden.

Perhaps Alan Stevenson had doubts about his own talent. Or could it be that he felt able to express his aesthetic talents through designing beautiful lighthouses?

As for example, Ardnamurchan, ornately decorated both inside and out with 'un-necessary' detail, such as a brass lion's head and writhing sea snakes?

MV The Sea of the Hebrides leaves Ardnamurchan and Mull behind. The ferry has a slight northwesterly direction, heading towards the little village of Lochboisdale on South Uist. In summertime the ferry is usually packed full. Now, in April, passengers are few and far between, and only five vehicles are parked on the salty, green-painted car deck.

A865

The hull of the big car ferry almost touches land on both sides as it enters the narrow fjord towards Lochboisdale on South Uist. Sharp rocks hide both below and above water, and they are notorious for tearing apart sailboats with ease.

As I drive onto land I choose to disobey the *Rough Guide*. It warns travellers not to make the mistake of driving only on the main road, A865, which runs the length of the island like a spine. I am trying to reach the ferry leaving from the little island of Berneray, further north, and I have no time for long detours

Smoking salmon, Hebridean smokehouse, North Uist

to the coast. No, today I'm going northwards, crossing the causeways over to the islands of Benbecula and North Uist to Berneray. There, a second CalMac ferry will take me to the home of tweed and stone circles, the Siamese twin islands of Harris and Lewis.

All I see as I drive along the A865 are freshwater lochs, peat bogs and hills to the east. Not a single glimpse, as I speed determinedly northwards, of the white sands along the coastline, and which the *Rough Guide* claims are among the most beautiful in the whole region.

Leaving Catholic South Uist, I continue over the causeway to the isle of Benbecula, which lies at the point of religious convergence between the southern Catholic island and the Presbyterian Protestant islands in the north. The *Rough Guide* has this to say about Benbecula: 'Blink, and you might not even notice the pancake-flat island Benbecula.' Reading on, the description does not become any more flattering: Many travellers just follow the main road through the island, which is just less than eight kilometres long. Not a bad idea, according to the guidebook, since the island has been thoroughly destroyed by the presence of the Royal Artillery after the war. Until recently, those working in the Royal Artillery made up half the population. Poor Benbecula.

I spent a couple of weeks on this 'destroyed island' in the mid-1980s, near Balivanich, the ugly, grey main town on Benbecula, again, according to the aforementioned guidebook. I have only good memories from the holiday. Driving through Benbecula now years later, I can endorse in many ways what the guidebook says. But what if the writers had spent some extra time here? Would they have seen anything else except the ugliness? Travelling in the Hebrides, like anywhere else, is not only about enjoying surroundings of natural beauty. A journey is also about memorable meetings with individuals; unexpected happenings which, when musing over the day in the evening, you conclude perhaps a little surprised, that yes, this *has been* a good day. In spite of rusty car wrecks, disintegrating tyres and ugly concrete houses. Even the cold war's grey military buildings fade away. For my own part, they were wiped from my memory.

According to a survey on the depopulation of the Outer Hebrides, the town of Balivanich is in fact one of the few places where people still seem to remain. They have reason to be very optimistic, say the folks staying in the ugly buildings they inherited from the British Air Force. Balivanich manages to attract young women, and this is the only place on the island where there are more women than men. Young women mean children, primary schools and a viable community. The recipe for Benbecula's success is cheap housing and employment opportunities for women, as for example at the hospital in Balivanich. On the other islands we find the opposite: a surplus of young men. The women leave, there are too few job opportunities, and the recreational activities are primarily adapted to the needs of men – it's few and far between aerobic workouts on the western seaboard.

Troublesome Conservation

From North Uist, a short causeway leads to little Berneray. The name is of Norse origin, perhaps 'Bjorn's Island' after a man, or 'Bear's Island.' When the road connection was opened in 1999 by the Crown Prince-in-eternally-waiting, Prince Charles, Berneray's home page announced: 'The prince, well known for his strong views on conservation and design, praised the way the causeway blended into its setting and the provision of facilities like otter culverts.' The prince had particularly noticed the otter tunnels built under the road to prevent the animals from being run over by cars. The shy creatures had even got their own traffic sign: a triangular warning with a picture of an otter.

It was not by coincidence that the prince had been invited to cut the ribbon. In 1987 he had visited the island for the first time, *incognito*, and had stayed with a farming couple in the hopes of understanding more of the lives of crofters. He planted potatoes, herded sheep, and cut hay. The prince was able to live and work in peace from journalists: Berneray looked after him. That must have been an unforgettable experience for the heir to the throne.

The same year that Prince Charles cut the ribbon, Scottish National Heritage (SNH), the government-based conservancy organisation, caused anger and resignation among the inhabitants of Berneray. SNH had proposed that three-quarters of Berneray should be categorised as 'A Site of Special Scientific Interest,' SSSI. Berneray has large areas of *machair*. From the month of May, the *machair* is transformed into a flowering carpet. Daisies, clover, wild orchids and buttercups bloom consecutively from May to September. The *machair* also has another advantage: When it is cropped short by grazing sheep, it's God's gift to golfers, and what must be the world's most unsnobbish of golf courses.

So why the interest in preserving the *machair*? The fragile grass carpet is a vital grazing ground for over-wintering Canadian barnacle geese and the local grey geese. Roots from grass and flowering plants on the *machair* also form an effective barrier, keeping the ever-expanding sand in check and preventing erosion. If the *machair* disappears, the blowing sands will take over valuable agricultural land, as is happening on the isle of Tiree. But the sparse, flowering carpet is constantly under threat from thoughtless walkers with tractor soles, cyclists with off-road tyres, and cars driving down to the beach. The local people and the SNH both agree that all this is not good. But from this to becoming a designated SSSI is just 'not on.'

So why the fight between SNH and the local population? Being a conservation area would mean, in practice, that most small farmers would have to comply with multiple restrictions as to how they must farm the land and use the grazing areas, and when and where they can plant. 'But why on earth should somebody come from the outside and teach us how to look after our own island?' ask the very upset islanders. No one knows the nature here better than us, and no one can

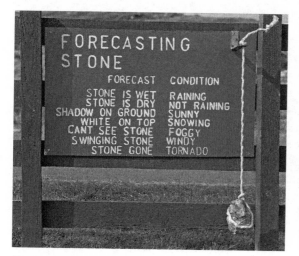

Signs, Berneray

look after it better. It's *because* of us, not in spite of us, that we have preserved the natural environment so well!

SNH tries to calm the crofters down. They will have special concessions, so they don't need to apply for permission every time they graze their animals or fertilise their fields. But the promises from SNH appear to fall on deaf ears and are met with suspicion. It seems that no sooner have the crofters finally got control over their own land, when they are confronted by a new threat: the nature conservancy aristocracy, which increasingly more makes the decisions in the Hebrides.

I have finally arrived at my destination: the ferry pier on Berneray. There's no sign of the CalMac ferry. It's raining and windy. Neither is there a single car queuing in the marked lanes. A saying in Gaelic goes: 'Those who wait long for a ferry will at one or another time get over to the other side.' A nearby little café, the Lobster Pot Tearoom, has unfortunately just closed. A cheery elderly couple, who I suppose must own the café, inform me that the staff went home at half-past four. They gave up. Not a single scone or cup of tea had found their way into waiting passengers.

Ferries on a Sunday

Berneray's home page informs tourists that public transport is non-existent on Sundays. Except for the ferries, which now sail on the day of rest in spite of many protests and a lot of fuss. On the 9th of April 2006, the ferry from Berneray to Harris undertook the first Sunday sailing. The reporter Milmo from *The Independent* reported that the passengers were met with a line of tape on their arrival at Harris: 'Caution Keep Out.' The pier was completely deserted. A strong protest and boycott by the many islanders on Harris who regarded the sailing as an insult against the Sabbath day. The sinful travellers were confronted by a poster when they landed: 'Exodus: Remember the Sabbath Day to Keep it Holy.'

The minister Andrew Coghill, from the Christian Lord's Day Observance Society, led the islanders' campaign against the CalMac ferry company. According to him, 90% of those who had expressed an opinion on the matter of Sunday sailings were against them. 'And,' he told *The Independent*, 'the notion that we need to move into the 21st century is a patronising stance that we're quite familiar with.' In the same article, Morag Monroe from Harris points out that 'It's not just church people who are opposed, but also those who have come to appreciate a day of relaxation and a chance to be together with their families for one day.' And, she added, 'in the end I see this as being detrimental to tourism because it will wreck the way of life which attracts visitors here.' Others, such as Archie Campbell from North Uist, lobbied *for* Sunday ferries. He told *The Independent*, 'People now have the choice to travel to Harris on a Sunday and they should have the right to exercise that choice. This is all about freedom of choice. It's a historic day.' Others on board saw the voyage as a victory against what they consider 'the stifling Christian fundamentalism of the Sabbatarians,' to cite the newspaper.

Finally, some cars join me at Berneray pier. It doesn't feel so lonely anymore and there's the little ferry coming as well. The captain must have intimate knowledge of the sound between Berneray and Harris. The ferry is confronted by an obstacle course, weaving among thousands of rocks, over and under water. They are accurately marked with buoys and lights.

On the crossing to Harris, I hear by their accents that many of the passengers are American. Perhaps they are returning to trace their roots with the help of the numerous heritage centres which have sprung up, generated by popular demand. There, for a fee, they can be helped in patching together fragments from their forefathers' lives. Old pictures. A letter on yellowing, fragile paper. A birth certificate. And if they're lucky, the Americans will return home with a clearer understanding of who they are and where they come from.

Sunlight and Quicksand

Leverburgh, Harris. The little township is named after Lord Leverhulme, who bought South Harris in 1919. He had big plans for the place. The entrepreneur employed local people, and built, among other things, a pier, a fish canning factory, a herring smoking shed, and houses. All this in spite of the many warnings from the local fishermen that it was too dangerous to fish in the rock-strewn sound. Lord Leverhulme died suddenly of pneumonia in 1925, the year after the first catch of herring was landed in the town, which had changed its name from Obbe, in honour of the business magnate. Today, the somewhat misplaced Scandinavianlooking wooden houses still stand as a monument to the optimistic visionary, and obstinate 'King of Sunlight,' Lord Leverhulme, founder of the international Unilever concern, and maker of those ubiquitous yellow bars of 'Sunlight' soap.

My landlady, Catherine Morrison, meets me on the pier and explains how I can find the house. 'Just go in. Everything is open.' This is one of the reasons why people move to the Outer Hebrides. Security. No locked doors, bicycles or cars.

The coastline along the west coast of Harris is spectacular. The ocean is more overwhelming than the Inner Hebrides. There is nothing to catch your eye: no 'skerries,' tiny rocky islands above or below the water. And no landmasses separate the Hebrides from the American continent, apart from small islands and rocks like St Kilda and Rockall. By Scarista Beach and the golf course which ends in the sand dunes, the rollers thunder in, white foam spewing over land and making fluffy dots on the huge beach. It's naked, beautiful, and disturbing. There's nothing to hide behind, and no calm hidden coves.

The door is indeed open when I arrive at Seilebost. A glassed veranda looks out on the tidal bay lying between the house and Luskentyre on the other side. At low tide, you can almost walk right across the bay. Well, that's what I thought until I tried it some days later. The water soon came up to my knees. My toes went white with cold and the rivulets which the tide had dug soon deepened to rivers. An Englishman I met the same day warned me there could be quicksand in areas like this. 'And do you know what you should do if you're stuck in quicksand?' He gave me a stern look. 'You lie back and shout for help.'

Luskentyre

The following day I cycle to Luskentyre. It's raining and windy. It is Sunday and deserted, deserted, deserted. Earlier today, there was a troupe of cars with men in suits and ties, and wives in their best coats, all on their way to the Sunday service. Around 40% are churchgoers in the Outer Hebrides, in comparison to 8% in the rest of the country. Not so long ago most people here began these rituals every Saturday, the day before the Sabbath: peat and water were brought into the house and the Sunday dinner was prepared.

I've met people who still follow this custom, in a modernised version. A sixty-year old woman told me that she was a member of the church society, *The Free Church Continued*. It separated from the mother church, *The Free Church*, some years ago, and according to her, the dissenters adhered more strictly to the Bible. She was brought up as a Catholic, but, she said enthusiastically, 'Catholicism is so complicated, but the teachings of The Free Church Continued are so simple. Everything is there, in the Book!' And according to the Book, the day of rest is holy. That's that. Thus she never did housework on a Sunday or made a meal, and the radio and TV were left in peace. With one exception. 'I listen to the Sunday service on the radio.' Her husband was also a member of the same church community but stretched the limits a bit more. 'My husband sometimes watches TV on a Sunday, but he's quick to turn it off if his mother is around. She would have been very upset.'

The road is still quiet. Maybe the churchgoers are having the supper which was prepared yesterday. The sandy bay at Seilebost suddenly and without warning transforms into a completely different landscape. Grey stones lie strewn on grey rock as if an angry giant had thrown around boulders in this moonscape. There is not a tree in sight, only brown heather and lichen-covered stone. The western sky lights up over sea, and at the same time the wind dies down. The mist rises, and the sheep, standing still in silent groups, gradually re-appear, as if they had been waiting for a change in weather. They have black faces; hardy Blackface sheep. Their white bodies are decorated, or mutilated, according to view, with blue and yellow paint. Sheep farmers identify their sheep from others by spraying their animals with gay spots of orange, red, blue or green.

The white, beautiful beach in Luskentyre is one of the most frequently mentioned places in the Outer Hebrides. All the houses around here are well maintained; there's not a single rusty old car wreck to be seen in any of the gardens, a common sight in both Uist and Benbecula. An article I read some years ago, about the difference between centre and periphery, claims that wherever you are in the world, you know you're in one of those places when car wrecks start appearing in the gardens. So what makes a place a periphery? Luskentyre is out of the way enough to be one, but lacks the obligatory car wrecks and old tyres. Could it be that those living here gradually come to see the landscape through the eyes of visitors from more central areas? Is this the process, transformation of periphery to centre?

An Encounter with a Weaver

'D. J. & M. D. Mackay Luskentyre Harris Tweed Company,' reads the text on a green sign next to the road, past the churchyard. Donald John and Maureen Mackay's loom shed and tweed outlet. Real Harris Tweed is stocked here. The weaver Donald John has just come home from New York where he attended a Scottish sales exhibition as part of Tartan Week.

A casual passer-by could be fooled into thinking that the modest premises indicate this is an insignificant local shop where the proprietor weaves to put food on his plate. But some years ago, Donald John received a call from the shoe manufacturer Nike. They wanted to make shoes—out of Harris Tweed. 'We need around 10,000 metres of material,' said Nike. Donald John could barely believe his ears.

Donald John has been a weaver all his life. Like his father. And his grandfather. And like all the others working in the craft trade on the islands, he claims that he never learnt the job. Watching the shuttle going back and forth was a part

Tweed weaver Donald John Mackay, Harris

of his upbringing. He is paid between £12 and £17 per metre, depending on the quality. Machine-woven cotton fabric is sold for a fivefold sum by interior design companies. 'Isn't it possible to get higher prices?' I ask in disbelief, indignant at the underpayment. 'Well, if you put up the price, then there's the risk that… I don't know, I don't know, we're holding on like this anyway, so…'

Hairy rolls of material lie stacked on wide shelves. A tweed jacket dangles from a coat hanger; tweed caps lie spread across a workbench. Shoulder bags in a classic black-and-white herringbone pattern hang on a hook. Donald John shows me the only pair of Nikes he has left. He did have two pairs but he donated one of them to an auction to raise funds for the victims of the tsunami in December 2004. The bidders queued up because the shoes had already become collectors' items.

Among the rolls of fabric, I recognise the Nike pattern. 'One moment.' Donald John fetches a magnifying glass and holds it up in front of the green tweed. On the other side of the thick glass, an undergrowth of thin, colourful threads shoots up.

I am taken aback and study the material without the magnifying glass. It looks green again. 'This is what makes tweed so unique,' says DJ, as he is known. 'Every thread of wool that's spun is in turn made up of five or six colours. It goes back to the times when wool was dyed with plants and people didn't have enough dyestuff to colour larger amounts than, say, five kilos. But then they maybe had to dye twenty-five kilos, so they had to spin yarn in different colours.'

Harris Tweed got its colour from the fearless flora that thrive in the Outer Hebrides. The roots of water lilies which float on the small *lochans,* or pools, give black; lichen scraped off grey rock make a rich, reddish tint; heather flowers provide a pastel green; the ribwort plantain yields blue; yellow groundsel serves up a lemon shade; while willow leaves offer a soft yellow. These plants, one sort at a time, naturally, ended up in a large three-legged pot, and were left to simmer with the wool until an experienced woman nodded and said, 'Yes, now we've got the right shade.' Then on to the next colour.

'What makes the fabric so special is its vividness, the *vibrancy,* it makes it *alive.'* Donald John's grey eyes become alive too, in step with his enthusiasm for the excellence of tweed. The combinations of colours were often kept as secret recipes. Traditionally, tweed was frequently either plain or undyed. It was only later that tweed became almost synonymous with the herringbone pattern, the black-and-white zigzag design.

Today there are over 700 colours to choose between, according to Donald John. Synthetic colours took over from vegetable dyes long ago. The vegetable dyes were too cumbersome, and besides you never really knew how they would turn out. Nobody could have full control over the plants' interaction with the wool.

From Famine to Catwalk

The 'Harris Tweed' brand was born out of hunger and poverty in the 1800s. The potato blight came in full force from 1846, and some years later, the *Inverness Advertiser* newspaper reported that the poor of Harris survived only thanks to the compassion of their neighbours and shellfish they gathered along the shore. But an extraordinary number of people had suffered sudden death. This aroused the journalist's suspicion: Were people actually starving to death out there on the edge of the ocean? The newspaper blamed the owner of Harris, Lady Dunmore, and Her Majesty Queen Victoria, for being completely unaware of the consequences of the famine.

How accurate was this assertion? The tweed industry was commercialised precisely around the time when Alexander and Catherine Murray, the Earl and Countess of Dunmore, owned Harris. But according to the 'bible' of Harris Tweed, the thick blue book, *The Islanders and the Orb,* by Janet Hunter, the facts end there, with different versions of the story taking over. A lesser-known version came from

Lady Dunmore's son. His notes report that starving women from Harris used to knock on the door of the Dunmore estate to sell their home-woven tweed to her ladyship. The material was inspected, weighed, measured and paid for, and in the autumn the rolls of fabric were sent to the mainland and distributed to dealers in England and Scotland. According to her son, this took place from 1839, before the great famine disaster that lasted from 1846 to 1850. So how could the *Inverness Advertiser* accuse Lady Dunmore of ignoring the people on her estate who were slowly turning into skeletons; the childrens' protruding knees, the elderly bedbound, and the mothers unable to breastfeed their newborns? If her son's version is true, Lady Dunmore was not unaware of the famine, and tried to raise funds for the hungry.

But it is not this version that has been mythologised, writes Hunter. The popular account of the birth of the Harris Tweed industry has been repeated, somewhat uncritically it could well be said, in books, articles and official reports, as well as by the islanders themselves. The story of the Harris Tweed industry has begun to live its own life; it has been repeated so many times that it has been taken as truth. And maybe it is. It goes more or less like this: In 1844, Alexander Murray, Earl of Dunmore, ordered large quantities of Murray tartan tweed, the pattern that identified the Clan Murray. He wanted to dress up the gamekeepers and other employees on the estate. If this is true, Hunter writes, the earl was one of the first estate owners to make his own uniforms for his ghillies, a fashion that soon caught on. When Queen Victoria bought Balmoral four years after the Earl of Dunmore had dressed up his staff, the cult of the Highlands and of tartan went into full swing.

I asked the genealogist Bill Lawson on Harris whether the Scottish clan system had any meaning at all in today's society. 'Only if you sell tartan!' Bill shook with hilarity but pulled himself together between the salvos of laughter. 'Maybe clans have some meaning in some parts of the mainland, if the clan chieftain lives locally,' he conceded. 'But not here. How much tartan do you see around you, except at weddings? Most tartans are made up anyway. Many were invented in the 1800s, and now even football clubs have their own tartans too!' He is right. Glasgow Rangers have their own tartan. So does Aberdeen Football Club.

So in the 1800s, the Highlands and the Western Isles were very popular, and summer guests from the upper classes spent weeks on estates and at castles. The ladies painted, went for walks or embroidered, while the men cut down bracken, stomped through the heather, and forced their way through the burns—'Ah! Such splendid clear air!'—and hunted grouse and deer, or fished for salmon in the rivers. 'Jolly fine tweed, sir,' they might have said, admiring the Earl of Dunmore's tweed suit. The ladies might have clasped their pale, well-manicured hands; they could quite fancy their husband wearing a suit like that! Soon tweed was in demand in both London and Edinburgh. Lady Dunmore was delighted; this meant earnings for the poor islanders knocking on her door and begging for help. Their problem was that they did not have the necessary means or contacts to sell their material. But she did, and she used them, gladly even, is the impression we get. She sold the material to friends in higher circles and established contacts with firms in the big cities. And the prices and the demand grew. The Harris Tweed industry had begun.

A Peculiar Odour

As mentioned, there are several variants of the story about how Harris Tweed found its way onto the catwalk in New York, Tokyo and Paris. In any case, it is indisputably true that tweed soon became popular in the British upper classes. The rough, warm and water-repellent woollen fabric in natural colours was well-suited to the image of a rugged hunter or fly fisherman. Tweed jackets, tweed trousers and tweed hats became standard attire, whether for grouse hunting or for the pursuit of political careers.

In Harris man Finlay J. MacDonald's nostalgic and realistic autobiography, *Crowdie and Cream*, he tells of the weak but unmistakable odour of wool and urine that spread throughout the upper house of the British Houses of Parliament on damp days. The smell emanated mostly from the eldest aristocratic members of the House of Lords. And no, they had not been caught short. The scent, which was discreet, it must be admitted, came from their high-quality tweed jackets, made in the old way and intended to last for their whole lives, at least. Perhaps the jackets were even inherited from their fathers, just like their titles and seats in the Lords. Now, readers may wonder what urine has to do with tweed. In *Crowdie and Cream*, MacDonald recounts how everyone in the family, as well as neighbours, guests and friends, were asked to use 'the tub' if they had to pass water. 'Where do you keep the tub?' was the Harris equivalent of the more mundane 'Excuse me, where is the bathroom?' The tub, a large tank that stood in the barn or the outhouse, was slowly filled up and the contents left to sit, until they reeked of a sharp stench that could chase a cat out to sea: ammonia. The foul-smelling liquid was ready for the job of dissolving the lanolin in the greasy, ready-woven woollen fabric, as well as fixing the vegetable dyes. On pre-war Harris, urine was the simplest and cheapest way of obtaining ammonia.

When the tweed leaves the weaver's loom, it is stiff and hard. For the material to be useable for clothing and blankets, the stiffness and excess oil has to be beaten out properly. By waulking. In his book, *Back to the Wind, Front to the Sun*, the late Angus MacLeod, from the neighbouring island of Lewis, tells his memories of waulking as the form of social gathering that it was. The women sat in pairs straight across from each other around improvised table tops, and the warm, wet and oily tweed, reeking of urine from the tubs, was beaten and kneaded to rhythmic waulking songs until it had been cleansed of superfluous oil, shrunk and twisted to the correct length and breadth, and softened so that it would be good to wear.

The shrinking would ensure that the tweed jacket never tightened on its owner's shoulders, even if it became damp. And if one day it *should* feel tighter, that could not be blamed on the tweed.

Today, waulking, urine in the tweed, and inherited titles in the House of Lords are all anachronisms, but perhaps a few lords still saunter around the Houses of Parliament wearing a hand-beaten tweed jacket from the interwar period, emanating a faint fragrance of urine.

The Orb

Thanks to its increasing popularity, Harris Tweed was literally copied in east and west. Soon 'Harris Tweed' jackets cropped up in Japan, and much later, when 'Harris Tweed' became a registered trademark, some Italians tried to sell 'Harrys Tweed.' When this was discovered by the Harris Tweed Association, which hovered protectively over the emerging brand, the Italian firm tried to register Harrys Tweed in Brazil instead. Without success.

Imitations had already started to appear at the end of the 1800s. Material from all over Britain was advertised as homemade, handmade 'Harris Tweed.' Only imagination, daring and business acumen set limits for the marketing of the imitations. In Glasgow, 'smelling-houses' were built, where peat fires were lit to give the tweed an authentic whiff of the Outer Hebrides. There, true enough, the peat smoke hung thickly under the roofs of straw and heather. A more modern version appeared much later: spray bottles with imitation peat-fragrance. You read correctly, spray bottles which showered the tweed jackets before they ended up in the chain stores.

If Harris Tweed were not immediately registered as a brand, the name would soon become a generic description the same as cheddar cheese, which could be made by anyone anywhere and to any quality standard. Thanks to the combined efforts of engaged people, the brand name of 'Harris Tweed' was registered in 1910, certified as 'The Orb.' The Orb design was, and still is, a globe surmounted by the Maltese cross. The first rolls of Harris Tweed stamped with The Orb mark came off the looms in 1911, guaranteeing the real thing and high quality. The original definition of the brand guaranteed that Harris Tweed had been hand woven in the weaver's home. The local virgin wool had to be hand spun and dyed in the Outer Hebrides. The Orb label could be used in all islands of the Outer Hebrides, not just Harris.

However, soon it was only the puritans who held strictly to the rule that the wool had to be hand spun. The Orb criteria were readjusted in 1934 to permit machine-spun wool. But the wool must still be spun on the Outer Hebrides, and must not be imported from the mainland.

Not everybody agreed with this adjustment, and there was a loophole in the law. It was still unclear, in a purely legal sense, whether or not one could call a material 'Harris Tweed' when the wool did not originate in the Hebrides. Such tweed would, true enough, not be covered by The Orb certification mark, but nobody owned the terms 'Harris' and 'Tweed.' And was it fair that the spinning factories on the Hebrides should have a monopoly on the sale of the wool? Wool from the mainland was cheaper, said some of the weavers, and they continued to sell the material as Harris Tweed without, of course, The Orb mark.

The conflict ended in court. The case started in 1960, at the same time as the Champagne producer J. Bollinger led a court case against the Spanish wine merchant Costa Brava Wine company, for selling 'Spanish champagne.' Several of the arguments used against Costa Brava were also applicable to the case of Harris Tweed. Even although it could be assumed that wine experts could differentiate champagne from the Champagne district, from champagne from Spain, less knowledgeable wine drinkers could easily be led astray. There was a considerable possibility that they would assume the bubbly golden drink they were swallowing was real champagne. Obviously, if what was happening in the Costa Brava was allowed to continue, very soon 'champagne' would be the generic name for an effervescent drink that had never seen France, let alone the Champagne district, in the same way that 'cola' or 'hoover' had lost their associations to the original product. Bollinger and the other producers won. The court case on Harris Tweed concerned exactly the same question: Did customers get what they thought they were paying for?

The judge, Lord Hunter, thought that the name 'Harris Tweed' had an aura of home-woven, handmade products. Those who bought a Harris Tweed jacket did not buy any old jacket! Wearing this piece of clothing gave the owner a sense of being part of a tough, romantic, exclusive, wilderness club; he even straightened up and walked about with more bravado than usual. Furthermore, many customers buying Harris Tweed felt that they were contributing to the welfare of the inhabitants of these distant islands. The weavers could augment their income, which they otherwise would struggle to glean from the infertile soil or the stormy seas. A sort of emergency assistance, in other words. The judgement in 1946 proclaimed that the name 'Harris Tweed' could be used only according to the definition from 1934 which had qualified The Orb trademark. The period of imported wool from the mainland was over.

Harris Tweed has always had an up-and-down career. The whole industry would probably have gone under long ago if it had not been for the various public donations during hard times when the market for tweed fell sharply. During the catastrophic year of 1975, the Harris Tweed Association concluded that machine-woven tweed was the only solution. The weavers thought that things had gone too far: degenerate into machine weaving! They voted against the proposal.

'What would have been the consequences if the weavers had voted for the machines in 1976?' I ask Donald John in Luskentyre. 'I'm in constant contact with the material; it's not rolling out at a hundred metres an hour,' he says. 'So it's much better than machine-woven material. The weaver notices details because the material moves slowly in front of him, so if something is wrong, he can correct it.' We are in the workshop in the green-painted corrugated-iron shed. There are two looms here. One is threaded with a multi-coloured warp. Donald John sits down at the other one, working the pedals of the Hattersly, the loom which was equipped with pedals after the First World War to provide armless soldiers with an income. The shuttle moves quickly backwards and forwards. A tiny knot appears and I understand what he means. Not a single flaw escapes his eagle eye, and the mistake is fixed before the shuttle goes off again. In a few minutes, he has woven several centimetres of new tweed material. 'Only two feet on the pedals! No electric looms, that's part of the deal,' says Donald John. 'Oh yes, yes, yes, very much so. The natural stuff always wins in the end.'

Emigration

Catherine Morrison, my landlady, also runs a bed and breakfast. When she was a child, she had to move to the mainland at the age of twelve to go to secondary school, as some children from the Hebrides still do. She went on to take higher education and worked for many years in a big city. Contrary to many others, she returned to make her home here in Harris. The question she now asks herself is: Who will take over her little business in the future? Her children and grandchildren live on the mainland. And who will care for her when the day comes she can no longer care for herself?

A research report, *Outer Hebrides Migration Study*, confirms that she is not alone regarding her concerns. The Outer Hebrides score high on some gloomy statistics: Young women, who often work in the caring sector and in old-age homes, are leaving the islands at a greater rate than young men. By 2019, the proportion of young women of fertile age is predicted to fall to around one quarter if something drastic is not done. There are, of course, some incomers to the islands, but over 70% are men and many are also pensioners who in turn will increase pressure on the already hard-pressed care services. The population of the Outer Hebrides has the highest proportion of elderly people in the whole of Scotland. In 2007 the average age was around forty-two years. In 2019 it will be over 45 if nothing short of a revolution happens. Catherine has every reason to question the future.

It's not only people disappearing from the Hebrides. Soon the sheep will probably be few and far between as well. One evening, sitting in Catherine's glass veranda, she serves me the Scottish national dish, haggis with prune sauce. The tidal bay outside changes shape and colour continually. Catherine and I are discussing a way of life that has been so important for the islands: sheep farming.

Gamekeeper Malcolm McPhail, Morsgail Lodge, Lewis

Previously, sheep dealers came to buy sheep from the local markets. Now there's an end to this practice, since the buyers must pay to transport the sheep back to the mainland. The business is no longer profitable. It's also not helpful that the price of wool is poor. The story from the 1800s is repeating itself, with a population which is in the hands of powers far outside the islands. The market. CalMac. EU. Nature conservationists.

Tarbert

In the meantime, the sheep work hard to keep the vegetation in check on the Outer Hebrides, both where they're welcome and where they are not: for example, when they break into Catherine's garden and help themselves to the green goodies. Before they are chased out, they manage to munch some of the brave young plants taking the risk of germinating in the spring weather.

The one-track road between Seilebost and Tarbert, the 'main town' of Harris, forces its way between boulders, *lochans,* and steely grey mountains. Finally, it dives down towards a sea loch to Tarbert, lying innermost in the bay. The little grey township melds with the barren hills. The CalMac ferry going back and forth to Skye is docked at the pier. The huge boat seems out of proportion against the backdrop of the little town. I park in the narrow main road, looking for a grocery store, and soon find the anonymous shop which has not bothered to advertise itself with a sign. 'Sorry, we don't have kitchen rolls and chicken today,' the lady at the counter apologises. 'They will come with the ferry on Wednesday.' Down at the harbour, I get a fishing rod and some nails from a ramshackle boathouse which serves as the ironmongers. The fellow who is serving me takes a handful of nails out of a huge sack, weighing them carefully on large old-fashioned scales. I ask for fishing hooks; he apologises, they don't really have a big selection of hooks right now: 'There was a storm, and the ferry carrying the hooks didn't come.'

A Bug on Stornoway Airport

Ferries are not the only means of communication which connect Harris to the mainland. Planes are also useful. That is if they actually get on their wings. When I returned from Tarbert, Catherine had bad news about the plane on which my travelling companion was to leave the following morning. He had booked the flight from Stornoway, the main town on the isle of Lewis, but now Catherine had heard on the local radio that the airport was closed because of a 'bug,' an illness affecting the personnel. A telephone call to British Airways on the mainland revealed that they were unaware of the airport shutdown far out to sea. 'The airport is CLOSED?? Because of a BUG??' shouted BA on the mainland, disbelievingly, over the telephone. BA phoned Stornoway but could not make contact. There was nothing else to do other than to travel to Stornoway the next day, a trip taking one and a half hours, to see if the airport had re-opened.

The following morning at the crack of dawn we set off, still not knowing whether the airport had opened again after the mini-epidemic among the ground staff. At Tarbert, Harris is almost cut in half; only a thin strip of land connecting South Harris with North Harris. And the name Tarbert means precisely that, isthmus. A piece of land over which folk, from time immemorial, have dragged boats to save them travelling long diversions. From the east, waves from the Minch roll in against the grey moonscape on Harris, which Stanley Kubrick chose as the location for *2001: A Space Odyssey*. From the west, the swell from the Atlantic crashes against the breakwater protecting the football field of Tarbert's junior school.

Leaving the town behind, we drive up into the impressive mountains of North Harris. Suddenly we find ourselves on a good two-lane road; these must be the best roads in the Hebrides. Soon a sign appears in the stony desert: 'Welcome to Lewis.' This in spite of the reality that Harris and Lewis are in fact the same island, separated from each other only by invisible borders drawn up by various landowners. Does this border mean anything in practice? According to the author Finlay J. MacDonald, there is apparently a difference: 'A Harrisman is a Harrisman, and a Lewisman is a Lewisman, and neither would have it differently!' So what then is a Lewisman? A joke about the men of few words from this island goes like this: 'Have you heard about the man from Lewis who loved his wife so much he almost told her.'

An hour later we are driving through Stornoway, the capital of Lewis, and the only real town in the Hebrides. The planes are flying! They are lifting from the runway, nose towards the east. The chap behind the desk assisting the queue, however, suddenly disappears as the passengers are about to check their baggage. Rumours abound; maybe he is in the toilet? He is gone for some time. The queue starts to get anxious, shuffling feet, glancing at watches—what on earth is happening? When he suddenly reappears, a passenger asks if he is standing in the right queue; there's no irony in the question. 'We're doing the best we can,' the man from the toilet barks. It is highly unusual to hear anybody from the islands talking like this. I forgive him on the spot, supposing that the bug is still on the rampage in his body. It must have been a powerful infection that attacked the airport.

For a while I lived in the delusion that the closing of the airport was an exceptional event, right until I discovered diverse readers' letters in the newspaper, *Stornoway Gazette*. The letters assert that the ground crew's continual afflictions by mysterious epidemics are giving Lewis a bad reputation, and that the unpredictable closures ruin the plans of everyone trying to run a business here. As if there weren't enough practical barriers on the Outer Hebrides already!

Cairns

From Luskentyre, a path runs right across Harris along a route marked by stone cairns. I have the Atlantic Ocean at my back, and follow a yellow-marked path rising slightly, heading eastwards. The mist lies low over the hills. The cairns mark the old route for funeral processions. It went from east to west. But why, one may ask, did they carry the coffins all that way from the east coast over to the churchyard in Luskentyre on the west coast? The answer is the Clearances. In the 1800s the inhabitants were forcibly evicted from the fertile *machair* landscape on the west coast, to the moon-like landscape of the east. Here, there was no churchyard of course. There was barely enough earth to grow a few potatoes in the shallow soil. Therefore, they had to carry their dear departed several kilometres over the hills to bury them. The cairns indicate where the funeral procession rested, lowered down the coffin, and had some oatcakes and whisky. Stories about funerals in Scotland could fill many books. Sometimes the bearers drank so much whisky before they started, that they even forgot to put the body in the coffin when the wake was over, and arrived at the churchyard empty-handed. Now and then, so much water of life was consumed as they rested by the milestones that they forgot to take the coffin along with them. Something seemed to be missing only when they reached the churchyard.

Today there are forces other than lairds and landowners which prevent people from living on the west coast. Large areas have been identified, by those advising the authorities, to be sites of special scientific interest, SSSI, just like Berneray. Nature is, of course, protected by those measures, but the lack of housing means that schools are closing one by one.

Problematic Farmed Salmon

Employment is the key to settlement on the islands. But is it realistic to think that investors are interested in and would be empathetic towards fragile local communities? Is it at all probable that values other than maximal profit would be considered? Scalpay is a little island connected to Harris by a bridge. In 2000, the Norwegian-owned Stolt aroused hope in the population of Scalpay when they opened the fish-processing factory, Stolt Sea Farms. The organisation Western Isles Enterprises (WIE), which supports initiatives contributing to economic growth in the Outer Hebrides, contributed funding towards a new factory building on the island. Catherine Morrison told me that every man, wife, daughter and son on Scalpay was working shifts in the fish-processing plant. Four years on, the good times were over. Stolt Sea Farms joined together with Norwegian-owned Marine Harvest. The factory moved to the mainland, and those employed lost their jobs. The cost of transporting processed fish to the mainland was apparently too great.

But as the people of Harris pointed out, 'Should not the owners of the factory have known this beforehand?' Instead of cheating the islands of millions!

Some of the anger was directed at WIE, which had in part financed the expensive buildings now being transformed into gigantic, empty ghost houses. In the *Stornoway Gazette*, the boss of WIE, Donnie MacAuley, responded to readers' questions as best he could. One of them went something like this: 'Why don't you just admit that WIE is incompetent to properly support and administer economic initiatives, and that it usually gets involved with firms which fail? Meanwhile, the people can't even get a little financial support to buy a PC.' Donnie MacAuley answered back that it was all a big misunderstanding, that WIE primarily works with economic support agreements. WIE advises those who want to start a business, and then invests in infrastructure. This is just as important. It's been a long time since cash alone was dished out as the main stimulus to business. And in any case, three-quarters of the businesses WIE supports are still going strong. That's above average for the country as a whole. The idea that we support businesses that don't function is just daft!

Some are also on the warpath regarding the way the salmon farming itself is run. The Salmon Farm Protest Group (SFPG) has a ten-point manifesto. The aim is to protect the genetic integrity of the wild salmon stocks in Scottish lochs and rivers against diseases among farmed salmon. In 2007, the SFPG publicised a list of the worst cases of escaped farmed salmon and of fish dying in the cages. Among the five worst firms, three were Norwegian. More than 1,000,000 salmon had escaped or died, according to SFPG. In many cases, the cause was destruction of the fish-farming sites due to Atlantic storms. The angry voice of SFPG's chairman, Bruce Sandison, shines through the text of the press release the group published: 'Farm salmon escapes seriously damage the genetic integrity of our wild fish stocks. Now, for the first time, the fish farmers who allow their salmon to escape will have no place to hide. They will be named and shamed in front of the whole world.'

Salmon farming is still a major enterprise on the Outer Hebrides, in spite of the closing down of the processing factory on Scalpay, and critics like Sandison. On the one hand, many are ambivalent about the fact that salmon farming in Scotland is in Norwegian hands. 'Would Norway have allowed Scotland to administer one of the country's most important natural resources?' ask many Scots. On the other hand, the Norwegian investments provide a lot of jobs. Important, local jobs. A manager of a fish farm had this to say about the ambivalence: 'You don't bite the hand that feeds you. The salmon farms have come to stay. At least,' to quote the honest manager, 'as long as there are enough white fish threatened by extinction in the sea to provide the fodder for the salmon.'

Scenic Cruises

There are, of course, stable business initiatives on Harris, such as the mini-cruises run by Hamish Taylor, the one-man enterprise, Scenic Cruises. Hamish lives in Flodabay on the east coast of Harris. Previously, he worked on oil tankers. Now he's a pensioner, and probably works harder than ever. At least in the summer months. His boat, the MV Catherine, glides silently around among the *skerries*, while Hamish gives the passengers a thorough introduction to the local history of Flodabay, the place where he grew up. He knows every bay, every ruin, and every rock.

When he was four years old, his father died while working in a gold mine in Arusha, Tanzania. The story of how Hamish's father died is the story of the Hebrides: Many have travelled far and wide over the generations. One day I sent an email to Hamish. He had just been to Cyprus and was off to New Zealand in February, planning to pop into Abu Dhabi on the way home to visit his son who works there. There are many stories of tourists visiting the island who, in patronising terms, address stalwart fishermen, weavers or uncommunicative peat-digging farmers as if the islanders didn't know about the discovery of the aeroplane. They are completely unaware that the fisherman, weaver or peat digger has just returned from a textile exhibition in New York. Or a holiday in Abu Dhabi.

Hamish is out in his boat most of the day with his cargo of interested people. 'I love being out with the boat but I don't know how long I will manage to do this. In the middle of summer, I'm out with tourists the whole time. I'm dead tired in the evening.' Hamish shares a fate with many on the Scottish islands. The peak season is short and intense. Even though some especially interested come April to June, and again September through October, the big crowds arrive in July and August. Then, from October to March, things get very quiet again. So when everyone else has summer holidays, Hamish has to keep going. In most of these one-person enterprises, like Catherine Morrison's and Hamish Taylor's, they are more or less on the go round the clock.

Seaweed-covered rocks poke up from the sea around the cement pier where MV Catherine lies at anchor. It's low tide. The seals are lying in their usual position, tails in the air, as if trying to avoid touching the slimy seaweed. They are shy, and when we cast anchor and approach the animals, they glide down into the safety of the sea. 'The water is unusually cold this year,' says Hamish. 'Usually the basking sharks and dolphins arrive in July, but we'll see what happens this year. Even lobsters are difficult to get hold of.' I told him I had just ordered a lobster from a fisherman. 'I know,' laughs Hamish, 'it was my son-in-law who delivered it. We know everything that goes on in this island.'

The Hurricane in 2005

The east coast of Harris is a multitude of bays, rocks and islands. A boat trip with Hamish is like going on a mountain hike with a geologist: We all see the same things, but the geologist sees so much more. The boat takes us out into the open sea. In the evening one can make out the lights on the Isle of Skye to the east. As we pass by an island with a sheer wall going straight down into the sea, Hamish points at a large cleft in the rock. 'It's the hurricane in January 2005 that did that,' he says. 'It was terrifying. It tore off the roof of my neighbour's house. My roof was also damaged by things flying through the air. We knew the storm was coming, but it lasted much longer than we expected.'

South Uist was worst affected. On the 11th of January 2005, the hurricane hit the low-lying west coast. The water level rose several feet. Perhaps because masses of sea water, which previously would have poured between the islands, were now shut out by the causeways, and confounded by a wall of boulders. Some think that those who constructed the roads between the islands did not properly heed the islanders, who had insisted that the causeways needed bigger tunnels to accommodate the mass of water passing through. Another explanation is that erosion of the coastline is causing tidal flooding of the roads.

Whatever the rights and wrongs, on that day in January the ocean kept on rising, and a family of five decided it was time to flee their home. The party consisted of Archie and Murdina McPherson, and their children Andrew, seven years old, and Hannah, five years old, along with Murdina's father, Calum Campbell. They fought their way out in the hurricane, to take refuge with Archie McPherson's family, only a short drive away. They drove off in a little procession of two cars, but never made it. The vehicles were swept out to sea. Campbell was found inside his car, while the couple was found three kilometres away. Many volunteered for the sober task of searching for the children. After a while, the daughter was found near her grandparent's home. The search had to be called off in the evening, but continued to look for the son the following day. Over 1,000 people in this closely-knit community participated in the funeral.

When I was on Harris three years after the tragedy, there were still many talking about the family from South Uist and the hurricane. They spoke of it as a traumatic experience touching everybody on the Outer Hebrides. 'We lost a family' was repeatedly said. It did not make any difference where folk came from, if it was Barra, Harris or any of the other islands. *We* lost a family. No one knows when such destructive powers will hit again. There are few places to shelter or escape to. 'The only thing that's sure,' say the old folks, 'is that there is more wind than before.'

White Slaves

Hamish manoeuvres the boat into a little bay, Finsbay. A colony of common seals lives here, with one or two grey seals amongst them. They stare unremittingly into the camera lens, with eyes which look heavily ringed with kohl. One particular face imprints on the retina because of its expression of endless sorrow. Maybe there *is* some truth, after all, in the Gaelic myth that seals carry the souls of drowned seamen.

In the autumn of 1739, the brig William sailed into Finsbay. Folk in the wee village crowded together, curious about what brought this big vessel to such a deserted place. The captain seemed like a nice fellow and they were invited on board to see the wares which were apparently on sale; there were also rumours of illegal spirits. Children, women, men, the old and the pregnant—when all were finally lured on board, they were then forced below deck. There they found sixty miserable people, whole families, all from the village of Bracadale on Skye.

The brig continued to Loch Portain in North Uist, where the same trick repeated itself and resulted in more kidnappings. However, it was soon evident that not all were welcome on board. The vessel called at the islands of Canna, Rum and Jura, to rid itself of individuals burdensome to the kidnappers: Ten children under five years were separated from their parents and left alone, in addition to an old, sick man, and two very pregnant women. With 111 persons aboard, the brig sailed on to Donaghadee in Ireland, to load supplies for the long voyage to the slave plantations in the British colonies in America.

When the brig anchored in Ireland, women and children were driven into a barn, the men chased into another. In spite of being guarded, or because the guards were bribed, the prisoners managed to escape. That is, those who were strong

194

enough. The old and sick were left behind. William Davidson, the captain of William, was furious, and reported the matter to the police. He ordered the immediate capture of the escapees. They were criminal, he asserted, and condemned to exile in the colonies, a popular punishment at the time. One could be exiled for many crimes: stealing, prostitution, poaching. The police, on the contrary, investigated the ship's log. Only six of the passengers had done something that could be called a crime, and even those breaches of the law were so trivial that they certainly did not qualify for exile. Arrest orders were issued, but not of the kind Davidson and his swain, the chieftain's son, Norman MacLeod of Berneray, had in mind. Now they were the hunted, but to no avail. They had already fled the country. Later there were rumours that two clan chiefs were behind the kidnappings and had tried to sell their own clans-folk as white slaves: Norman MacLeod of Dunvegan and Alexander MacDonald of Sleat.

When slaves from the African continent were taken to the British plantations in droves, they worked side-by-side with white slaves, who were being transported there as far back as the 1600s. Some were being punished for criminal offences. Others were just kidnapped. Children too were slaves, sold by parents no longer able to support them. Perhaps they either turned a blind eye, or hoped for the best for their children. The slave profiteers had told them the children would work as servants in the big house on the huge plantations. An occupation with a future, they were assured.

The Boat Builder John MacAuley

Hamish steers the Catherine back to Flodabay. His cousin, the boat builder and local historian John MacAulay, is in full swing sanding his sail boat. I met John the first time I was in Harris. Or to be more precise, I looked him up. I knew he built boats and was an expert on *birlinns*, the boats used by the clan chiefs to sail around their own territories or visit neighbouring chiefs. *Birlinns* were more or less exact copies of the Norwegian Viking boats called *karver*, specifically designed to sail in shallow, restricted waters. However, the *birlinn* differed from the Viking boats on one important feature: the rudder. The Norwegian boats had side rudders, while the Scottish boats had made an advancement and placed the rudder at the stern.

John invited me to his boat workshop lying opposite his home on the other side of the road. The workshop was a tunnel-shaped leftover from World War II, with walls of green-painted, weathered corrugated iron. The Scottish blue and white flag waved from the roof, and over the door was a sign saying 'Boat builder.' Behind the double door was a beautiful boat in larch wood. John was also working on a bigger project, when time allowed. Outside the workshop stood the beginnings of what would become a true copy of Spray, the boat in which Joshua Slocum was the first to sail solo around the world. The voyage lasted three years. In 1909, both Slocum and Spray disappeared without a trace, leaving many unanswered questions as to what had gone wrong.

We crossed the road to John's lovely stone house, one of the few old well-preserved buildings still in existence in the Outer Hebrides. In contrast to several of the islands in the Inner Hebrides, where many old white-washed cottages are preserved, the architecture on the Outer Hebrides is somewhat lacking in charm, what with all the newer, but drier and more comfortable, bungalows. As we sat in the garden, the conversation turned quickly to the *birlinns*. John gave me a booklet he had written about St Clement's church in Rodel, south on Harris. John MacAulay is interested in the church for a very special reason: A particularly fine carving of a *birlinn*, as they looked once upon a time, is set in a panel over one of the graves in the church. 'Look here,' John said enthusiastically and pointed to an enlarged copy of the *birlinn* from St Clement's, 'you can even see the rope work which goes behind the sails.' Nowadays, no such vessels exist. After the Battle of Culloden in 1746, the clan chiefs were given the order to destroy their *birlinns*, leaving behind no Scottish versions of the Norwegian Gokstad and Oseberg Viking ships.

St Clement's Church

I had visited St Clement's church some days before my boat trip with Hamish. Stormy blasts of wind made it difficult to open the car doors. The stone church is formed as a cross, with a square tower on the west side. The door was unlocked. Inside it was cold and dark. It took some time before my eyes adjusted to the faint light the leaded glass windows grudgingly allowed to filter in. The church is not in use, so there were no carpets, no pews, no pulpit nor electric lights to indicate that I was in the 21st century. Alongside the walls stood two stone coffins. Others were buried under gravestones on the floor. St Clement's is 'the Westminster of the Isles,' the resting place of generations of MacLeod chiefs who once owned Harris, as well as parts of Lewis and Skye. MacAuley writes in his book about St. Clement's that the church could have been built by the first MacLeod chief of Harris, Tormod. His father was Leod, son of Olav the Black, a Kinglet of Man who ruled over Lewis and Harris in the 13th century. When Tormod died, his two sons, Torquil and Tormod, were given the lands of Lewis and Harris, respectively. This, writes MacAuley, could date the building as very early 14th century.

Also according to MacAuley, the oldest known illustration of the church is a relief on a so-called 'beggar's badge.' These badges were usually made of metal, such as lead or copper, and gave poor people license to beg. According to Balfour Paul's book from 1886, these beggar badges were first mentioned in a law passed by the Scottish Parliament in 1424, when strong and artful beggars flooded the country in such huge hordes that begging had to be regulated. The law differentiated between deserving and less deserving vagabonds—those who, through no fault of their own, were poor due to ill health or disability, and those whom the law defined as parasites, 'who, besides other inconveniences which they daily produce in the commonwealth, procure the wrath and displeasures of God for the wicked and ungodly form of life used among them, without marriage or the baptising of a great number of their bairns.' The scroungers were invariably gypsies, fortune-tellers, male and female, wandering university professors, musicians, and the likes. The beggar badge had to be worn so that it was clearly visible, pinned to the outer clothes. People who were caught begging without the badge were to be imprisoned for as long as they could pay for themselves. If this was not an option, their ears were cut off before they were exiled. And if this severe punishment did not work, and the beggar was caught again, he was immediately hanged.

The *birlinn* in St Clement's church is built into the wall, a relief on a stone tablet over the coffin of the eighth MacLeod chieftain, Alasdair Crotach, 'the humpback.' The very one who organised the big outdoor banquet on Skye and, according to oral history, is blamed for the massacre in the Eigg cave in 1577. But by that time, blessed Alasdair had already rested in his stone coffin for many years.

In John MacAuley's opinion, the relief in St Clement's church is probably the best depiction of a *birlinn* existing today. In the darkness I can just make out a square sail, and the holes in the hull indicate that the boat could use seventeen pairs of oars. The *birlinn* was perfect for the waters surrounding the Hebrides. It was easy to navigate in the deep, narrow sea lochs and over the shallow sandy bays. The rowers, writes John in the booklet, fed themselves on a kind of pudding used by fishermen right up until the 1900s: 'a mixture of oatmeal and fish liver which was packed into a part of a sheep's intestine and secured with a knot at each end.' This surprise package was neither boiled nor fried; the rowers just sat on it. The best results were achieved by energetic rowing, when heat and friction generated by warm behinds imparted itself to the contents. Due to the constant kneading, the contents were transformed to a sludgy consistency, which could then be sucked out through a wee hole. Invigorating and healthy.

Ljodhus

The name of the island of Lewis derives from an Old Norse name: Ljodhus, from Leod, or Ljotr, whom the MacLeod clan claim as their founder. On Lewis, about 80% of the place names are Norwegian, but it was a continual struggle to hold on to the Norse colonies. In 1098, King Magnus Barefoot set out on a campaign to reassert his kingship over the western isles: the Hebrides, Orkney and Shetland. Originally, the king had sent ambassadors to the local chiefs to emphasise that on no account should the colonies consider breaking away. But the temptation for the ambassadors, led by Ingemund, was too great. He established his headquarters in Lewis and summoned the chiefs to demand their loyalty. This was a very stupid thing to do. The chiefs would not be dictated to in this way; indeed, they were so disgusted with this self-imposed tyrant that they set fire to his house one night. Those who were not swallowed up by the flames were put to the sword.

Doubtless, Ingemund was a traitor; perhaps he didn't deserve better. But Magnus Barefoot was very displeased that the Norse-Gaelic chieftains had taken the law into their own hands. Therefore, gripping his sword, he sailed from Norway with a large fleet. First he stormed Orkney and imprisoned the two earls who were in charge of Shetland and Orkney, respectively. He appointed his son Sigurd as a kind of local regent, before he continued on to the Hebrides. Through fear, fire and blood, the Scottish islands would be compelled to loyalty. The attack on Lewis and the Hebrides is recorded in the saga of Magnus Barefoot:

In Lewis Isle with fearful blaze
The house-destroying fire plays;
To hills and rock the people fly...

Chessmen

There are few concrete traces left of the Vikings on Lewis, apart from the place names. But on an early spring day in April 1831, Malcolm 'Sprot' MacLeod, from the village of Pennydonald on the west coast of Lewis, made a remarkable discovery. The story was recorded by the minister, Mackenzie, that same year. In a little stone casket, buried in the dunes on the enormous beach of Uig, he found a number of chessmen, almost enough for four sets. They are known as the Lewis chessmen. The seventy-eight pieces still looked new, as if they had never been used, but were on their way to some or other distinguished customer. The solid small sculptures were made of walrus and whale tooth, and some were over ten centimetres tall. A few were really comical, their bulging eyes sending stolen glances aside, instead of staring the player straight in the eyes. Some wore the same clothes as the *berserks*, those famous Norse warriors who fought with great frenzy, and yet others, for some unknown reason, bit into the top edge of their shields. MacLeod displayed them in his barn, but perhaps folk had other things on their minds, or perhaps he thought he could make money from them. In any case, they were soon up for sale and a middleman sold them on. The chess pieces which had kept together for 700 years parted company. Some went to a private buyer; others were sold directly to the British Museum in London, where they remain to this day.

Naturally, nobody knows how the chessmen, which probably originated from the Norwegian city of Trondheim in the 1100s, came to be under the shifting sands of Uig. According to the local museum in Uig, there could be a modicum of truth in an old local story. It is said that a young French seaman was rowed to land in Uig. Perhaps he was a member of the crew on one of the French ships in

Cal Mac ferry, Stornoway, Lewis

the vicinity when Prince Charles made his bid for power in Scotland in 1746. Anyway, when the seaman landed, he met a local farmer looking after the land-owner's cattle. Would it be possible for a homesick fellow who had jumped ship to be taken to the nearest harbour? Of course, said the farmer, but how are you going to pay the journey? The Frenchman pointed to a package: I think I have more than enough to compensate you! What a mistake. The fellow from Lewis was a notorious criminal, and murdered the young seaman that very night when the twosome stayed in the mountains on the way to a fictitious harbour. He stole the chess pieces and buried them for the time being in the sand in Uig. So why were they still there? Well, the story goes, the murderer was caught and hung in Stornoway and confessed on his way to the gallows. No-one believed the story of the chessmen and they were left in peace for 200 years.

In 1920 Roderick Mackenzie from Lewis was walking in the same mountain-ous area. Sheltering from the rain under a rocky shelf, he suddenly caught sight of something white in the faint light. He reached out to explore the object. A skull. The first thing that struck his mind was that perhaps he had discovered the truth about the local legend of the murdered French seaman.

The Stone Circle of Calanais

Long before the Vikings colonised the Hebrides, the islands were inhabited by another people who also had their own religion and rituals. If little is known about how the Vikings lived on Lewis, this is even more true of the way of life of those who lived there long before the peat bogs came to be, when huge trees still graced the landscape. But these people left their mark: gigantic standing stone circles.

Calanais village west on Lewis in itself is an unremarkable little place, if it weren't for the fact that the larger of the two circles is the Hebrides' answer to Stonehenge. Every 18.6 years, the moon is in a unique position in the sky. It dances low over the hill formation called 'the old hag from the bogs,' south of Calanais. The moon concentrates its beams on the stone circle, lighting up the field between the standing monuments. An old myth says that the stones were once giants which had a spell cast on them, condemning them to stand here for eternity.

The site in Calanais is formed like a cross with a stone circle in the middle. Inside the circle, a huge stone rises, over five metres tall, beside a grave. The stones are of local black- and white-speckled Lewis gneiss, one of the oldest types of stone on the planet. This more than 3,000,000,000-year-old stone was formed even before the time of fossils.

Around 5,000 years ago, a civilisation on the Hebrides enjoyed a milder and drier climate. Around Calanais, where today there are peat bogs and lochs, there were swaying fields of barley. There was every possibility of living a good life there: fish and shellfish from the sea, fish in the rivers, and good grazing for deer, sheep and cattle. There were even trees: groves of beech and hazel provided fuel and building material. Then slowly, slowly, it became colder and wetter. Organic material no longer decomposed completely, but lay as a half-digested, thick, acid soup, which grew ever deeper over time. Peat slowly but surely covered large parts of Lewis and the rest of the Scottish island groups. At first unnoticeably, one millimetre a year is not much, but gradually the fertile fields were blanketed by a wet, cold shawl, rendering them useless for cultivation. The black peat also crept round and up the stones of Calanais.

In 1857, Lord Matheson, who owned Lewis, ordered the excavation of the stone circle. Over one and a half metres of heavy wet peat had to be removed before the diggers hit the bases to which the stones were fixed. In the stone circle they also found the burial chamber, hidden and preserved for several thousand years. It was partially destroyed, and contained human bones and a blackish, fatty substance which the archaeologists thought might be human remains. Was the grave simply abandoned and then gradually decayed, or was it purposely destroyed around a thousand years before Christ? Perhaps new ideas and religions were spreading in the Bronze Age?

The main question, however, remains unanswered: Why, between 4,000 to 5,000 years ago, did the inhabitants feel compelled to invest so much time and resources to create projects such as Calanais, Stonehenge, or Brodgar in the Orkney Islands? Stone circles and standing stones were erected all over Great Britain. Why? The theories abounded, and when a plausible one was launched, it became almost impossible to dispel. Martin Martin visited Calanais around 1695. He was told by the local inhabitants that Calanais was, in ancient times, used to worship heathen gods, and that a Druid priest usually stood in the middle of the circle preaching to his congregation. Martin communicated the Druid theory, which became very popular in the intellectual circles of the time. Scientific papers asserted, for example, that it was the Druids who were behind Stonehenge in southern England. During the Romantic period in the 1800s, the Druid cult experienced a renaissance. As for Calanais, a certain Henry Callender repeated the theory in an academic article, illustrated with devoted Druids staring up at the North Star.

So who were these Druids? The answer is that nobody really knows. Julius Caesar, in constant conflict with the Celts, recorded that Druids were priests of high status. They were exempt from taxes and military service. They also acted as judges, and the most feared punishment they could mete out was to be excluded from the community. This Gallic society disappeared in the first centuries after Christ. Speculative and imaginative theories unfolded about how the Druids lived their lives before the age of radiocarbon dating. Today, one thing is quite certain: Whoever the Druids were, they almost certainly did not exist 2,000 to 3,000 years before Christ.

It is a well-known phenomenon that those with an attraction 'in their own back yard' often have not seen it with their own eyes. This tourist-native paradox means that visitors see more of, let's say, Lewis, than many of the local inhabitants do. But is it a mere coincidence that many Lewis folk have never set foot inside Calanais' stone circle? No, according to the journalist Lesley Riddoch, this is more than simply indifference to an attraction in their midst. The stones can provoke hostile emotions. Some god-fearing islanders ask themselves: How is it possible for New Age followers from all over the world to flock to these heathen stones, worshipping them, embracing them enthusiastically with both arms, trying to sense their energy, while at the same time still deny the very existence of God?

The Free Church

No, God is the only true source of strength. The majority of people on Lewis have no time for the New Age. Quite the contrary, most of them want to hold on to the old age and keep modern times at arm's length.

It's Sunday on the Aird of Uig. The spiky palm leaves in the garden shiver in the northeasterly wind. The raindrops blow horizontally. Aird is a strange little community. I am staying in an abandoned military camp which the RAF sold cheaply to incomers who were willing to do up the reinforced, bunker-like houses, with broken windows and where sheep sheltered from the rain. Some of those living here can best be described as overwintered English hippies. Nice folk who sit round the fire in the light summer nights playing their instruments and passing cheap whisky and home-made 'cigarettes' around. The culture of the incomers in the previous military barracks is very much in contrast to that of the local church community. A community which has and still does dominate Lewis to such a degree, that some folk even decide to move out. I am talking about the breakaway church, which refused to bow down to the power of the Church of Scotland.

It's not far from Aird to the Presbyterian Free Church at Valtos, but it takes time to drive the narrow road which twists and turns over bridges, through gates and cattle grids, and continues through the narrow, steep Valtos cleft, the sheep sauntering lazily in the middle of the road. It's just as if they are in touch with the pulse of the island and know it's the Sabbath day. Seven to eight cars stand parked outside the kirk. I don't know quite what to expect, but I admit to having lingering prejudices.

The Free Church. Those who hold the Sabbath so holy that it's rumoured they insist the swings in the play parks should be padlocked on Sundays. And who raised noisy religious objections every time someone wished that the ferry to Lewis could sail on Sundays—which it now does. The issue became national news. BBC covered the event with the headline 'Sunday ferry makes first sailing.' On Sunday the 19th of July 2009, a small group of demonstrators gathered on the harbour in Stornoway to express their opinion on the ferry MV Isle of Lewis sailing to Ullapool on the mainland. Their banner said: 'Remember the Sabbath day to keep it holy.' A number of women wiped away tears as they prayed for a return to the Lord's commandments. The demonstrators appealed to the Scottish nation to 'turn its back from to sin and wickedness.' The ferry company CalMac took the whole thing calmly, for even worse was being accused of differential treatment of the islands. Religion or beliefs were not valid reasons for failing to run the ferry, they asserted. However, it was not only the demonstrators who were there. When the ferry sailed out from Stornoway, several hundred people gathered to applaud and wave to the passengers on board. Jubilation erupted: life had become a bit easier, visiting relatives no longer needed to break the weekend on Saturday, and tourists would find their way to the island. But feelings of triumph probably also rumbled under the surface because the church had been forced to step down in the years-long conflict for control of the ferry.

The Free Church is more than just free. It is also strong. It fights against Sunday service for ferries and planes, Sunday-open restaurants, and even Sunday-open public toilets. It does not give up as long as there's a breath of life in the grey-haired congregation. Like the one in Valtos church. Three elderly gentlemen welcome me at the doorway, shaking my hand. I'm given an English Bible. The King James I version, that the king himself commanded to be translated. It was completed in 1611. According to the Free Church, King James's version is the one most faithful to God's Word.

The church is flooded by neon lights, as if we were in a storage hall. Not a single cross indicates that we're in a church. The only object hanging on the walls is a clock. Is this an ominous sign? I've forgotten to ask how long the service will last. What if it goes on for three hours? Can I walk out on a service? That would seem like a protest, since we are only about twenty people on the wooden pews. A pulpit stands at the opposite end of the doorway, and in front of it again is a similar pulpit in a miniature version. The 'Elders,' the three senior gentlemen who greeted me, are seated against the wall. The church is partly led by these laymen, which has been the case ever since the Free Church separated from the Church of Scotland. For how could a real church have a king or queen as its head?

The minister, dressed in a white shirt and dark suit, opens with a few words. Then the precentor takes over. He begins to sing a psalm, and soon the congregation joins in. Somewhere behind me a beautiful, strong bass voice joins in the singing. The congregations in the Free Church sing only psalms, because they come from God, virtually directly from the Bible. Hymns, on the other hand, are composed by people; they do not originate from the Word. No matter how beautifully they praise God, they are of human making and cannot be sung in the Free Church.

Gaelic Gospel

The congregation sings without instruments—no organ or piano. Only voices. Instruments interfere with the praise of God. Ministers from bygone days have many bagpipes and violins on their conscience. Where other countries were burning books, the Highlands and islands burnt music. Instruments and worldly music were sinful.

Professor Ruff stresses that the Free Church has nevertheless contributed to the history of music in its own way. According to him, the manner in which these congregations sing, responding to a caller who initiates the psalm, is the forerunner of Gospel music. 'They have always assumed that this form of worship came from Africa,' says Ruff, an Afro-American professor of music, to the newspaper *The Independent*. 'Black Americans have lived under a misconception. Our cultural roots are more Afro-Gaelic than Afro-American. Just look at the Harlem telephone book,' he points out; 'it's more like the one from Edinburgh or the Uists.' He continues: 'There is a notion that when African slaves arrived in America, they came down the gangplanks of slave ships singing gospel music—that's just not true.' What *is* the case, however, is that some Scot emigrants became slave owners in the American deep south. For many years the slaves on these plantations spoke Gaelic, not English. In a newspaper from 1740, Ruff found, for example, that a generous reward was offered for an escaped African slave. He was easy to identify, it informed, 'because he only spoke Gaelic.'

It was not before professor Ruff visited Scotland that he really became convinced about the connection between American gospel and Gaelic psalm singing.

'I was struck by the similarity, the pathos, the emotion, the cries of suffering and the deep, deep belief in a brighter, promising hereafter,' he tells *The Independent*. And why shouldn't the slaves have adopted the Scottish music? They were given their names, religion, and many of their customs, all with a Scottish reference. There are more descendants of Gaelic Scots in the USA than there are Gaelic Scots in Scotland, according to Ruff. And many of them are black.

Suddenly my attention is sharpened. In his sermon, the minister is talking about international politics—that people from all over the world want to come to Europe—about them risking their lives in boats and trailers and paying smugglers to get them over the borders onto the European continent. I prick up my ears. At last I'm going to witness the radical roots which, after all, this church is founded upon, from the time it supported the crofters against the landowners in the fight for rights and homes. The Hebridean answer to liberation theology. The church community also reacted immediately when the famine hit in the 1840s, the same decade when the Free Church broke dramatically away from the Church of Scotland. During the famine, the new church spoke on behalf of the islanders and got emergency help to them. It became enormously popular. These were the times! That period when the church gathered hundreds, thousands, of enthusiastic followers. Sometimes services were held below the high-water mark on the beach—the seabed was free for all—or in caves or barns, because the church community was forbidden to build churches. Now I'm about to hear the present-day church's fight for the boat refugees and the poor.

But the sermon takes a different turn. 'It's understandable as human beings that those people want to have a better quality of life,' says the minister. 'That they want to come into our kingdom. But how many of them want to enter the Kingdom of God?' Is it me he's staring at so intensely? I stand out; I haven't quite got the dress code right. I've tried to hide myself far at the back and am painfully aware that I'm the only woman bareheaded. All the others, on the whole elderly women, have hats. There is a family with children in the church, two girls who are more under the pews than over them, but they are also properly dressed with covered heads.

The minister continues: 'Some will go to Heaven. But what happens with the rest who won't get in?' I wait apprehensively; maybe this includes me. 'I would not be doing my duty if I refrained from telling you this,' the minister continues. 'If you don't get into Heaven, you go to Hell.' I start. This is really not politically correct nowadays, is it? Do the children understand what he's saying? Is it truly possible to assert that children have religious freedom if they hear statements like this every Sunday? On the other hand, freedom of religion is perhaps not an issue for the parents who take their children to these sermons. What would come of that? What kind of parent is so negligent bringing up his or her children that they could end up in Hell? In this particular world, surely that would amount to serious child abuse?

The pews are beginning to feel hard. The sermon has lasted for about three-quarters of an hour unbroken by a single psalm. I steal a look at my watch. It's an hour since the service began. Fifteen minutes on, I suddenly hear the minister welcoming people to the six o'clock service tonight. Everyone stands up abruptly; there's no small talk, no murmuring, and the churchgoers move quietly towards the exit. The elders shake my hand politely, one after another. 'You will be coming to the service tonight, too?' they ask. 'Maybe,' I lie.

Out in the car park the minister strolls towards me, greeting me. 'So nice of you to stay throughout the whole service,' he says with a warm smile. 'Most of those who come by leave after a few minutes.' Times have really changed; now the ministers thank the churchgoers for not leaving the service. And this in a church that once gathered whole villages, every Sunday. What will happen the day when the grey heads have gone? Who wants to hear about eternal damnation? How many want to hear about Hell nowadays?

Arnol Blackhouse

It is not only the influence of the church which has changed in the Hebrides over the course of the previous two generations. In the little community of Arnol is a 'blackhouse' museum. A blackhouse was a traditional house used in several places well into the 1900s. The houses were sooty inside because they did not have chimneys. The smoke curled upwards from the fireplace in the middle of the floor, collecting under the roof, and rendering everything black. Some now protest against the English term 'blackhouse,' especially since Gaelic pride is growing stronger. They find the name derogatory. Why not simply use the original Gaelic name for the low, chimney-less buildings? *Taighean*, or 'house,' if you will. In any case, they were first called blackhouses to distinguish them from the newer 'whitehouses,' with their posh white mortar and a pipe to carry smoke up and out through a chimney.

Whatever one chooses to call them, they were just perfect for the Hebrides: water- and wind-proof. Originally, whole villages lay on sloping terrain whenever possible to prevent the rain from collecting around the foundations. Wisely, the door was placed away from the prevailing winds. The oldest houses had rounded corners; the low walls were straight. Usually, the long house was divided in three. A bedroom. A living room with an extra bed. And a byre which sheltered cows and wintering lambs in the farthest end of the house. The houses were similar to the Norwegian longhouses from Viking times. Angus MacLeod relates in a book from Lewis, *Back to the Wind, Front to the Sun*, how the pile of animal manure grew during the winter so that finally the animals were almost hitting their heads on the beams of the byre. At last, when spring arrived, the muck was dug out and the whole family was busy carrying the manure to the potato beds.

The houses had double walls, one and a half metres thick. The roof rafters rested on the inner wall, leaving a broad ledge running round the house where grass grew on top of the thick walls. This was a favourite place for grazing sheep, or for curious children. The cavity between the inner and outer walls was filled with earth, sand or gravel, so that water and damp was filtered downwards and created a damp, insulating barrier around the whole house. This prevented heat inside the house from escaping, and stopped the flow of raw cold air from outside. The inside walls were often plastered with clay, and as time went by, the more fashionable houses lightened their walls with a white lime powder one could buy at the village shop. Those who were most fashion conscious put canvas on their walls and papered them with newspaper and, when it became available, real wallpaper.

The roof was composed of heather, ferns or marram grass, but preferably of barley straw. 'They do not cut the barley, they pull it up,' wrote Dr Johnson from his travels in the Hebrides. He does not explain why they did this, so the reader could be made to believe that the natives were so backwards that they used primitive harvesting methods. Far from it. The reason for this apparently lazy practice was that the bottom end of the straw, with roots intact, was especially suitable for thatching. After the roof was covered in straw, an old herring net was laid over it to stop the wind from carrying it off in a storm. The net was fastened by ropes pleated of heather which went back and forth across the top ridge and were anchored at the roofline with heavy stones. The windows, or slits, were often set in the roof: sometimes of glass, at other times simply an opening which let in light. 'At one time,' according to MacLeod, 'there was a tax levied on windows.' Few could afford the luxury of ordinary windows in their walls.

What about the floors? 'The floor...,' relates MacLeod, 'is often referred to in the media in a derogatory manner as "beaten earth".' The truth is that the floor was constructed scientifically and with due care. Firstly, all of the earth was removed from the site right down to the bare rock. A shallow drain was dug in the middle of the floor for the full length of the house and was then covered over by flat lintel stones. It ended at the far wall at the byre. The next step was to fill in with small, clean stones, allowing any water to escape through the internal drainage system. Then a quantity of good pliable clay was mixed into a mortar and a liberal covering was applied to the surface of the floor. If a newly-wed couple moved in, there was a tradition of holding a dance in order to stamp down the clay. MacLeod comments that a floor like this would keep you warm and cosy, in contrast to a cement floor that was cold and uncomfortable.

The house at Arnol was built in the 1880s and the last occupant was an elderly woman who moved out in 1964. I am alone inside it. It's dark and smells intensely and wonderfully from the peat fire glowing in the middle of the floor. Light filters in from a slit in the roof, transforming the thick grey smoke into a slanting pillar of light over the fire. The chairs around the fire are low so that one can sit below the hovering smoke. The woman who lived here made food on a griddle, or in pots hanging from a chain over the quietly burning peat. Now a large, sooty water kettle hangs from the rafter, as if the old woman might suddenly return to make herself a cup of tea after milking the cows housed under her roof. Maybe she would have fetched a cup from the cupboard standing against one of the walls, with porcelain plates and cups from English factories stowed inside. The cupboard is made of driftwood found on the shore. The floor is covered with well-worn linoleum.

In the bedroom, the traditional *box beds* are fully-enclosed homemade wooden sleeping alcoves. The tops of the beds are slanted slightly towards the wall so that raindrops which might sneak in change their minds and direction. The beds have curtains in front, allowing the occupants a degree of privacy. Usually several family members slept in the same bed: the boys in one, the girls in another, and parents and babies in a third. The bed in the sitting room usually belonged to a widowed grandparent.

Timber and planks were valuable materials on these islands, which grew practically no trees. Thus the beds were built so they could be easily dismantled and packed flat if, or when, folk were thrown out by the landowners. The walls, of course, had to be left standing, but the rafters could be carried away since they belonged to those who lived in the house. On some islands it was common practice to present newly-weds with a ridge-pole.

An elderly man enters the room. He presents himself as Donald Morrison and works at the Arnol museum. 'You know, our parents grew up in houses like this,' says Morrison. 'And they miss the way people got together in the old days; that disappeared when the new houses came. Now we go to German or Spanish courses, or the cinema, to while away the winter.' In those days, winter was a good time. The outdoor work was done; it was time to relax and enjoy oneself. If visitors came by, you shared what you had, even if it was only a few potatoes. 'You see,' he continued, 'they knew what it was to be hungry. If a guest had gone without food for a long time, they knew how he felt.' It was life on the edge, which could easily tip either way.

Morrison lets me into the secrets of the thatched roof. Once a year the villagers formed work groups. They removed all the straw to get to the layer lying innermost and nearest the smoke from the peat-fired hearth. That straw was impregnated with soot. The black straw was recycled as valuable potato fertiliser, and supplemented with manure and seaweed. The rest of the old straw, untouched by soot, was laid back again and topped up by a new, fresh layer of straw on top. A blackhouse was in fact a finely-tuned ecological system. When many chose to modernise the old houses by letting the smoke out, the straw suddenly began to rot much more quickly.

Morrison changes the subject, and asks where I come from. 'Here, many take pride in their Norse heritage, especially the elderly. They don't really care about how the Vikings behaved, but admire them for their skills as seamen—that's what's important to them.' Today's seamen of the Hebrides joke that any seasick Vikings abandoned ship early, on Shetland and the Orkneys. Only the most seaworthy of them made it to the Hebrides, say their proud descendants.

The Year the Tweed Disappeared

In areas exposed to rough weather, the inhabitants always have to multi-task to get by. The crofters farmed the land and fished during the summer months. In wintertime, they wove tweed. It has always been like this. Up until an Englishman almost destroyed the entire traditional tweed industry. This is the story about the 'Year the tweed disappeared' and of a mill which arose from the dead.

A.M. Rae MacKenzie, the sales manager at Harris Tweed Hebrides, is sitting in an improvised office in the container-like buildings which the sign says is 'The Office.' The tweed mill in Shawbost west on Lewis started up in 2007, but from this MacKenzie the line goes straight back a hundred years to his grandfather, Kenneth MacKenzie, who started the big spinning factory in Stornoway at the beginning of the 1900s. Lady Dunmore is given much of the honour for establishing the tweed industry, but it was Mackenzie's factory in Stornoway which led to tweed becoming a fashion article worldwide. His grandson, now sitting in front of me at the desk in his office, has indeed tweed in his blood. The telephone rings. MacKenzie apologises, picking up the receiver. It's a weaver on the line. He says that he is empty. 'Is it your head or your loom that's empty?' asks MacKenzie in a friendly tone before noting down the order for the yarn.

Harris Tweed Hebrides was established as a rescue operation. The story goes as follows: In 2006, the Yorkshireman Haggas bought KM Group, a firm which owned both the remaining woollen mill in Stornoway and the one in Shawbost. But Shawbost had closed some months before the takeover, so that it would be more attractive to the buyers to make a bid for the brand name KM. The result was that Haggas bought the rights to the KM name and the mill in Stornoway, but not the machines and buildings of the Shawbost mill which had closed down. Haggas then held the monopoly on delivering yarn to the tweed weavers of Harris and Lewis. This would not have been so bad if he had upheld the tradition of spinning wool in all the colours of the rainbow. But Haggas had other plans. He wanted to spin wool to make only four patterns, and produce all the items himself. Men's jackets were to be sold online. Designers and tailors in Paris, London, Milan and Tokyo were informed they could no longer buy rolls of tweed.

Four patterns! Not hundreds as it always had been. Four. And then they were to be made into jackets only for men between fifty and the grave. Tweed clothes for women were a non-starter for Haggas. His plans caused a lot of turbulence in the market, felt on several continents. The mills on Lewis had sold material to individual tailors the world over for a hundred years, sewing jackets, trousers, hand-

The Orb trademark

bags, sixpences, and the like. That time is now over, announced Haggas, mailing letters to companies in Europe, Japan, the USA and Australia. We no longer sell our Harris Tweed. We make our own men's jackets and sell them online.

MacKenzie was the sales manager in the Stornoway mill when Haggas launched his plans for the future, and he tried to get the factory owner to rethink his plan. It might be all right in theory, but was utterly hopeless in practice. 'You're right,' said MacKenzie, its true tweed articles are classic, but they are also a fashion item. That means that the industry has to keep abreast with current fashion—non-stop! Cut and colour have to be continually updated; customers don't want just four jackets to choose from, as if they were Chinese suits made to fit all. Haggas did not agree. He asserted that tweed clothes were classic. That's it. In other words, the very same jacket could be sold as a standard piece of clothing year after year. MacKenzie pointed out that customers in Italy don't want the same jacket as those in Japan. They want different numbers of buttons, exclusive splits, and various lapels. Not to mention different taste regarding pattern and colour! Fancy, young Japanese simply have different preferences to middle-aged Germans, MacKenzie insisted. And what happens when customers flaunt their newly-bought, very expensive jacket and meet someone else with the exact copy? Exclusiveness, right out the window. The tweed jacket will become a mass-produced item.

MacKenzie also objected that the new plan for the tweed industry would fail all those customers who had based their businesses on sewing cloth bought exclusively on the Outer Hebrides. They would either have to close down or find other material. It was one thing for Calvin Klein, Vivienne Westwood, Chanel and Adidas, who would naturally manage just fine without Harris Tweed. But lesser customers would be in trouble if they could no longer buy material from their mills. Not to mention all the small local enterprises on the island which survived by sewing handbags, purses and other small items. Local workplaces would be lost. Well, maybe, said Haggas, but that could be compensated by the weavers now having to work all year round. That would be novel, because weaving had always been seasonal, during quiet periods in the autumn and winter months. Online sales could mean that production was kept going throughout the year. This argument did get some support from individual weavers—it wasn't a bad idea. MacKenzie gave up trying to persuade Haggas to abandon his plans. He pulled out of the KM Group. Beginning in the summer of 2007, KM in Stornoway bought only mass-produced patterns from the weavers. The brand name 'Harris Tweed' was in the process of becoming extinct, and the issue was on everybody's lips.

In every fairy tale, either the good fairy or a prince on a white horse magically pops up just when things are about to go really wrong. The prince arrived in the shape of a rich American investor, Ian Taylor. In November 2007 he bought the buildings and machines of the closed-down mill in Shawbost. Around the New Year of 2008, Shawbost received its first orders, and by May it was in full production. When autumn came, the mill was able to sell rolls of fabric in any colour whatsoever.

For a whole year, tweed as the world had known it had disappeared off the market. A black hole in the history of the industry. Of course it had experienced many ups and downs, but nothing so serious as 2007. 'I suppose it took some time to re-establish its good reputation?' I ask. MacKenzie nods. Harris Tweed Hebrides mill participates annually in a big trade fair in Paris, Premier Vision. All the main fashion houses are there, as well as producers of furniture and textiles. The revived firm got a warm welcome. The old customers were assured that now everything was the same again. Others thought that the firm in Shawbost was a newcomer, and had to be informed that this was in fact an old established enterprise, and that the majority of those working there were highly experienced craftsmen. A Swedish dealer was confused. She insisted that she had received a letter saying that she could no longer order more tweed. 'Don't worry,' MacKenzie said, 'everything is back to normal.' Max Mara, GAP, Prada. All back on the customer list.

Now, Harris Tweed Hebrides produces over 90% of the world's tweed. So what happened with Haggas's mill? It went the way many had forecasted. Haggas was left with 70,000 jackets he tried to sell at reduced price. Nobody wanted run-of-the-mill jackets in four patterns. Now it is Shawbost which administers the inheritance from Lady Dunmore and Kenneth MacKenzie.

Sheepdog trial, Shawbost, Lewis

Sheepdogs and Uncooperative Sheep

The mill lies on the outskirts of the little village of Shawbost. The Old Norse name reveals that once upon a time there was a settlement here: *Saebolstadr*. Sea farm. A sign points to the right: 'Sheepdog trial.' The narrow road ends in the *machair*. Pickup trucks, several of them with dog cages piled on the back, stand facing a field which, for the occasion, has become an arena for a traditional sheepdog competition. Some of the dog owners are leaning back in director chairs; others stand in groups staring intensely at a Border collie which has raced off to fetch three sheep. The dog is herding the sheep towards us in zig-zag movements. If the co-operation between the shepherd and dog goes well, the sheep are persuaded to go through the gate into an enclosure. A good sheepdog must behave gently. If the sheep become too frightened, they lie down or become stressed, disoriented, and difficult.

Difficult? Does that mean there are easy as well as difficult sheep? 'No,' says an elderly participant with an English accent, sitting a couple of chairs away from me. He leans heavily on his crook; the handle is made of sheep horn. 'There's no such thing as difficult sheep. Only bad dogs.' This fellow is clearly on the side of the sheep. 'And,' he assures me, 'in spite of their reputation, sheep are not at all stupid. They size up the shepherd and the dog and decide if they are worth co-operating with.' Another chap beside me joins in the conversation. 'Don't listen to

Traigh Shanndaig beach, Lewis

him when he says there's no difficult sheep.' My neighbour, another Englishman, grips his coffee cup. 'He can shepherd all kinds of sheep,' he continues, nodding towards the chap who champions the sheep, 'but for we who do this as a hobby, there is definitely something called "difficult sheep".' Later I get to know that the man who can 'shepherd all kinds of sheep' is the sheep farmer, Jim Cropper. He has participated in competitions since he was twenty-five years old. He is England's most famous shepherd, and his experiences are published in his biography, *The Dog Man*.

'What are the rules?' I ask my neighbour with the coffee cup. He leans back, watching the dog trying to get the sheep through the gate. He's from Lancashire and speaks in dialect, so I get hold of only half of what he's saying. As far as I understand, you start with a hundred points and lose points every time the sheepdog makes a mistake. The sheep must be herded in the straightest line possible, not here and there in exhausting detours. The signals from the owner, high-frequency whistles or flute tones, instruct the dog what to do next.

The Border collie has a set time to complete all the tasks. Fetch the sheep, herd them through the gate, and get them into the enclosure, all in close teamwork with the owner. Then it's out of the enclosure again; this time, a single sheep must be separated from the other two. 'Why?' I ask. 'The farmer has to do this when a sheep has problems giving birth and needs help to deliver her lamb. Then you have to get her away from the flock. Also, sometimes a sheep has wandered over to a neighbouring herd and has to be fetched back again,' says my neighbour in the director chair.

The competition in Shawbost is part of The Hebridean Circuit, an annual competition which lasts for a week. It starts on the island of Skye and journeys to the Outer Hebrides for four days, before the dogs and their owners get on the ferry and return to the final competition on Skye. The dog who wins the cup gets the honourable title of 'Lord of the Isles.'

A car horn toots. The judges are seated in a big delivery van out in the field. Time is running out. The dogs are herding the sheep out of the area and they jump with surprising agility over a wall and into an enclosure of Leca blocks. A tall, blonde lady shepherd sits down nearby. 'She's Swedish,' says my neighbour. She and a couple of her countrymen, including the Nordic champion, have taken a little trip, as they put it, to the Hebrides with their dogs. They are not the only ones who have come from afar. An American woman has brought her dog with her all the way from the USA.

My neighbour is #23. Right now, #19 is on the field, but he's still calm and collected. 'I won the cup last year,' he says. 'Do you want to see it?' He gets the silver cup from his car, polishing it on his sleeve. His name, Steven Duckworth-Tom, is engraved on the challenge cup.

Now it's Duckworth-Tom's turn. He fetches his dog, Tom, and waits until participant #22 is finished. Last year's 'Lord of the Isles' makes a good start. The black-and-white collie rushes, jaws open, towards the far-off enclosure to fetch his sheep. Blackface sheep with coarse, stiff wool and black faces. The very ones which once provided wool for the weavers. Their wool is no longer soft enough for today's customers. 'Is it only the Blackface sheep participating in today's competition?' I ask. No, Cheviot sheep, with their large white heads, which also thrive in the salty, blustering Atlantic wind, can take part in sheepdog trials. So what's the difference between the two races as competitors? Those with black faces run in a flock; they stay more together, says one participant. What decides who gets which kind of sheep in the competition? Good or bad luck.

Something is going wrong for the Tom and Duckworth-Tom pair. The sheep refuse to go into the enclosure, and stand stubbornly outside the gate huddled together. The shepherd tries to coax them through the gate which he's holding open with a rope. The sheep hesitate. One of them makes a break for it. Duckworth-Tom whistles commands and Tom tries to chase the reluctant escapee back to the other two. But the latter are by no means standing patiently waiting for the dog and the third sheep. They grab the opportunity to escape—away from the gate and Duckworth-Tom. He gives up and leaves the field.

'What happened?' ask the others as he returns to his chair and coffee cup. The sheep were too stressed; they lost their heads and became unmanageable. 'But there's a new chance this afternoon, with dog number two,' says Duckworth-Tom. However, the Cup is about to wander out of his keeping and over to a new worthy winner of the Hebridean Circuit: Jim Cropper and his dog Fleet.

213

St Kilda—the Myth at the End of the World

'Know how to fasten this?' Each of us gets a lifebelt and skipper Angus Campbell gives an overview of the safety procedures. It's April on Harris. I am heading eighty kilometres further west of the Outer Hebrides to an island in the Atlantic Ocean. Beyond lies the American continent.

I arrive at the pier in Leverburgh just before eight o'clock in the morning. My fellow passengers are already on the deck, each sleepily clutching their plastic coffee mugs. We are a group of ten on our way to the mythical group of islands known as St Kilda. The trip will take about three hours one way.

It is almost ominously windless today, and sunny, the kind of weather that doesn't last. The wind might build up at any moment. The boat chugs slowly out of the harbour, leaving Leverburgh behind, but soon the powerful engines pick up speed. Best to cling on for support; it's getting difficult to stand upright. Soon we are out in the open sea and, despite the lack of wind, rocked by the huge Atlantic rollers.

One of the best-known travel descriptions of St Kilda, *A Voyage to St Kilda*, was published at the end of the 17th century by Martin Martin, who was associated with important scientific institutions such as the Royal Society in London. On a calm day, the 29th of May 1697, Martin Martin sets off for St Kilda. He is accompanied by the minister John Campbell, who has some business to attend to in these most westerly islands. Martin is fully aware that this is a unique opportunity. 'This occasion I cheerfully embraced.' Campbell and Martin hire a crew on Harris, seamen who can master an open boat. Here, on route to these windswept and relatively uncharted islands, Martin Martin's famous tour of the Hebrides could well have come to a watery end. The little expedition drifts at the mercy of the wind. No land is sighted for sixteen hours. A storm blows up. The crew lose all hope of survival, convinced that the devil has taken over control and that Satan is trying to prevent the minister from reaching St Kilda. Finally the wind dies down, the crew are given a new round of spirits to boost their morale, and they reach St Kilda on June the 1st. The journey from Harris has taken them about three days. Three hundred years later, we take three hours.

But it is the same heaving ocean that is bearing us forward. I decide to seek shelter, and find a poor chap sitting at the entrance to the wheelhouse, bent over a paper cup. I can't help but give him some good advice: 'If you go up on deck and get some fresh air, you'll feel better!' 'Thank you,' he says in polite English fashion. He gives me a wan smile but continues to stare forlornly into his cup. I totter further into the cabin to have a chat with the skipper, who has the same name as Martin's travelling companion: Campbell. He has greying hair and wears a freshly ironed, blue short-sleeved shirt and jeans. His face cuts a clear profile against the light as he sits in front of the broad instrument panel with screens, levers and knobs. He's more like a pilot than a skipper. A boat like this is a considerable investment. It has capacity for up to ten to twelve passengers. The cost of our day ticket barely covers that of the fuel. So can he make a living out of these tours? Campbell grips the wheel firmly, his eyes fixed ahead on the endless swell. He shakes his head. 'I work as a fisherman when I'm not sailing to St Kilda. High winds often lead to cancellation of crossings, so usually I can only make the trip once or twice a week during the summer season.' Campbell has, however, ordered a new boat from Ireland that withstands rough seas and should enable him to make more trips during the summer. Between October and April, there are no trips.

This pattern of working is typical for the people of the Hebrides and other more remote communities. Most multi-task to make ends meet. In an economic analysis of *Innse Gall,* the Outer Hebrides, it was found that about 20% work in the tourist trade, a risky undertaking out here in these ocean-bound lands and limited by the short summer season. Many enterprises, such as Campbell's boat trips, are limited too by the sometimes violent forces of nature. To give an example: When the engineers were working with Stevenson to design a lighthouse on the Atlantic seaboard of Scotland, they found that the lighthouse tower had to be twice as high and able to withstand twice as much pressure as similar structures in the North Sea, which, in comparison, was like a calm pond.

The economic analysis also found that fewer than 4% earn their living from agriculture and fishing. Fewer than 4%? Yet everywhere the eyes rest in the Hebrides, it's likely to be on a sheep. They are everywhere, grazing out on the hills all year round or lying dead in the ditches. Others are busy munching the forbidden green treats in windblown kitchen gardens when somebody forgot to shut the gate. But why then does sheep farming amount to so little? And surely sheep do not demand much investment? Perhaps the biggest cost is all the barbed wire fencing dividing one pasture from another, a serious challenge to those who like to wander around freely. Fishing, on the other hand, needs a considerable financial investment. I note that the economic analysis table has columns showing how many people fish and how many are involved in farming as *main sources* of their earnings. The tables are designed to reflect how people on the mainland normally earn their living and cannot capture the diverse and seasonal types of activities the island people are engaged in. Tell me: How can the reality of a postman, who delivers mail in the morning, then becomes a scallop fisherman while running his bed and breakfast establishment, be adequately classified on graphs and in tables?

I ask Campbell what he fishes for. 'Mostly shellfish, scallops, sometimes lobster. Most of the catch is sent to Spain.' Spanish trailers are filled to the brim with scallops, soft-shelled crabs, lobster and scampi. Paradoxically, it is almost impossible to find fresh seafood for sale in the Hebrides. However, most absurdities have an inbuilt logic, in this case, an economic one; these fresh delicacies are not sought after by local people, at least not in economically viable quantities.

The space between sky and sea is suddenly filling up with birds. They seem to appear from nowhere. We are approaching one of Europe's biggest colonies of seabirds. The gannets are among those flying farthest from their nests. Wonderful birds, whiter than seagulls, with apricot head feathers and blue eyes. They can easily fish for a whole day, scanning the sea between St Kilda and Harris. They speed into the waves with characteristic dive-bomber tactics, forming their bodies into missiles which enter straight into the sea.

Gannets were a prized catch on St Kilda. The former inhabitants made shoes of the neck and head skin, hooks of the beaks, meals of the carcasses, and fertiliser of the remains. Martin Martin's writings describe an easy method the inhabitants of St Kilda used to capture their favourite food. A herring on a little wooden raft was launched into the rolling waves. The gannet dived, its beak piercing the herring and boring itself into the wood. The bird remained transfixed to the raft which was pulled to land, where a waiting islander broke its white neck and hung the bird from his leather purpose-built belt.

Noa Words

We are rapidly approaching St Kilda, a volcanic archipelago made up of four islands. They were never called by their correct names by the inhabitants. Superstition regarded it as too blasphemous or dangerous to call certain things by their real name. Instead, they were identified by 'noa' words: descriptive terms or nick-names. Coastal, hunting and fishing cultures often have a large store of noa words. A fisherman I met on the way to the Hebrides told me that seamen and fishermen on the islands still use noa words at sea. 'Can you give me some examples?' I asked. 'Well, you have *red fish* for salmon, *long neck* for swan, *curly tail* for pig and *long tail* for rat.'

Superstition has always thrived in the Scottish islands, but many have met with shut doors and silent islanders when they have tried to explore the theme. Who wants to be presented as exotic and primitive? A little further in our conversation, I asked if he thought it would be possible for me to get out on a fishing boat. The fisherman hesitated: 'That may be difficult.'

'Would I be in the way?'

'Well, noooo, *that's* not the problem. Some are a bit unwilling; they think that it's unlucky to have women on board.'

I wonder now what skipper Campbell thinks of the whole matter, and decide to find out. 'So it's bad luck to have women on board fishing boats?' Campbell gives an embarrassed laugh and glances at Seamus, his young right-hand man on board.

'Aye, it's bad luck with women. And ministers too!' Now they both laugh.
'Why?'

'Well, the thing about women is really an excuse to avoid having them on board,' says Campbell.

'And why are ministers so unpopular?'
They look at each other, laughing, imitating whisky-drinking movements.

Hirta

On my map, there are no noa words. The islands of St Kilda archipelago are called Hirta, Boreray, Soay and Dun. The first three have Old Norse names. The Reverend MacAuley observed as late as the middle of the 1700s that the inhabitants of St Kilda spoke a somewhat strange form of Gaelic, since the language also included some Norse words.

We are drawing closer to the biggest island, Hirta, or Hiort, as it is also called. This is the only island in St Kilda where there has been a permanent settlement. The historian and archaeologist Andrew Fleming reckons that Hirta has been inhabited for at least 5,000 years, but nobody knows exactly how long people have lived here.

The boat sets anchor in Village Bay and we climb down into a little rubber dingy. Today it is perfectly calm in Great Britain's most far-flung island. Hirta looks idyllic on this fine spring day, but not long ago conditions forced a researcher to stay here for an extra two weeks. The weather would permit neither helicopter nor boat to approach the island. On an average, winds reach storm strength once a week, according to Calum Ferguson in the book, *St Kildan Heritage*.

The stone pier is slippery because of the low tide; the difference between high and low tide is at least three metres. We are received by the Swedish ranger, Annelie Mattisson. 'Welcome. I'm the ranger on the island. I want to let you know about some of the rules.' She goes on to tell us that this is a UNESCO World Heritage site, one of the few which has joint status for both its natural and cultural qualities. It is also a bird sanctuary. 'You must not take anything with you from here, nor leave anything behind. Behind you, you can see the village. Some houses have been restored. Researchers and others working here are living in them; please respect their privacy.' But we can visit the little museum, and behind the village, the churchyard. 'And over there,' she says drawing her breath, pointing, 'you can climb up the valley to the highest cliff. But be careful not to go too near the edge. In a moment of distraction ... seagulls diving or a strong gust of wind ... it's over 300 metres down.'

After being informed about what we can, and mostly can't do, she comes over and has a chat with me in Swedish. Annelie is working in conservation biology. She is certainly in the right place, for on St Kilda there are abundant cultural and natural treasures to preserve and protect: both against wear and tear of human activity and the forces of nature itself. Annelie returned to St Kilda after participating in a so-called 'work party,' organised by the National Trust for Scotland (NTS) some years ago. The work parties are composed of people from all walks of life who pay for their own board and lodging while working voluntarily. So can anyone join a work party? 'No special skills are needed, but you must be in good physical shape and have a sense of humour!' The work parties are open for all between eighteen and seventy-five, according to NTS's website.

Houses

The houses in Hirta's little village line a broad, well-worn grassy path, 'The Street.' The name is appropriate because this is the only street on the island. The houses were built in two periods during the 1800s. Previous to this, the islanders lived in underground homes made of turf and stone. These abodes provided safe and effective protection against the southeasterly storms and hurricanes, but also became a source of various diseases. The dwellings were shared by both people and animals. Writings by early tourists and visitors expressed shock, disgust and concern regarding the unhygienic conditions. The minister Neil MacKenzie, for instance, came to St Kilda in 1829. He describes how he had to crawl *down* into the houses, over piles of animal dung and the carcasses of dead birds. When he finally got into the home, it was impossible for him to stand upright. In the spring the waste was dug out through the door and used as compost on the small patches of barley. MacKenzie noted that the houses gained a good yard in height inside after the spring cleaning.

Another visitor was Sir Thomas Aceland, who in the year 1838, as a friend and benefactor of St Kilda from the mainland, returned on his yacht. On one of his previous journeys he had been so shocked over the condition of the houses that he had decided to donate money to encourage the islanders to build new living quarters.

The new generation of dwellings made promising progress. They arose from the ground, stretching towards the light and the sky, but not without risk. There is not a single tree on St Kilda: not then, not now. Everything above ground is exposed to the unhindered wrath of winds straight off the Atlantic Ocean.

Aceland donated money for 'blackhouses.' Thus from 1838, St Kilda was brought into line with the rest of the Hebrides and large parts of the Scottish mainland. Most people in the countryside lived in low, dry stone buildings with thatched roofs. Humans and animals continued to live together as they did in the earthen dwellings, but at least the new houses had a wall separating the family from their livestock. The cottages had small windows but they were of glass that Aceland had provided. There was also more height between ceiling and floor. And more space. The roof was supported by a framework of poles recycled from the earthen dwellings. The houses became black with soot inside: *black*houses. The islanders breathed, slept, and lived their lives in an ever-present bluish fog of smoke, as did almost everybody else in the Hebrides at that time.

Every house along The Street owned a strip of land stretching towards the sea. When the houses were built in the 1830s, every family was given a piece of land.

Hiertachs, as the islanders from Hirta called themselves, decided the ownership of each small farm by lottery and moved in. Most decisions on St Kilda were made in this egalitarian way, working towards consensus.

The ruins of the houses from those years are still lying along the broad, hard-packed grassy path, and I stop to take a close look at their rounded corners, where the wind cannot get a hold. There is at least one metre between the outer and inner walls. In some houses, this airspace between the walls was used as a sleeping alcove.

October 1860. Homes on the west coast of England and Scotland are devastated by hurricanes. St Kilda is also hit. The ruined blackhouses are replaced by modern houses, long before such dwellings were common in the rest of the Hebrides. The reason for this trailblazing was that information about the situation on St Kilda reached the newspapers on the mainland. People began to demand action on behalf of the homeless islanders, indicating that there was already a special affection for St Kilda among the population. The landlord and owner of St Kilda, MacLeod, who lived on Harris, gave generously. If he had not done so, doubts would have arisen about his commitment to the wellbeing of his tenants.

The new houses from the 1860s had chimneys and larger windows. *White-houses*. Now the smoke was led up and out. Finally, the animals had to move out and into the old blackhouses, side by side with the new ones. The builders decided to use corrugated iron on the roofs instead of thatch; it was too damned old-fashioned and inconvenient with thatch! When the rain poured down at night, it now sounded as if somebody was playing marbles on the roof. In the name of modernity, the inhabitants had to tolerate many sleepless nights. The new roofs also leaked. One of the tenants complained in a letter: 'whenever it rains the rain in is nearly the same as it is out [...]' The double walls in the old houses which kept the warm air in and the rain and damp out were replaced with a single and relatively thin stone wall. The letter continues: '[...] and the wind is blowing in through the wall.' Progress?

The Evacuation

Each house in The Street is fronted by well-worn flagstones. Little streams bubble under the stones, draining the land around the cottages. Some of the buildings are restored, thanks to voluntary work parties. The other cottages are in ruins; the roofs have disappeared. Gone with the wind. Entering one of them, a stone among the weed reads: *No.12. 1930. Empty. Formerly Ewan Gillies.* The floor is covered by stinging nettles, the plant which indicates previous human habitation. There is a fireplace in each gable wall. Once peat fires were burning here night and day, and the spinning wheel and loom stood ready during the long winter months. The windows, now without glass, face towards the sea, the shore, and the little bird island of Dun.

Everybody who comes to St Kilda knows how the story ends. That's exactly why most people come here. After the First World War, the number of islanders fell to half the original, and the rapidly dwindling population asked to be evacuated. In the spring of 1930, the islanders gathered for a meeting. There were now thirty-six persons living on St Kilda. Everybody agreed. They understand that they must sell their animals and leave their homes to the forces of nature. A letter was written and sent to the officials.

> We, the undersigned, the natives of St Kilda, hereby respectfully pray and petition HM Government to assist us all to leave the island this year and find homes and occupations for us on the mainland.

They know that they will lose everything. Old men cry openly. The evacuation draws a lot of attention in the British press. St Kilda has long had the status of a mascot. *The Lost Paradise.* But the paradise is no longer sustainable. Many of the men have already been working on the mainland for several years. There is a surplus of women but too few children are born. There are not enough families to maintain the population. Once up to 200 people lived here. An extremely high infant mortality, coupled with emigration, led to a large reduction in the population between the mid-1800s and 1900s. When the decision to evacuate is finally undertaken, poverty and hunger have taken their toll on the resilience and morale of what was once a self-reliant community.

There is something poignant about deserted villages. The absence of what was. Hammering, chattering, and Gaelic singing, as folk went about their work. At the same time, it is not difficult to understand the choice they made in 1930. The postal service on St Kilda was so unreliable that the inhabitants also used a form of bottle post to communicate with the outside world. Little boat-like constructions, with sails and bottles fastened to them, with the request: 'St Kilda Mail Please Open.' The bottle-boats were carried by the Gulf Stream. Occasionally they arrived more or less at their intended destination. Sometimes the bottles drifted all the way to Norway. One such boat was found in Haugesund in 1899; another was picked up on the Norwegian coast as late as 1930. A curiosity when seen through the lenses of our time, but for the inhabitants who became acutely ill and did not have transportation, communication with the outside world around them was a matter of life or death.

Soay Sheep

I clamber up the slope behind the village, a steep cleft in the hillside lying between the mountains of Ruival and Oiseval. Norse names again. Red Mountain and East Mountain. On the way up I pass hundreds of stone huts, called 'cleits,' from

Cleits, storinghuts for birds, peat and egg, St Kilda

the Norse word *klettr*, meaning rocks, scattered on the hillside. These small huts topped with turf have been described as the drying machines of the Stone Age. As the wind blew through cracks in the walls, it dried the carcasses of birds, as well as peat for fuel. The eggs were stored in ash to protect them against the raw damp.

I peer into one of the cleits and pull back immediately. There is a smell of death. Gradually, as my eyes become accustomed to the darkness inside, I see a swollen, dead, black sheep. A Soay sheep, named after Soay, or *Saueey*, in Norse, 'Sheep Island.' The race goes back to the Bronze Age and doesn't behave like other sheep. Its members are not flock animals, so they run in all directions when startled. Thus the inhabitants of Hirta needed specially trained sheepdogs which did not become confused by this strange behaviour. The dogs raced after the sheep and held them in their jaws. Their teeth were filed so as not to harm their prey. Now it is forbidden to bring dogs to St Kilda. The sheep are to be left in peace.

Until the last century, Soay sheep were isolated on the small neighbouring island of Soay. That is until some were transported to Hirta in the 1930s. Researchers are now studying the animals' DNA because the ancient race has the rare characteristic that it has not been crossed with any other races. As if in a Darwinian laboratory, Soay sheep look after themselves, breed, eventually reaching peak numbers, before many die of starvation following a hard winter. Slowly the flock increases again until the next crisis in seven to eight years' time, and so the cycle continues. During a talk given to us by Bill Lawson, the local historian from Harris, he dryly remarked that if ordinary crofters had treated their sheep in this way, the animal protection folk would have been after them long ago.

One of the DNA researchers approaches me. She is carrying a sheep over her shoulders. 'She's rejecting her lamb,' she says. 'She won't let the lamb suckle. We're going to get her to change her mind.' It seems that somebody is keeping an eye on things after all.

I gaze at the sheep from a distance. Woolly, black, sinuous and skinny, with spiral horns. They stare back, yellow labels clipped to their ears. Each has its own number. I remember Annelie's warning not to go too near the sheep. They have lambs and want to be left in peace.

Feathers and Oil

Nearing the top of the valley, I am all alone. The village lies far below me like an aerial photograph. The sun is scorching; this spring in the Hebrides has been wonderful. I pause and take a gulp of water from my bottle, then tackle the last leg through marshy areas dotted with more cleits.

The valley ends abruptly in Britain's highest coastal cliffs, the nesting sites for seabirds. 'Don't go near the edge. Remember the loose edges and sudden gusts of wind,' I remind myself. I wriggle gingerly on my stomach towards the edge. To the west lies the bird island of Boreray, or North Island in noa language, separated from Hirta by six kilometres of ocean. A small cloud has settled on its highest point. These islands generate their own cloud formations.

White specks are wheeling hundreds of metres below: nesting fulmars. Some are also hovering right over my head, warning me. These plump birds don't like intruders, so I pull back. Fulmars have a habit of defending themselves by squirting out nasty-smelling oil with a pervasive stench. I recall Bill Lawson telling us how the smell had remained on his watch strap for years. The inhabitants of St Kilda, however, highly prized this fluid, which they used in their oil lamps and also for medical purposes. Like cod liver oil, it is rich in vitamins A and D. The oil was an important part of the diet and also a popular export item. Fulmar feathers were also exported, and provided income for St Kildans in the 1800s. The British army bought sacks of evil-smelling feathers, removed the worst of the odour as best they could and stuffed them in pillows and mattresses. The smell kept the lice at bay, but after three years it came back with a vengeance. The soldiers complained, and the feathers were cleaned once again.

Nowadays, nobody collects feathers or oil. But the inhabitants of St Kilda climbed down this very cliff. Originally, each man went bird-hunting alone. He secured himself by fixing a stake in the rock, then lowering himself with the rope down the cliff wall—a dangerous undertaking. The stake could work loose or he could have problems on the way up. According to a classic book on St Kilda, *Island on the Edge of the World*, the men took fewer risks during the 1800s and the death rate was greatly reduced. The fulmar gatherers started to work in pairs. One held the rope while the other let himself down. The birds were caught by snares fastened to the end of a pole. The fulmars lay faithfully on their nests, not leaving them despite the approach of their most dangerous enemy. As the noose slipped over its head, the bird fluttered wildly, tightening the line. Finally, the hunter wrung its neck and fastened the bird to his belt.

Grief

There are no accurate statistics to tell how many men lost their grip or foothold, and plunged into the sea. Many of the Gaelic songs from St Kilda are composed by bereaved widows and sweethearts. Sometimes mothers, no longer able to feed their children, had to give them into the care of foster parents.

Many of the laments are translated into English. One of them was written by a woman who was twice widowed. The first time she lost her husband when he was capturing birds. Her second husband was drowned just outside Village Bay. Following these calamities, unable to feed her children, she gave them over to a foster mother.

> Because of what happened, your babes
> No longer have your support:
> Being forced to place them with others
> Makes me very sad
> [...] Now cared for by a woman disinterested
> And not fully committed to them.

Do people grieve less over the loss of their loved ones in situations where death always hovers nearby? Can one become accustomed to losing one's nearest and dearest when their death is a strong statistical probability? Does this tendency affect the process of grieving? I pore over the many songs in the book, *St Kildan Heritage*. I'm in no doubt. These bereaved are deep in sorrow or perhaps even depressed. The islanders themselves did not call their state 'depression,' but what else could it have been?

> Thoughts of death
> Invade my mind each day;
> I've avoided my friends
> Since the day you were buried.

We never get used to loss. But perhaps we can lose the energy to grieve. The cliché that one has no tears left to cry was perhaps first born on places like St Kilda.

The stories of loss on this little archipelago are many. One of them could function as a philosophical dilemma on the issue of making a choice. Two friends are climbing down a cliff to catch birds. They share the same rope. The rope frays just above the climber hanging uppermost. He makes an instant calculation. 'The rope is just about to break. It can't bear the weight of both of us. If I cut the rope below me, the weight on the rope will be halved. I might just make the top before the rope breaks. If I don't cut the rope, it will break and we will both die. I must cut the rope.'

I start downwards, heading towards the little churchyard behind the village. An oval stone wall embraces the mostly small, unmarked gravestones leaning in all directions. There's not much room here. It almost looks as if the dead have been buried in layers, in grassy mounds. Once, somebody knew who lay where. Now, only the newer stones tell us who remained behind on the island when the living left for good.

Sickness of the Eighth Day

The small churchyard was in frequent use. In the 1860s seven out of ten newborn babies died of tetanus. I re-read the figures: seven out of ten died. The midwife herself had lost twelve of her fourteen children in this way. 'Sickness of the eighth day' they called this recurring disaster. Eight days with painful cramps which often began in the jaw area, resulting in the baby having a permanent grimace. A punishment from God, pronounced one of the resident ministers in the 1800s. The west coast of Scotland cowered under this form of grim Christianity.

One evening, shortly before the trip to St Kilda, I went to the little township of Tarbert on Harris to hear a talk by Bill Lawson, the local historian, who said that the neglectful care of the sheep on St Kilda amounted to animal abuse. He runs 'Seallam!'—a heritage centre—with his wife Chris from Lewis. Every island has one. For a fee, Australians, Americans and Canadians are assisted in tracing their Scottish ancestry. The couple also run their own publishing firm which prints Bill's books. He has a particular interest in St Kilda, and when the tourists arrive in the spring, Harris Hotel arranges weekly talks in co-operation with Bill.

It was a lovely spring evening. I ordered a beer, forgetting to specify lager, and ended up with a pint of Guinness. I paid for the flat, dark beer and wandered into the lecture hall, where I found Bill preparing a slide show. A motley bunch of tourists, ten in all, were gathered in the hall. Some may have been interested in St Kilda; others, perhaps, thought it was a bit quiet in Tarbert and were grateful for any diversion. Bill introduced a young girl who was to entertain us in the intervals with Gaelic songs.

One of the themes of his lecture was that of infantile tetanus. In 1889, said Bill, the minister Angus Fiddens settled in St Kilda. He was shocked by the high infant mortality rate and contacted a friend who was professor of gynaecology at Glasgow University. The determined minister taught himself elementary birth hygiene, and tried to persuade the midwife to change her practices and start cleaning the stump of the umbilical cord with antiseptic solution. His efforts were to no avail. Semmelweis all over again. The babies continued dying until the death of the midwife. Only then did Fiddens manage to convince the expectant mothers to change the old traditions.

So why was this disease so prevalent on St Kilda and some few other places? Bill Lawson mused over different theories in his talk. One main hypothesis is that the supposed practice of anointing the umbilical cord with fulmar oil infected the babies with tetanus. The oil was said to have been stored in dried fulmar stomachs. In that case, asked Lawson, why did they have such high incidences of tetanus on other islands where there were no fulmars? I left the talk recognising that the mystery of the tetanus infection was still unsolved. However, much later I came upon an article written by a paediatrician called Stride, who pointed out that tests for tetanus bacteria in fulmar oil were all negative. The 'oil theory' had arisen from a Dr Gibson, who had made only an *assumption* that the umbilical cord stump was smeared with oil. A rather dubious assertion, in other words. On the other hand, tetanus bacteria have been found in the soil in and around the old houses and cleits on St Kilda. Stride asked: Could the infection have come instead from the dirty clothes the babies were wrapped in? Were dirty knives used to cut the cord? Or horsehair to tie the little stump left after the cord was cut?

Priscilla

The population on St Kilda was also vulnerable to disease because of its residents' isolation from the rest of the world. Lack of immunity to diseases could be fatal, as was experienced in 1852 when the frigate Priscilla set sail from Liverpool on course to Australia. On board were thirty-six emigrants from St Kilda. In common with the rest of the Hebrides, the islanders immigrated to new continents during the 1800s. Facing a passage of several months, it was an ill-fated voyage. Half of the emigrants from St Kilda never arrived; they died of measles on board.

I study the passenger list from the Priscilla which appears in St. Kildan Heritage. Among the emigrants is the MacCrimmon family. The parents Donald and Anna have their four children with them. They plan to start a new life, far away from poverty and infertile land. The passenger list tells a different story.

Donald (32) died of dysentery, 14. October, 1852
Anna (32) died of exhaustion, 25. January, 1853
Marion (9) died of dysentery and measles, 23. October, 1852
Mary (6) died of dysentery and measles, 22. October, 1852
Donald (5) died of dysentery and measles, 22. October, 1852
Christina (1) died of dysentery and measles, 27. October, 1852

Baby Christina is the last child to die; protected, perhaps for a while, by the antibodies in Anna's breast milk. Anna loses her husband and four children in the course of two weeks. One by one they are lowered into the ocean, enclosed in sackcloth. The ceremonies must have been simple. These were, after all, daily events. A prayer; tears; fear in those left behind. The journey took a toll of forty-one lives. Anna stops eating. The frigate reaches Australia in January 1853 but Anna is not allowed to disembark. She is transferred to a quarantine boat. A shadow of her old self, she survives for only six days. The official cause of death is starvation. Or was it a slow suicide? Anna must have died of a broken heart.

The Myth of St Kilda

Susceptibility to disease was real, but to what degree was St Kilda really isolated and marginalised? Was it a community living completely isolated from the rest of the world, as myth and the tourists of the 1800s wanted to portray it?

MacKenzie, the minister who lived there in the 1830s, describes how the inhabitants deliberately exploited the myths about themselves. When a yacht with tourists arrived, the people went on board to sell wool stuffs, birds' eggs, and diverse souvenirs. They pretended that they thought polished brass was gold and flattered the owner; he must be a man of some standing! They picked up bits of coal and pretended surprise that they could not eat the black lumps. When they saw themselves in a mirror, they backed away and feigned amazement that there was no one behind the mirror. Another visitor writes: '[...] a moment's observation would have shown anyone they had that very morning shaved before a looking glass [...].'

One may ask: What was the reason behind this theatrical performance? The islanders had found that the charade made the tourists give them things which were better than those they already possessed. And why disappoint them by not living up to the myth of wild and primitive islanders if it made both parties happy? The urge to experience the untouched and original was the very reason St Kilda became a mascot. In Victorian times, the 'Age of Improvement,' the tendency of tourists to develop the natives was, no matter where in the world they were, particularly well developed. And the natives said 'Yes, please,' and joined in the game.

The writer and archaeologist Andrew Fleming maintains that modern writers also participate in perpetuating the myth of St Kilda. An archetypical one is that of the people who had to give up the struggle against nature, as in the classic, *The Life and Death of St Kilda*. Another myth is that St Kilda was so special, so isolated, that the islanders were unable to adapt to modern society, as portrayed in the book, *Island on the Edge of the World*. As a kind of counter-argument to this, Fleming wrote the book, *St Kilda and the Wider World*. He argued that islands which we today think of as isolated, were in fact ports of call on the ocean highways of bygone days, places of trade or to settle in. And aren't small islands frequently depopulated without any drama whatsoever? Fleming asks. 'Why did St Kilda become such a drama queen? So written and re-written about, so loved and visited?'

The Myth that Took UNESCO

On UNESCO's list of world heritage sites there are names of buildings, constructions, and areas which have special significance for all mankind: the Taj Mahal, the Great Wall of China, Easter Island, and the pyramids. And St Kilda. UNESCO has even gone to the exceptional length of giving the islands the status of a dual World Heritage Site, first for nature, then for culture. The seas around St Kilda are also included on the list. Has the global organisation allowed itself to be misled by the myths of the Victorian age and writers from bygone times? Or was the appointment fully deserved? John Randall reflects on the inscription in his article, *St Kilda – Myth and Reality*. In the revised application to UNESCO in 2003, the Scottish authorities wrote: 'For many, St Kilda is the epitome of an idyllic community, living in harmony with nature for hundreds, if not thousands, of years, but ultimately seduced by the comforts of modern life.'

According to the Scottish authorities, the island community disintegrated because it was influenced and drawn to the modern outside world. Before this, the island was an idyll. Randal calls this myth the 'Noble Savage.' Innocence was corrupted. The inhabitants became greedy. A perfectly harmonious community ends in turmoil. Values are destroyed. It is not only St Kilda which has been viewed in this way. Similar myths abound about indigenous communities where drunkenness and suicide appear in the wake of transition to modernity. But is it really true that the islanders were 'seduced by the comforts of modern life,' or is that just one more myth? The myth of the evacuation of St Kilda?

The Parliament

Leaving the churchyard, I return to The Street. I take some photographs but am not happy about them; there is no life in the pictures. I try to conjure up imagines of the people living in the houses in front of me, the people I have seen in old pictures. The women with their hair centre-parted and with bare feet or homemade shoes made of gannet skin. The married women wearing white lace hair bands instead of a wedding ring. They are always working. Knitting or spinning. Carrying large baskets on their backs filled with peat. Several pictures show the men standing gathered on the street outside the houses. The 'Parliament,' these gatherings were called. The early travellers were wont to believe that it was here laws and important decisions were made. In reality the Parliament did not amount to more than a gathering of men meeting to share out the day's tasks. In the pictures the bearded men wear rough woollen trousers and waistcoats, a flat cap on their heads. Some walk barefoot; some wear leather shoes. All with at least one dog each. The children are barefoot and look well nourished, dressed in clothes of homespun tweed. The girls have scarves of light-coloured wool. They too have centre partings in their hair. All look gravely into the camera. It is easy to come to the conclusion that people were more serious in the past. Both children and adults in old photographs look as though life were a sad necessity. But after the button was pressed and the shutter closed, the playing, laughter and chatting continued, never to be captured on a glass plate.

It's time to leave Hirta and gather on the pier to board Campbell's motor boat. On the 29th of August 1930, all the inhabitants collected on this same pier for the last time before boarding the steamboat HMS Harebell. Some glanced up at the little village, the churchyard, and the dead friends and relatives left behind there. Others were unable to say farewell; they went on board without looking back. In the deserted houses, where the peat still smouldered in the hearths, the Bible lay open at the 2 Book of Moses: Exodus. They had chosen to go, but nevertheless felt forced to leave St Kilda. Perhaps the children had mixed feelings. They saw their parents' grief, but were excited about going on the steamship. Suitcases were carried on board, but most possessions were left behind. Beds and tables. Hunting equipment. Bird snares had no place in their future lives.

Ironically enough, many of the evacuees got work as foresters on the mainland. Some of them had never seen a tree before, never mind a forest. The old folks especially would come to long for their homes and feel like refugees in their own country. Internally displaced. The islands which had been inhabited for several thousand years were abandoned to the gannets, the sea mists, and the wind. The roofs caved in and once more the sheep moved into the houses.

Boreray

The journey is not over. The boat sets course for the most dramatic of all the islands of St Kilda, Boreray, with its two 'stacks,' great pillars of rock rising clean out of the waves: Stac an Armin, and Stac Lee, the highest in Great Britain, 191 and 165 metres high, respectively. Both are blindingly white with bird droppings, just as if someone had painted them as beacons. The two stacks are, together with Boreray, home to the world's largest colony of gannets. Slim-bodied, diving seabirds. White snowflakes against black cliffs.

Once, the men and boys of St Kilda climbed up these slippery, steep walls in the dark to catch gannets. The first man to scale the cliffs had no rope to hold on to. If he fell into the water, the next fellow had to try. The ability to tolerate heights and sure-footedness were vital for survival on St Kilda. Perhaps not surprisingly then, a young man who had asked for the hand of his sweetheart had to prove himself through a test of manhood before being accepted. The young suitor invited the

Boreray and the seastacks Stac an Armin and Stac Lee, St Kilda

rest of the village to witness his skills on a famous rock, called the 'Mistress Stone.' Martin Martin describes the performance in the book, *A Late Voyage to St Kilda,* from 1697. The would-be husband had to go to the top of the Mistress Stone and stand in an especially demanding position until those observing were satisfied, and could pronounce him mature enough for the role of breadwinner. Dizzy men lived their lives as bachelors.

One of the islanders insisted that Martin should also try his hand before departing from St Kilda; it would bring him good fortune to perform the daredevil rituals. Martin retorted dryly, 'I told him that such practices would have the opposite effects on me, that I would lose both my life and my sweetheart in the same moment.'

As we sail below Stac an Armin, I remember the story about the smallpox epidemic. In 1726, an islander from St Kilda travelled to Harris and was infected by smallpox. He died and was buried there. The following year his clothes were returned to St Kilda in a ship's chest. The chest was opened and the books and clothes unpacked. As was also the smallpox virus. Almost all the inhabitants of Hirta died, except one adult and eighteen children. In addition, three men and eight boys who had gone to Stac an Armin to collect feathers, just before the outbreak began, also survived.

The hunting party on Stac an Armin were unaware of the tragedy unfolding on the other side of the sound. When they had collected enough feathers, they signalled as usual that they wished to be fetched. But no boat came. The eleven hunters were stranded on the stack for nine months, from August to May. They

229

survived on fish and birds, making hooks of rusty nails. How they managed to survive throughout the winter in this inhospitable environment defies understanding, even while seeing this place on a warm spring day.

It is equally difficult to put oneself in the situation of the only surviving adult on Hirta who was left behind with eighteen children and the many dead. All the burials. All the orphans. All the grief and fear. The hunger. The thin, stony earth of the little churchyard, the anonymous gravestones. All the children who must suddenly grow up and fend for themselves.

Heavy Metals

Gannets, fulmars, and puffins swarm around the boat, diving for food. I put on the hood of my anorak to protect me from airborne bird droppings. In the brochures and books one can read that the St Kilda archipelago is Europe's largest nesting site for puffins, with around one-quarter of a million birds. Now, there are nesting sites with more puffins than St Kilda, and I wonder if the Scottish brochures really mean the largest nesting place in the EU. Easy to mix them up, Europe and the EU. However, the puffins are starving and dying. The sea temperature has increased, and perhaps that's the reason the puffins' favourite food, the sand eel, has immigrated to cooler waters.

Man's destruction of nature has probably had consequences for St Kilda for much longer than first supposed. Martin Martin described the island as a grain store. In spite of this account, food production decreased throughout the 1800s. Researchers from Aberdeen University think they know how this paradox could have happened. On the basis of soil sample analysis, they found that the inhabitants unknowingly contaminated the soil with metals such as lead and zinc. The lead came from the practice of using peat ash as a soil improver, and the zinc from discarded food, in particular bird carcasses. I read on: The metals probably came from industries on the mainland; it leached into rivers and on into the sea, poisoning the fish and accumulating in the birds eating the fish. During the 1800s, agriculture, and therefore the use of fertilisers, intensified on St Kilda. Tens of thousands of birds were captured yearly so there were plenty of carcasses to use as fertiliser. This led to an accumulation of zinc which poisoned the soil, rendering it less capable of feeding St Kilda's population.

Supper

Skipper Campbell turns the boat eastwards. We are three hours away from Harris. The Englishman has got on an anti-seasick plaster and has a slightly healthier tone in his still pale skin. I make for the cabin. After all, it's only April and there is not much warmth in the afternoon sun.

As we are putting in to the pier on Harris at seven o'clock in the evening, Campbell exchanges some Gaelic words with a fisherman mooring his boat. I ask if it's possible to buy a lobster. 'Of course it's possible! How many do you want?' asks Donald MacLean. I really want only a couple, for supper. The fisherman holds up two lobsters, their claws bound together with an elastic band. 'You can have these two for £20. And this bag of crab claws free.'

Campbell gives me a hike back to Seilebost. We drive through the *machair* landscape with overgrown strips of old 'lazybeds,' ancient potato fields which once provided food for a much bigger population than today, and look down at some of the most beautiful beaches to be found. 'Why do so few people live here?' I muse, half to myself, half to Campbell. 'We have tried to get a house here for years but have almost given up. It's almost impossible to be allowed to build because of environmental protection. They think it will wear down the *machair* and then the sand will spread.'

The strange thing is that it was here, on the fertile west coast of Harris, that folk lived before the landowners forced them to the east coast in the 1800s. The eastern side has its own beauty, beset with a rocky coastline dotted with little islands, but it is very sparse. Now the people want to return to the western seaboard but they are unwanted, now as before. Is it then true what Ian Mitchell, the author of the controversial book, *Isles of the West*, says? That non-government organisations and national authorities send bureaucrats on yearly contracts, from the towns, to instruct the people how to look after their environment? Do they make decisions with a mixture of arrogance and lack of knowledge? It's difficult to take sides in this silent war going on in the islands.

I thank Campbell for the run back, fetch the seafood from the boot, and wander down to the house by the tidal strand. My body still thinks I'm at sea. Nautical vertigo.

■

Works cited

Barnard, A. (2008). *The Whisky Distilleries of the United Kingdom*. Edinburgh: Birlinn Limited.

Bathurst, B. (1999). *The Lighthouse Stevensons*. London: Harper Collins Publishers.

BBC News. (2009, 19 July). *Sunday Ferry makes first sailing*. Retrieved 31 March 2011, from http://news.bbc.co.uk/2/hi/uk_news/scotland/high-lands_and_islands/8157570.stm

Black, R. (unknown). *The Dun Hill*. Retrieved 1 April 2011, from http://www.macaskillsociety.org/History_files/The%20Dun%20Hill.pdf

Bond, R. (2007). Hitler's British Girl, *Channel 4*. Documentary.

Boston Daily Globe (6 November 1905). Special Feature. In General Mood. Mark Twain Talks to Newspaper Men. Has Much of Interest to Say on Various Topics. Humorist Reads Some of His Latest Aphorisms. Retrieved 31 March 2011, from http://www.twainquotes.com/inter-views/Interview6Nov1905b.html

Braun, E. (1935). *The diary*. Retrieved 1 April 2011, from http://www.evabraun.dk/evabraun6.htm

Burt, E. (1998). *Burt's Letters from North of Scotland*. Edinburgh: Birlinn Limited.

Byron, G.G. (27 February 1812) *Speech in the House of Lords*. Retrieved 5 April 2011, from http://eve-rything2.com/title/Lord%2520Byron%2520Sp eaks%2520to%2520 Parliament

Cameron, A. (1988). *Bare Feet and Tackety Boots*. A boyhood on the island of Rum. Edinburgh: Luath Press Limited.

Canmore (2001). *Eigg, Uamh Fhraing*. Retrieved 1 April 2011, from Canmore http://canmore.rcahms.gov.uk/en/site/22183/details/eigg+uamh+fhraing/

Comhairle nan Eilean Siar (unknown). *Berneray Causeway-Opening*. Retrieved 1 April 2011, from http://www.cne-siar.gov.uk/eriskay/berneray.htm

Comhairle nan Eilean Siar (2007). *Outer Hebrides Migration Study*. Final report. Retrieved 31 March 2011, from http://www.cne-siar.gov.uk/factfile/population/documents/OHMSStudy.pdf

Cowell, A. (2002, 22 July). Dunvegan Journal; For Sale: Mountains Entwined in the Scottish Soul. *The New York Times*. Retrieved 31 March 2011, from http://www.nytimes.com/2002/07/22/world/dunvegan-journal-for-sale-mountains-entwined-in-the-scottish-soul.html

Crichton, T. (2003, 2 March). Harris buys into its own freedom. *Sunday Herald*. Retrieved 31 March 2011, from http://findarticles.com/p/articles/mi_qn4156/is_20030302/ai_n12581149/?tag=content;col1

Currie, J. (2000). *Mull. The Island and its People*. Edinburgh: Birlinn Limited.

Davies, N. (2000). *The Isles. A history*. Basingstoke & Oxford: Papermac.

Dean and Chapter of Westminster (2011). *David Livingstone*. Retrieved 1 April 2011, from http://www.westminster-abbey.org/our-history/people/david-livingstone

Den katolsk kirke (2008). *Den hellige Kolumba av Iona*. Retrieved 1 April 2011, from http://www.katolsk.no/biografi/columba.htm

Discover Tiree (2011). *History & Heritage*. Retrieved 1 April 2011, from http://www.isleoftiree.com/history-sky.html

Donelly, J. (2011). The Irish Famine. *BBC*. Retrieved 31 March 2011, fromhttp://www.bbc.co.uk/history/british/victorians/famine_01.shtml

Dressler, C. (2007). *Eigg. The story of an island* (2 ed.). Edinburgh: Birlinn Limited.

Ezard, J. (2002, 28 November). MI5 wary of Mosley's 'dangerous' wife. Memos highlighted close contacts with Hitler. *The Guardian*. Retrieved 31 March 2011, from http://www.guardian.co.uk/uk/2002/nov/28/freedomofinformation.art-sandhumanities

aithfull, J. (2004). *The Ross of Mull granite quarries.* Iona: The New Iona Press.

erguson, C. (2006). *St Kildan Heritage.* Stornoway: Acair Limited.

leming, A. (2005). *St Kilda and the Wider World. Tales of an Iconic Island.* Bollington: Windgather Press Limited.

rank, R. (1984). *Viking atrocity and Skaldic verse: The Rite of the Blood-Eagle.* Retrieved 6 April 2011, from http://ehr.oxfordjournals.org/content/XCIX/CCCXCI/332.full.pdf+html

Geikie, A. (1904). *Scottish Reminiscences.* Glasgow: J. Maclehose and sons. Retrieved 8 April 2011, from http://www.ebooksread.com/authors-eng/archibald-geikie/scottish-reminiscences-ala/page-12-scottish-reminiscences-ala.shtml

Harman, M. (1997). *An Isle called Hirte. A History and Culture of St Kilda to 1930.* Isle of Skye: Maclean Press.

Hirst, C. (2005). *Back to the wind, front to the sun. The Traditional Croft House.* Isle of Lewis: The Islands Book Trust.

Hoge, W. (1997, 6 June). Island Tenants Triumph: They're the Lairds Now. *New York Times.* Retrieved 31 March 2011, from http://query.nytimes.com/gst/fullpage.html?res=9800E1DE163CF935A35755C0A961958260

Hompland, A. (2000, 25 February). Bygdedyret er dødt! Leve Bygdedyret! *Dagbladet.* Retrieved 31 March 2011, from http://www.dagbladet.no/kultur/2000/02/25/195988.html

Horwell, V. (2003, 14 August). Diana Mosley. Obituary, *The Guardian.* Retrieved 31March 2011, from http://www.guardian.co.uk/news/2003/aug/14/guardianobituaries.thefarright

Hudson, J.D. & Allwright, E.A. (2003). *The Geology of Eigg.* Isle of Eigg: Isle of Eigg Heritage Trust.

Hunter, J. (2000). *Last of the free. A History of the Highlands and Islands of Scotland.* Edinburgh: Mainstream Publishing Company.

Hunter, J. (2001). *The Islanders and the Orb.* Stornoway: Acair Limited.

Hutchinson, R. (1998). *Polly. The True Story Behind Whisky Galore.* Edinburgh: Mainstream Publishing Company.

Jefford, A. (2004). *Peat smoke and spirit. A portrait of Islay and its whiskies.* London: Headline Book Publishing.

Jennings, A. & Kruse A. (2009). *From Dál Riata to the Gall-Ghàidheil.* Retrieved 31 March 2011, from http://uhi.academia.edu/AndrewJennings/Papers/175149/From_Dalriata_to_Gall-Gaidheil

Johnson, S. & Boswell, J. (1984). *A Journey to the Western Islands of Scotland and The Journal of a Tour to the Hebrides.* London: Penguin Group.

Kelbie, P. (2003, 20 September). Gospel truth: Hebrides invented church spirituals. *The Independent.* Retrieved 31 March 2011, from http://www.independent.co.uk/news/uk/this-britain/gospel-truth-hebrides-invented-church-spirituals-580565.html

Kelbie, P. (2005, 23 July). Castle playground of the idle rich may be turned into flats. *The Independent.* Retrieved 31 March 2011, from http://www.independent.co.uk/news/uk/this-britain/castle-playground-of-the-midle-rich-may-be-turned-into-flats-199905.html

Kemp, J. (2008, 25 November). Tartan and home truth. *The Guardian.* Retrieved 31March 2011, from http://www.guardian.co.uk/education/2008/nov/25/centre-study-scottish-diaspora-controversy Lamb, J. (2011). Captain Cook and the Scourge of Scurvy. *BBC.* Retrieved 31 March 2011, from http://www.bbc.co.uk/history/british/empire_seapower/captaincook_scurvy_01.shtml

Love, J.A. (2001). *Rum. A landscape without figures.* Edinburgh: Birlinn Limited.

MacArthur, E.M. (2002). *Iona. The living memory of a crofting community.* Edinburgh: Polygon at Edinburgh.

Macdonald, D. (2004). *Tales and Traditions of the Lews.*

Edinburgh: Birlinn Limited.

Macdonald, F.J. (1994). *Crowdie and Cream and other stories. Memoirs of Hebridean childhood*. Warner Books: London.

MacIntosh, A. (2004). *Soil and Soul. People versus Corporate Power*. London: Aurum Press Limited.

MacKenzie, A. (2002). *Tradition of North Mull*. Edinburgh: Birlinn Limited.

MacKenzie, D.W. (2000). *As It Was / Sin Mar a Bha: An Ulva Boyhood*. Edinburgh: Birlinn Limited.

Mackinnon, F.E. (1997). *Tiree Tales*. Isle of Tiree: The Author.

Maclean, C. (2006). *Island on the edge of the world. The story of St Kilda*. Edinburgh: Canongate.

Marshall, G. (2007). *The Accrington folly. A story of the town, a family and an island*. Pen Press Publishers Limited.

Martin, M. (1999). *A description of the Western Islands of Scotland ca 1695. A voyage to St Kilda*. Edinburgh: Birlinn Limited.

McCrum, R. (2009, 10 May). The masterpiece that killed George Orwell. *The Observer*. Retrieved 31 March 2011, from http://www.guardian. co.uk/books/2009/may/10/1984-george-orwell

McIntosh, A. (2011). Letter to Laird Schellenberg of Eigg. Retrieved 1 April 2011, from http://www. alastairmcintosh.com/articles/1992_beseech-ment.htm

McPhee, J. (1998). *The Crofter and the Laird. Life on an Hebridean Island*. Isle of Colonsay: House of Lochar.

Meharg, A.A., Deacon, C., Edwards K.J., Donaldson, M., Davidson, D.A., Spring, C., Scrimgeour, C.M. & Feldmann, J. (2006). Ancient manuring practices pollute arable soils at the St Kilda World Heritage Site, Scottish North Atlantic. *Chemosphere*, 64, ed. 11, 1818-1828.

Milmo, C. (2006, 10 April). Silent protest greets first Sunday ferry as South Harris defends its way of life. *The Independent*. Retrieved 31 March 2011, from http://www.independent.co.uk/ news/uk/this-britain/silent-protest-greets-first-sunday-ferry-as-south-harris-defends-its-way-of-life-473596.html

Milne, M. (2000, 13 February). Prince Charles' favourite islanders fight conservationists. *Sunday Herald*. Retrieved 31 March 2011, from http:// findarticles.com/p/articles/mi_qn4156/ is_20000213/ai_n13946112/

Mitchell, I. (2004). *Isles of the West*. Edinburgh: Birlinn Limited.

Orwell, G. (1971). *The collected essays, journalism and letters of George Orwell. Vol IV. In front of your nose 1945-1950*. Middlesex: Penguin Books Limited.

Paul, J.B. (1886-1887). On Beggars' Badges, with Notes on the Licensed Mendicants of Scotland. In: *Proceedings of the society of antiquaries of Scotland*.Vol.21. Edinburgh: Neill and Company. Retrieved 31 March 2011, from http://www. archive.org

Peterkin, T. (2001, 9 September). Highland owners 'should end apologies'. *The Telegraph*. Retrieved 31 March 2011, from http://www.telegraph. co.uk/news/uknews/1340088/Highland-own-ers-should-end-apologies.html

Ponting, G. (2002). *Callanish and other megalithic sites of the Outer Hebrides*. Wales: Wooden Books.

Randall, J. (2007). *St Kilda: Myth and Reality*. In: B. Lawson, J. Lowe, J. Randall & M. Robson (red.). St Kilda. Myth & Reality. Lewis: The Island Book Trust.

Reynolds, P. (2003, 14 November). Nancy Mitford spied on sisters. *BBC*. Retrieved 31March 2011, from http://news.bbc.co.uk/2/hi/uk_news/ magazine/3263733.stm

Richards, E. (2002). *The Highland Clearances*. Edinburgh: Birlinn Limited.

Riddoch, L. (2007). *Riddoch on the Outer Hebrides*. Edinburgh: Luath Press Limited.

Roberts, J.L. (1999). *Feuds, forays and rebellions: history of the Highland clans 1475-1625*. Edinburgh:

Edinburgh University Press.

Robertson, A. (1791-1799). *Statistical Account of Scotland*. Account of 1791-1799, vol.11, Kildalton, County of Argyle. Retrieved 31. March 2011, from http://stat-acc-scot.edina.ac.uk/sas/sas.asp/?monospace=&twoup=&nohighlight=&account=1&transcript=&sessionid=047ee8bcb435cd6e2aeddf9f7ca0dbdb&naecache=6&accountrec=641 8&navbar=&action=publicdisplay&parish=Kildalton&county=Argyle&pagesize=

Ross, D. (2008, 14 March). Should Harris become a national park? It is up to the islanders. *The Herald*. Retrieved 31 March 2011, from http://www.heraldscotland.com/should-harris-become-a-national-park-it-is-up-to-the-islanders-1.876572

Ross, J. (2005, 14 January). Island's anguish for drowned family. *Scotsman*. Retrieved 31 March 2011, from http://news.scotsman.com/scotland/Islands-anguish-for-drowned-family.2594990.jp

Scotch Whisky Association (2009, 2 Desember). *The Scotch Whisky Regulations 2009*. Retrieved 31 March 2011, from http://www.scotch-whisky.org.uk/swa/files/ScotchWhiskyRegGuidance2009.pdf

Sir Arthur Conan Doyle Literary Estate. (2000). *Sir Arthur Conan Doyle Biography*. Retrieved 1 April 2011, from http://www.sherlockholmesonline.org/biography/biography15.htm

Somers, R. (1848). *Letters From The Highlands Or, The Famine of 1847*. London: Simkin, Marshall & Co.

Spartacus Educational (2011). *The Luddites*. Retrieved 1 April 2011, from http://www.spartacus.schoolnet.co.uk/PRluddites.htm

Speel, B. (unknown). *Egyptian Style*. The website of Bob Speel. Retrieved 1 April 2011, from http://myweb.tiscali.co.uk/speel/group/egyptian.htm

Stevenson, R.L. (1994). *Kidnapped*. London: The Penguin Group.

Stevenson, R.L. (2002). *The complete stories of Robert Louis Stevenson. Strange case of Dr. Jekyll and Mr. Hyde and nineteen other tales*. (ed.). Barry Menikoff. New York: The Modern Library.

Stornoway Gazette (2005, 7 July). *WIE Chief answers your questions*. Retrieved 31 March 2011, from http://www.stornowaygazette.co.uk/news/local-headlines/wie_chief_answers_your_questions_1_115797

Storrie, M. (1997). *Islay. Biography of an Island*. Isle of Islay: The Oa Press.

Stride, P. (2008). St Kilda, the neonatal tetanus tragedy of the nineteenth century and some twenty-first century answers. *J R Coll Physicians Edinb* 2008:38:70-77.

Sturlason, S. (2009). *Snorre Sturlasons kongesagaer*. "Stormutgavene". (ed.). Finn Hødnebø. Oslo: J.M. Stenersens forlag.

Swinson, A. (2005). *Scotch on the rocks. The True Story Behind Whisky Galore*. Edinburgh: Luath Press Limited.

Walters, K. (2004). Law, "Terror", and the Frame-Breaking Act. Economic History Society. In the program to *The Economic History Society*. Annual Conference, 2-4. April. Royal Holloway, University of London.

Wolcott, J. (2007, February). Why Are British Sex Scandals So Much Better than Ours? *Vanity Fair*. Retrieved 31 March 2011, from http://www.vanityfair.com/culture/features/2007/02/wolcott200702

Wordsworth, W. (1838). *The Sonnets of William Wordsworth*. London: Edward Moxon. Retrieved 31 March 2011, from http://www.literaryhistory.com/19thC/WordsworthPrimaryBib.htm

Wright, G. (1993). *Jura and George Orwell*. D.G.B. Wright: Isle of Jura.

Wright, G. (2003). *Jura: a guide for walkers* (3rd ed.). D.G.B. Wright: Isle of Jura.

HEBRIDENE

Butt of Lewis
Swainbost
Flannan I.
Stornoway
Lewis
Turnpan Hd.
The Minch
Ru Stoer
K. Wrath
Portskerry
Ben Clibreck 908
961 30
Ben More 996
Morven

S:t Kilda
Harris
Glas I.
Shiant I:s
Ullapool
Dornoch
Tain
Ness
Trodday
Gairloch
Ben Wyvis
1109 29 1045
Dingwall
Beauly
Inverness
Loch Ness

N. Uist
Monach I.
Benbecula
S. Uist
Little Minch
S. Rona 749
Portree
Raasay
Skye 986
Cromelarry
1182 Cairn
Eige
Broadford
Glenelg
Ft. Augustus 28
Caledonian

Barra
Mingalay
Barra Hd.
Ushinish
Canna 810
Rum
Eigg
Mallaig 1039
Ft. William
889
Ben Nevis 1343
Ballachulish
Grampians
Blairgo
1214 88
Killin

Coll
Tiree
Staffa I.
Iona
Mull 971
Ben More
Oban 17 983
Inveraray
Lochgilphead
L. Lomond 742 14
Stirling
13 Falk

Skerryvore
Dubh Artach
K. of Lorn
Colonsay
Stanton Bank

Rudda Mhail
Jura 583
Tarbert
Greenock
Dumbarton
Paisley Glas
Rothesay 15
Hamilton
Saltcoats 8
Lanark
Kilmarnock
Ayr 7

Islay
Bowmore
Arran 874
Kintyre
Firth of Clyde
Plada
Malin Hd.
Inishtrahull
Campbel town
Mull of Kintyre
Sanda
Ailsa Craig 701
Girvan
Merrick

Tory
Fanad Pt.
Inishowen 615
Rathlin
Ballycastle 77
Buncrana
ody Foreland

Made in the USA
Charleston, SC
06 November 2016